Excel

T0359317

Revise in a Month

Years 4–5
Opportunity Class
and Scholarship Tests

Get the Results You Want!

Lyn Baker
Kristine Brown
Sharon Dalgleish
Tanya Dalgleish
Allyn Jones

PASCAL
PRESS

Completely new edition incorporating early 2021 Opportunity Class test changes

ISBN 978 1 74125 704 5

Pascal Press
PO Box 250
Glebe NSW 2037
(02) 8585 4050
www.pascalpress.com.au

Publisher: Vivienne Joannou
Project Editor: Mark Dixon
Edited by Mark Dixon and Rosemary Peers
Answers checked by Peter Little and Dale Little
Typeset by Grizzly Graphics (Leanne Richters)
Cover and page design by DiZign Pty Ltd
Printed by Vivar Printing/Green Giant Press

Acknowledgements
The publisher wishes to thank the people and organisations who gave their kind permission to reproduce copyright material. Specific acknowledgements appear under each text.

All efforts have been made to gain permission for the copyright material reproduced in this book, but we have not been successful in contacting all copyright holders. The publisher welcomes any information that will enable rectification of any reference or credit in subsequent editions.

Table of Contents

About the Tests

The NSW Opportunity Class Placement Test comprises three test papers:

- Reading (25 questions in 30 minutes)
- Mathematical Reasoning (35 questions in 40 minutes)
- Thinking Skills (30 questions in 30 minutes).

There is no Writing test.

The ACER Scholarship Tests (Primary Level 1) consist of three test papers.

- Reading and Viewing (25 multiple-choice questions in 30 minutes)
- Mathematics (20 multiple-choice questions in 30 minutes)
- Writing (two short extended responses in 40 minutes).

Reading Test

The NSW Opportunity Class Placement Test and the ACER Scholarship Tests both include questions that ask you to read written texts and then answer questions to show how well you understand them.

The Opportunity Class Test has four sections and the question format changes for each section.

The ACER Scholarship Test Reading and Viewing section only uses multiple-choice questions requiring you to choose the right answer from the options given.

How much time will I have?

Both the NSW Opportunity Class Placement Test and the ACER Scholarship Test give you 30 minutes to answer 25 questions. You will have to work very quickly in all sections.

What type of questions will be in the test?

Both tests use multiple-choice questions. However, the NSW Opportunity Class Test also includes other question types which change from section to section. At the time of writing the format is as follows:

Literary texts—multiple-choice questions about two different texts or about different stages of one text

Poetry—multiple-choice questions about one or more poems

Factual texts—a cloze task which asks you to place sentences or phrases into an information text in a way that makes sense

Varied short texts—matching statements to four short texts on the same general theme.

What kind of texts will I have to read and understand?

Both tests include a variety of types of texts. You will definitely have to answer questions about narrative stories, poems and factual texts. The factual texts could be, for example, reports, instructions or explanations, biographies, interviews or diary entries. In the ACER test you might have to understand texts which also include visual information.

In this book the texts have been organised into four categories—literary texts, poetry, factual texts and varied short texts—to match the content, organisation and question types of the Opportunity Class Test.

What will the texts be about?

The texts cover a wide range of topics, including personal feelings and experiences, family life, different cultures, animals and plants, history, the environment, science and technology, art and music.

Do I have to study these areas before the test?

No. The topics will be general interest and all the information you need to answer the questions will be in the texts. The questions test how you read, not how much you know.

What kinds of questions will I be asked?

The questions cover a range of reading skills and strategies.

Some will ask you to find particular facts. Some will ask you to work out the meanings of a word or phrase. Some will require you to think about main ideas. Others will ask you to draw a conclusion based on what you have read. This means the answer won't be clearly given to you in the text—you will have to use the text to work out the answer (e.g. to predict what is going to happen).

Some questions may ask you to look more at the way the text is written (e.g. to identify words that express emotion or opinion).

Do I have to answer all the questions?

Yes, you should try to answer every question but you may run out of time. You will have to work very quickly to answer all the questions. If you can, put an answer for each question.

How can I make the best use of my time?

Here are some tips to help you with the Reading comprehension questions and to make the best use of your time.

- Quickly skim the text to get a general idea of the topic and type of text (e.g. instructions, story, description) and then quickly look at the questions.
- Read the text carefully but quickly.
- For multiple choice, choose the answer you think is best. Cross out the ones that look obviously wrong as soon as you see them.
- For the new question types in the Opportunity Class tests, you will find advice in the Key Points for those sections.
- Be sure to look back at the text to answer the questions. Don't just answer it from memory!
- Also, look again at the question to make sure you have not made a silly mistake when reading it.
- Don't waste too much time on any one question. If you are not sure, guess the answer but mark it so you can come back to it later if you have time. If it seems impossible to choose, select the answer you first thought was right.
- If you have time to spare, go over your answers. Sometimes you will realise the correct answer to a question after answering other questions.

Thinking Skills Test

Many of the standardised tests include a Thinking Skills test component. This is different to testing knowledge: it tests your reasoning ability—how well you can think through problems. All tests are generally of the same format.

How much time will I have?

The NSW Opportunity Class Placement Test for Thinking Skills has 30 multiple-choice questions to be completed in 30 minutes. You will be given four choices and you'll need to choose the best answer. The test assesses your ability to think critically and problem solve.

What kinds of questions will be in the test?

Thinking skills questions will test your ability to think and reason. They cover the topics of literacy (language skills), numeracy (mathematics), spatial awareness (visualising) and logic (reasoning), and often integrate some basic general knowledge. To answer critical-thinking questions you need to read and understand the information provided in the texts and understand the language of the questions, including the grammar.

You might use a mixture of the following thinking skills:

- identifying the main idea in an argument
- drawing a conclusion from information provided
- identifying an assumption that has led to a conclusion
- identifying a mistaken assumption
- assessing evidence
- applying reasoning as well as detecting errors in reasoning
- eliminating conclusions that cannot be correct because the evidence does not support them
- evaluating statements in order to judge the ones which strengthen or weaken arguments.

Problem-solving questions will test a wide range of reasoning skills and strategies based on general literacy, numeracy and visualising shapes, patterns and relationships. They will also require students to manipulate words, numbers and shapes. There may also be questions about something completely unusual or different. These will require you to use logic and apply common sense.

Do I have to study these areas before the test?

No. There is no body of knowledge to study for the Thinking Skills test. You need to work out the answer from the information provided. Practising with the sample questions in this book will help you learn about the types of questions you can expect in the test and how to work out the answers.

Do I have to answer all the questions?

Yes, you should try to answer every question but it is quite possible you will not have time to do them all. You will have to work quite quickly to answer all the questions.

How can I make the best use of my time?

Thinking Skills testing depends on speed. The smarter the student, the faster they will be able to reason correctly and do the test, and the higher their score will be.

The questions and tests in this book provide you with the opportunity to maximise your speed in answering Thinking Skills questions by making you familiar with the style and format, and with some of the types of questions you may encounter in such tests.

Here are some tips to help you with the Thinking Skills questions and to make the best use of your time.

- Read the questions carefully but quickly. Make sure you know what the question is asking. Don't jump to conclusions based on a word or phrase you recognise.

- Attempt the questions one at a time and choose the answer you think is best.

- Look again at the question to make sure you have not made a silly mistake when reading it. There are answers that seem correct if you have not read the question carefully.

- Don't waste too much time on any one question. If you are not sure, make an intelligent guess but mark the question so that you can come back to it later (if you have time). If it seems impossible to choose, choose the answer you first thought was right.

- Answer every question. Don't leave any out. You'll have a one in four chance of getting the right answer, even if you guess. You do not lose marks for incorrect answers.

- If you do have some time to spare, go over your answers. Sometimes you will realise what the correct answer to a question is after answering other questions.

Mathematical Reasoning Test

Both the NSW Opportunity Class Placement Test and the ACER Scholarship Tests include a Mathematical Reasoning component.

All tests are generally of the same format. Mostly you will be given information and asked one question about it. Sometimes you might get more than one question.

What kinds of questions will be in the test?

All tests use multiple-choice questions. This means you are given a question and have to choose the best answer from four or five possibilities. The tests vary in the way you record your answers but most ask you to mark your answers on a separate answer sheet. You don't have to write any words.

What do I need to bring to the test?

As the tests are multiple choice, you will need pencils and erasers. Calculators, rulers and geometrical instruments are not allowed, so you need to be good at mental calculations and estimating length and angles.

What mathematics topics will be covered in the test?

The tests include questions involving Number, Patterns, Measurement, Geometry, Statistics, Probability and Working Mathematically. This means you will be familiar with the topics covered in the test but the questions may be more difficult or of a type you may not have seen before.

Do I have to study these areas before the test?

No. The best preparation is to know what to expect on the day of the test and to practise the types of questions in the test.

What kinds of questions will I be asked?

You will be given some information and asked one question about it. The information might be given in words or might involve a diagram, graph or table.

You will be familiar with most question types from classroom work and from other tests you have done, such as the NAPLAN tests.

Where can I do my working?

Most tests have a question booklet and a separate answer sheet. Many of the questions are so difficult you will need to write down some working to help you find your answer. You can use space on the booklet near the question.

Do I have to answer all the questions?

Yes, you should try to answer every question. However, it is possible you will not have time to do them all. Some questions will take less than one minute to answer, while others will take longer. You will have to work quite quickly to answer all the questions. Many students don't manage to do this.

How can I make the best use of my time?

Here are a few tips to help you get through the test, and to make the best use of your time.

- Don't waste too much time on any one question. If you are not sure, guess the answer but mark it so that you can come back to it later (if you have time). If it seems impossible to choose, select the answer you first thought was right.
- Answer every question. Don't leave any out. You'll have a one in four (or five) chance of getting the right answer, even if you guess.
- If you do have some time to spare, go over your answers. Sometimes you will realise the correct answer to a question after answering other questions.

Writing Test

You only need to do the Writing sessions in this book if you are doing the ACER Scholarship Tests. The NSW Opportunity Class Placement Test does **not** ask you to do any writing so you don't need to do these sessions if you are doing only that test, although you may do them if you wish.

How much time will I have?

The ACER Scholarship Tests give you 40 minutes to do two pieces of writing—20 minutes for each piece. You won't have time to prepare, draft, revise and proofread as you usually would, because there is not enough time.

How much should I write?

You will be given a booklet to write in but there is no set length. Generally, in such a short time you would not be able to write more than 150–200 words (about one page). The important thing is how well you write, not how much you write.

How will I know what to write?

You will be given words or pictures to respond to. This is called the stimulus material. For example, you might be asked to write about a photograph, a drawing, a comment or a question.

Will I have a choice of what to write?

The ACER Scholarship Tests give you two questions to write about. You must do both.

One question will ask you to tell a story. You can usually choose to write a true story or an imaginary one. The other question will ask you to give your opinion on a topic. The topic will be something of general interest to children of your age—you don't have to study anything before the test to do this writing.

You won't have a choice for either question. There will only be ONE story question and ONE opinion question. You must be sure to write on the topic or question you are given. However, both questions will usually be quite general and open-ended, and give you plenty of opportunity to write about something of interest to you. You could write about something completely different from the next student and in a completely different way—and both of you could do well. So, in a way, you always have a choice of what to write.

You may also have a choice about **how** to write. For example, you might write your story as a diary, a poem or a letter. You might write your opinion as a letter to a newspaper, or as a speech to your classmates. Sometimes, however, you might be told the writing form. For example, you might be directly instructed to write a letter to someone.

Look at the question below.

This question could lead one student to write a true story about finding a key to a sister or brother's box of treasures. Another student might write an imaginary diary entry about finding out someone's secret. Another student might write about receiving a very special box for her birthday. All would be acceptable.

How can I make the best use of my time?

- Read the stimulus material and study any pictures very carefully. You need to be quite clear what you are being asked to write about.
- Brainstorm some ideas on the topic. Don't waste time thinking of a million different possibilities. Think of two or three at the most, and then choose one.

- Organise your ideas into a logical plan—basically an introduction, body and conclusion. You may not stick to your plan but it helps to have one.
- Start writing and keep going!
- If you have time, read through your writing to make quick improvements to wording and to proofread for spelling, grammar and punctuation.

How will the markers judge my writing?

The markers are looking for clear, lively and interesting writing. They are looking for:

- what you have to say (the quality of your ideas)
- how well you organise your ideas
- the language you use (how well you express yourself).

Try to make your writing as interesting as possible. Your story might be funny or strange or exciting or sad. It might be written in an unusual way or form. However—most importantly—don't try to rewrite something you have prepared. The markers will pick up on this.

In your opinion piece, make sure you back up your opinion with reasons. Write clearly in a way that will convince your reader that your opinion makes sense. Again, don't write something you have prepared.

Finally, write in a way that can actually be read! No matter how brilliant your ideas are, if the markers cannot read your handwriting, they will not be able to give you a good mark. So, if you know your handwriting is not always clear, take time now to improve it.

Important!

This information was correct at the time of writing but make sure you check the information you get about your particular test.

Follow this plan to revise for the NSW Opportunity Class Placement Test and the ACER Scholarship Tests!

Introduction

The content of this book is organised into days of the week—four days each week. Each day covers the maximum you should do on one day. You do not necessarily need to do every section, topic or task. You should focus on the parts you need to practise. Of course you can do all sections, topics and tasks if you wish to.

Times are **suggested** for each section. These are **guides only**. You may take more or less time than other students.

In Each Week

Day 1

On Day 1, you will practise one Reading comprehension topic. Each topic covers a different category of text. For example, in Week 1 Day 1 you will look at literary texts.

Each topic will have the following parts:

- **Key Points** gives you an overview of these kinds of texts, common types of questions asked, and tips and clues on answering questions.
- **Practice Tasks** give you practice reading these kinds of texts and answering questions of the kind you will meet in your test. Read the texts and answer the questions. Then go to the Check your Answer section at the back of the book for the answers and useful tips. While there is time set, this is just a guide. You do not have to complete the task in that time. However, you will have to work quickly in the actual test so you should try to improve your speed as you go through the book.
- **Real Test** allows you to practise answering questions similar to those in the real test under a strict time limit. This time you should work faster and keep to the time limit or even try to beat it. Again, answers and explanations are given at the back of the book.

Day 2

On Day 2, you will cover three topics from the Thinking Skills component. For example, in Week 1 Day 2 you will cover:

- Identifying the main idea
- Assessing the impact of further evidence to strengthen an argument
- Assessing the impact of further evidence to weaken an argument.

Each topic will have the following parts.

- **Key Points** gives a summary of the topic, as well as examples and sample questions.
- Three **Real Tests** allow you to answer questions like those in the real test. Time yourself doing these questions. Answers are given at the back of the book.

Day 3

On Day 3, you will cover two topics from the Mathematical Reasoning test. For example, in Week 1 Day 3 you will cover:

- Whole numbers and money
- Fractions and decimals.

Each topic will have the following parts.

- **Key Points** gives a summary of the topic, as well as examples and sample questions.
- Two **Real Tests** allow you to answer questions like those in the real test. Time yourself doing these questions. Answers are given at the back of the book.

Day 4

On Day 4, you will practise one Writing topic. For example, in Week 1 Day 1 you will cover writing an 'Imagine if ...' story. The four types of writing chosen are the most useful to revise and practise before the tests. However, there is always more than one way to shape these basic types. Some possible forms are:

- a letter to the editor
- a personal letter
- an advertisement
- an information report
- an essay
- a speech
- an interview
- a personal recount
- a letter to a person in authority
- a diary entry
- a magazine or newspaper article
- instructions and rules
- a poem
- a conversation
- an imaginative recount.

Each of the four Writing topics will have the following parts.

- **Key Points** gives you a summary of the type of text, common types of questions, and tips and clues on answering questions for that type of text.
- **Sample** gives you a model question and response for the type of text. The model response has clear notes showing you the appropriate structure and language for that type of text.
- **Practice Tasks** give you a variety of tasks to allow you to develop skills for writing the type of text. Follow the instructions to complete the tasks. Answers and explanations are given at the back of the book.
- **Real Test** allows you to practise answering questions similar to those in the real test under a strict time limit.

Sample Test Papers

- **Sample Test Papers** appear at the end of the book. They are very similar to the real NSW Opportunity Class Placement Test and the ACER Scholarship Tests (Primary level).
- Before attempting the Sample Test Papers, make sure you have done the **Real Test** for any topic you were unsure of and that you worked through the answers for any questions you answered incorrectly.
- Set aside the **time allowed** for each Sample Test Paper and complete the papers under **test conditions**—no sneaking a look at your earlier work or class books! That way you will be better prepared for the real tests.
- **Answers and explanations** for the Sample Test Papers are given at the back of the book, on pages 228–240.

Let's start to revise!

Week 1

This is what we cover this week:

Day 1 **Reading:** Literary texts

Day 2 **Thinking Skills:**

- ◎ Critical thinking—Identifying the main idea
- ◎ Critical thinking—Assessing the impact of further evidence to strengthen an argument
- ◎ Critical thinking—Assessing the impact of further evidence to weaken an argument

Day 3 **Mathematical Reasoning:** ◎ Whole numbers and money

◎ Fractions and decimals

Day 4 **Writing:** 'Imagine if ...' story

- In your test, you might be asked to answer questions about **extracts from short stories, novels, folktales or fables**. These are all examples of literary texts. Literary texts usually aim to make us laugh or cry, or be frightened or intrigued by something. Some aim to teach us about the world and ourselves.

- Some **literary texts** are very descriptive, while others focus more on action and events. Others are mostly about what people say or think, and these contain a lot of dialogue.

- Always **read a literary text right through** before answering any questions about it (unless you run out of time). This is because ideas about a person, an event or an experience may be spread across many paragraphs or even the whole text. You may have to pull these ideas together to come up with one main idea.

- Sometimes the answer will not be obvious—you will have to search for hints and clues here and there to work out an answer—to **draw a conclusion or make a sensible guess**.

- You might be asked about, for example:
  - the **subject or topic** of the writing or part of the writing (e.g. friendship, families, growing up)
  - the **characters**—what the characters did or said, and how they felt
  - the **setting**—where the events take place and how they are described
  - the **atmosphere**—the feeling or mood created in the writing (gloomy, tense, exciting, hopeful, depressing, frantic)
  - the **plot**—the events that happened or the order in which they happened
  - the **writer's feelings** about the topic they are writing on (e.g. the writer might be making fun of something or showing admiration for something)
  - the **meanings of words**. Writers of literary texts often use unusual words; you will have to really use your brains to work out the most likely meaning. You will mainly need to use context clues hiding in the words and sentences before and after the word.

Practice Task 1

READING
Literary texts

10 min

Use this first practice task as a guide. Try to answer the questions without looking at the answers. Then look at the answers for tips about how to get the answer right. Don't worry if you don't get every answer right. Try to do it in 10 minutes but don't worry too much about this. The point is to help you understand the kinds of questions you will find in the test and how to answer them.

Carol and I sat perched in the peppertree near the fence. The wind had dropped and the powdery dust on the road lay undisturbed. Occasionally, a ute or motorbike from one of the nearby farms would approach and pass, clouding the air around us. Slowly, as the dust settled, the landscape would return to its hazy monotony. A few puffy clouds drifted over the low mountains, but didn't come close enough to give us any relief.

Carol climbed higher in the tree and swung backwards and forwards on the thin branches.

'Watch it, you stupid thing', I called. 'It'll break and then you'll know it.'

'Something's coming', Carol called back, ignoring me. 'A truck.'

'Who is it?' I asked without moving.

'Dunno', said Carol. 'Too far away to tell. It's not from around here, though.'

'How do you know?' I called, suddenly interested.

'You can tell', she replied. 'It's not from around here. Anyway, there's a few of them.'

She was right. In the distance a convoy of trucks moved slowly towards us. I climbed higher up the tree. As the trucks laboured down the dusty road I began to make out details—they weren't any that I knew. And there was music!

I scrambled down out of the tree followed closely by Carol, almost falling in our eagerness to get over the fence and onto the roadside. The trucks ground up the road towards us—little flags fluttered above the cabins and there were pictures painted on the sides. Then I saw where the music was coming from. Lounging on a bundle of tarpaulins roped tightly together above the cabin of the first truck, was a woman with a trumpet raised to her lips and aimed at the sky, playing a dance tune! Carol and I stood speechless as the truck slowed down and, with a groan, pulled up in front of us. The woman blew a last long note, then sat for a moment with the trumpet still at her lips, like she was draining a bottle of its last drops. The other trucks were still struggling up the road towards us.

The woman held the trumpet to one side and tipped her sunglasses down her nose. She looked at Carol and me with a grin.

'Bloomin' hot', she said. 'You kids got any water?'

From 'Dad, Mum, the circus and me' in *Through the Web and Other Stories* by Ian Steep, Harcourt Brace Jovanovich, Sydney, 1992

1 How would you describe the feeling of the narrator (a boy) for his sister Carol?
   A   He cares for her but does not want to be with her.
   B   He enjoys being with her.
   C   He hates everything about her.
   D   He wishes she were a boy.

2 Which statement best describes the weather?
   A   A storm is approaching after a hot day.
   B   There was a wind but now it is very hot and still.
   C   It is warming up after a cool morning.
   D   It is very hot and windy.

3 What can you tell about where the children live from the description of the scene?
   A   They live in the middle of a busy city.
   B   They live in a busy country town.
   C   They live in a boring suburb where nothing much happens.
   D   They live in a country area where nothing much happens.

4 What do you think is the main reason Carol is so sure the truck is 'not from around here'?
   A   because she can see it has a strange name on its side
   B   because there are a few trucks together
   C   because she knows all the trucks around there and it isn't one of them
   D   because it looks like a truck from the city

5 How would you describe the way the trucks moved?
   A   slowly and with difficulty
   B   slowly and smoothly
   C   very quickly and easily
   D   slowly and carefully

6 The word 'speechless' conveys the children's
   A   fear for the woman's safety on top of the truck.
   B   interest in what the woman was doing there.
   C   surprise about where the woman is and what she is doing.
   D   excitement that they might get to see a circus.

☞ **Answers and explanations on page 195**

Practice Task 2

READING
Literary texts

`10 MIN`

Read the text carefully and answer the questions. Circle the correct answer for each question. Try to keep to the time limit. When you finish, check the answers. If you did not choose a right answer or if you were unsure about it, read the answer explanation. Don't worry if you don't get the answer right—the aim is to give you practice with the types of texts and questions you will find in the test.

I'd waited for over an hour with Mum and Dad to see the specialist. On previous visits I'd read all the comics, and I didn't believe all that stuff about goldfish being soothing and relaxing to watch. Today, I was really frightened.

'Well, I'm afraid I can't help you any more.'

Perhaps I was going to die or be sentenced to life in my room, bedridden with my own special, incurable disease. My face and arms used to break out in heaps of tiny, itchy blisters. I couldn't stop scratching my red and lumpy skin. Scratching made the problem worse; the blisters became infected sores.

'None of the medicines or creams appear to be working', said the specialist, her bifocals stuck on the the bulb at the end of her nose. 'Whatever chemical it is, is in the smog, and gives Stuart a very nasty allergy, indeed. The only thing I can now recommend is a change of climate.'

Outside, Dad mumbled something about witchdoctors wasting his money.

So my chemical engineer dad, my schoolteacher mum, my big brother (he's got a disease too, Dad says it's puberty) and me, and the pink tizz (they're my two little sisters) moved to the country. Since there aren't many jobs for chemical engineers in country towns, Dad became the local 'Mr Fixit': changing tap washers for the elderly, mowing lawns, pruning roses and clearing sparrows' nests from under roofs and out of gutters.

We swapped our unit overlooking the harbour for a flaky weatherboard farmhouse overlooking a dry creek bed. The leaky gutters were overflowing with peppercorn leaves. The water tanks were filled with smelly green algae. Mice lived in the walls, a possum lived in the ceiling, and the fruit trees guarding the house hadn't been pruned for yonks. The house was a picture of tangled neglect.

'Lots to do here!' said my excited father, yearning to unpack his tools and put things right.

'Why couldn't we live in town like normal people? You've always got to be different', muttered my not-so-pleased mum.

From 'Dad nil: the pelican four' by Paul Williams in *Through the Web and Other Stories*, Harcourt Brace Jovanovich, Sydney, 1992

Practice Task 2

READING
Literary texts

1 What was Stuart's medical problem?
A an incurable disease
B a skin allergy
C an abnormal fear of goldfish
D an eye problem

2 What was the cause of his medical problem?
A chemicals in the city air
B skin creams
C puberty
D unknown

3 Stuart's dad
A was very grateful to the doctor for her advice.
B thought the doctor was charging too much money.
C was annoyed that the doctor had not found out what the problem was.
D was annoyed with his wife for choosing the doctor.

4 How many times had the narrator been to the doctor?
A only once before
B never before
C many times
D There is no way of knowing this.

5 Which of these statements is **not** true?
A The dad had to change his job after moving.
B The dad was happy about their new home.
C The mum was happy about their new home.
D Their new home was very different from their old home.

6 Which of these statements best describes their new home?
A untidy, overgrown and uncared for
B untidy but in good condition
C neat and tidy and well cared for
D pretty and charming but a bit neglected

☞ **Answers and explanations on pages 195-196**

Practice
Task 3

This time try very hard to do the task within 10 minutes. If you can, do it in less. You will have to work very quickly in the test to complete this section in under 10 minutes.

When Merlin, the most famous magician of legend, was young, he seemed unlike an ordinary boy. People said that he was half-fairy and were rather afraid of him. He never did wicked or cruel things, but he would often rock his sides with laughter for what seemed to be no reason at all. Sometimes he would disappear for a week or two. It was whispered of him that he would catch and ride the wild stags, and that all the pretty does and their young followed him, so that the forest glades seemed alive with flying herds of deer. The gossips said, too, that the fairy people were building a house for Merlin in the deep green places of the woods—a house with seventy windows and sixty doors—where, as

soon as he was old enough, he would live quite alone. But when Merlin was stared at because of these things, he only laughed to himself, as usual, and, unconcerned, went about his business.

Then, one day, a party of horsemen came riding along toward the palace in which Merlin had been born. They asked all they met where they could find a certain handsome youth of whom many strange tales were told. The things they mentioned were exactly the stories that were told about Merlin; so, of course, many people told them where Merlin could be found. And, curiously enough, as the riders drew rein before the gate of the city, there stood the slender boy with his laughing mouth and eyes so clear and wild and free.

One of the horsemen sprang down, seized Merlin, and flung him on his own saddle. Then he sprang up behind, set spurs to his steed, and galloped off in company with his friends. Merlin neither struggled nor cried out. He just laughed to himself as usual, for ever since he was a baby he had known that this would happen to him.

Adapted from *King Arthur and his Knights*, made for JG Ferguson Publishing Company by Holt, Rinehart and Winston, 1927

Practice Task 3

1 What did people say about Merlin as a youth?
  A He was a magician.
  B He was wicked and cruel.
  C He was half-fairy.
  D He laughed too much.

2 Where was Merlin born?
  A in a fairy house in the forest
  B in a palace
  C with the wild deer in the forest
  D outside the gates of the city

3 How did Merlin react to people staring at him?
  A He stopped whatever he was doing and stared back at them.
  B He laughed at them and walked away.
  C He became very angry and upset.
  D He laughed to himself and went on doing whatever he was doing.

4 Why didn't Merlin try to get away from the horsemen who were looking for him?
  A because he knew it was his destiny to go with them
  B because he knew they would hunt him forever
  C because he knew they would kill him
  D because he knew he was not strong enough to escape them

5 What does 'set spurs to his steed' mean?
  A patted and stroked the horse
  B buttoned down the saddlebags
  C dug boots into the horse to make it move
  D spoke to the chief horseman

6 Which statement is true?
  A Merlin used to disappear from time to time.
  B Merlin used to ride wild stags.
  C Fairy people were building a house for Merlin.
  D Merlin was going to live alone when he was old.

☞ Answers and explanations on page 196

Real Test

Now test your reading skills within a strict time limit. Don't work beyond the time limit. If you can finish in less than 10 minutes, that is even better. Circle the correct answer for each question and then check your answers. If you get an answer wrong, read the explanation carefully and check the text again.

I remember him as if it were yesterday, as he came plodding to the inn door, his sea-chest following behind him in a hand-barrow—a tall, strong, heavy, nut-brown man, his tarry pigtail falling over the shoulder of his soiled blue coat, his hands ragged and scarred, with black, broken nails, and the sabre cut across one cheek, a dirty, livid white. I remember him looking round the cove and whistling to himself as he did so, and then breaking out in that old sea-song that he sang so often afterwards:

'Fifteen men on the dead man's chest—
Yo-ho-ho, and a bottle of rum!'

Then he rapped on the door with a bit of stick and when my father appeared, called roughly for a glass of rum. This, when it was brought to him, he drank slowly, like a connoisseur, lingering on the taste and still looking about him at the cliffs and up at our signboard.

'This is a handy cove,' says he at length; 'Much company, mate?'

My father told him no, very little company, the more was the pity.

'Well, then,' said he, 'this is the berth for me. Here you, matey,' he cried to the barrow man; 'bring up alongside. I'll stay here a bit,' he continued. 'I'm a plain man; rum and bacon and eggs is what I want, and that head up there for to watch ships off. What might you call me? You might call me captain.' And he threw down three or four gold pieces on the threshold. 'You can tell me when I've worked through that,' says he, looking as fierce as a commander.

And indeed bad as his clothes were and coarsely as he spoke, he seemed like a mate or skipper accustomed to be obeyed or to strike. The man who came with the barrow told us the mail had set him down the morning before at the Royal George, that he had inquired what inns there were along the coast, and hearing the Admiral Benbow well spoken of, I suppose, and described as lonely, had chosen it from the others for his place of residence. And that was all we could learn of our guest.

He was a very silent man by custom. All day he hung round the cove or upon the cliffs with a brass telescope; all evening he sat in a corner of the parlour next the fire and drank rum and water very strong. Every day when he came back from his stroll he would ask if any seafaring men had gone by along the road. At first we thought it was the want of company of his own kind that made him ask this question, but at last we began to see he was desirous to avoid them. For me, at least, there was no secret about the matter. He had taken me aside one day and promised me a silver fourpenny on the first of every month if I would only keep my 'weather-eye open for a seafaring man with one leg' and let him know the moment he appeared.

How that personage haunted my dreams, I need scarcely tell you.

Adapted from *Treasure Island* by RL Stevenson

Real Test

1 Where does the story take place?
   A on a ship stranded at sea
   B at an inn called the Royal George
   C in a house close by the sea
   D at an inn called the Admiral Benbow

2 Based on what is written in the extract, we know the main character is a
   A pirate.
   B man with one leg.
   C sailor.
   D sea captain.

3 Which of these statements is **not** true?

   The main character is looking for somewhere to stay where he can
   A be on his own.
   B be in the company of others.
   C get a good view of the sea.
   D get good food and drink.

4 What does the word 'connoisseur' tell us?
   A The main character might not be the rough man he first appears to be.
   B The main character is a drunkard.
   C The main character fears he will be poisoned.
   D The main character has no manners.

5 'You can tell me when I've worked through that' suggests the main character
   A wants to spend all his money.
   B wants to be treated well.
   C does not have much money.
   D has plenty of money.

6 The main character could be described as someone who
   A likes to tell people what to do.
   B is used to other people doing what he tells them to do.
   C is afraid of talking to other people.
   D is kindly and shy despite his rough appearance.

☞ **Answers and explanations on pages 196-197**

- The main idea is the **conclusion** the creator of the text wants you to accept.
- The main idea can be **anywhere in the text**.
- The main idea will be **supported by the rest of the text**.

Example

Instead of being driven to school each day, students should walk. This would ensure that all students start the day with fresh air and exercise. It would bring many benefits to health as well as to learning. Research shows that exercise prepares the brain for learning and helps children concentrate.

Which of the following best expresses the main idea of the text?

A   Fresh air and exercise bring many benefits.
B   Students should walk to school instead of being driven.
C   Some students live too far from the school to walk.
D   Exercise helps children concentrate better in class.

Steps to work out the answer

1   Read the text carefully. Ask yourself: What does the creator of this text **want me to accept**?
2   Underline the sentence you think is the **main idea**: Instead of being driven to school each day, students should walk.
3   Check: Does the rest of the text give you reason to **believe** this underlined sentence?
4   Decide which of the statements listed in the question **best expresses the main idea** you found.

B is correct. The text wants you to accept that students should walk to school instead of being driven. You can check this is the main idea by seeing if the rest of the text gives you reason to believe it. In this case, the rest of the text gives information about the benefits to health and learning from fresh air and exercise. So this confirms the main idea and B is the statement in the list that best expresses it.

Incorrect answers

A and D are incorrect because they support, or are a reason to believe, the main idea that students should walk to school instead of being driven.

C is incorrect because it is extra information not stated in the text, so it cannot be the main idea.

Checklist

Can you:

1   *read a text carefully and think about what the creator of the text wants you to accept?*
2   *underline the sentence you think is the main idea?*
3   *check that the rest of the text gives you reason to believe this main idea?*
4   *from a list of statements given, find the one that best expresses this main idea?*

Real Test 1

THINKING SKILLS
Critical thinking—Identifying the main idea

10 MIN

1 Medieval knights were expected to live by a code known as chivalry. This code of chivalry meant knights had to be loyal, fair, respectful and truthful. It also meant knights had to protect the weak and defenceless. The word chivalry comes from a French word *chevalier*—which simply means a person who rides a horse.

Which of the following best expresses the main idea of the text?

A Knights had to live by a code of chivalry.
B The word chivalry comes from a French word.
C Knights protected the weak and defenceless.
D A chivalry is a person riding a horse.

2 Guinea pigs need a rich environment that allows them to exercise and express natural behaviours. It is important for their physical and psychological wellbeing. Some of these normal behaviours are interacting with other guinea pigs, running, jumping, exploring, tunnelling, playing with toys, chewing and hiding. Be sure to provide your guinea pigs with plenty of stimulation.

Which of the following best expresses the main idea of the text?

A Guinea pigs need a stimulating environment.
B Guinea pigs like to interact with each other.
C Guinea pigs have a lot of natural behaviours.
D Guinea pigs make great pets and are fun to watch.

3 Around the world, people in different countries and cultures celebrate birthdays in different ways. In Canada the birthday person might have butter smeared on their nose, while in Jamaica they might have flour thrown on their head. In China the birthday person should eat long noodles to symbolise a long life. In Mexico the birthday person gets to bite into a creamy cake but they are not allowed to use their hands, and after the bite their face will be pushed into the cake.

Which of the following best expresses the main idea of the text?

A Eating noodles on your birthday symbolises a long life.
B Every culture celebrates birthdays in the same way.
C Different countries and cultures have different birthday traditions.
D People from some cultures do not give birthday presents.

4 Brush turkeys have a reputation for destroying gardens by constructing large mounds of vegetation, earth and mulch to incubate their eggs. In fact brush turkeys can be good for the garden. They love to eat insects so will keep your garden bug numbers under control. They also eat seeds and, as they scratch about, they help distribute the seeds of many native plants. So if a brush turkey wants to move into your garden, consider leaving a corner near a tree where you are happy for their wild construction to go ahead.

Which of the following best expresses the main idea of the text?

A Brush turkeys build their mounds under trees.
B Brush turkeys destroy gardens.
C Brush turkeys eat insects and seeds.
D Brush turkeys can be good for gardens.

☞ **Answers and explanations on pages 197-198**

Real Test 1

5 There are so many fascinating facts about elephants. They are the largest land mammals in the world with an average life span from 50 to 70 years. They have 150 000 muscles and tendons in their trunk—which is a long nose they use for smelling, drinking, trumpeting and picking things up. When elephants see each other they say hello by wrapping their trunks together. It's not true that elephants are afraid of mice. But they *are* terrified of bees!

Which of the following best expresses the main idea of the text?

A Elephants are terrified of bees.

B There are many amazing facts about elephants.

C An elephant's trunk has many uses.

D Elephants live long lives.

6 Venus is a planet of similar size to Earth. Its surface has craters, thousands of volcanoes, rivers of lava and mountain ranges, as well as smooth flat plains. Venus would not be hospitable for human life. For a start there's no oxygen in the air on Venus so humans couldn't breathe. Also, it's hot enough at the surface to melt lead and the rain would burn human skin like acid in nanoseconds. Venus might be an interesting planet to study but it isn't somewhere humans could live.

Which of the following best expresses the main idea of the text?

A Venus would not be hospitable for human life.

B Venus might be an interesting place.

C There's no oxygen in the air on Venus.

D Venus is a planet of similar size to Earth.

7 *The Secret Garden* by Frances Hodgson Burnett was first published as a book in 1911 and has been made into a film and also a stage play. The story tells of an orphan, Mary, from a privileged background who is sent to live at her Uncle's estate on the English moors. When we first meet her, Mary is sour, spoilt and demanding. She eventually discovers the secret garden of the title and her cousin, who also seems spoilt and demanding. *The Secret Garden* is a wonderful story about friendship, family and love. I highly recommend it.'

Which of the following best expresses the main idea of the text?

A *The Secret Garden* was first published as a book in 1911.

B The writer highly recommends *The Secret Garden*.

C *The Secret Garden* is a wonderful story about friendship, family and love.

D *The Secret Garden* was written by Frances Hodgson Burnett.

8 My family is moving house to the other side of the city. We are moving to a nicer house, which is great but I will have to go to a different school. I love this school. All my friends are here. I like the teachers. I really don't want to move to a different school.

Which of the following best expresses the main idea of the text?

A Phillip prefers his new house to his old house.

B Phillip doesn't want to change schools.

C Phillip doesn't want to move to the other side of the city.

D Phillip is angry with his parents for making him change schools.

☞ **Answers and explanations on pages 197-198**

9 The term 'swamp' is often used negatively to imply a horrid, wet place but swamps, along with other types of wetlands such as marshes, mudflats, mangroves and billabongs, are vitally important for the environment. These wetlands provide habitats and nurseries for fish and other animals as well as migrating birds. They trap sediment and filter nutrients to help sustain healthy rivers.

Which of the following best expresses the main idea of the text?

A A swamp can have fresh water, salt water or brackish water which is somewhere in between.

B Swamps provide habitats and nurseries for fish and other animals.

C Wetlands include marshes, mudflats, mangroves and billabongs.

D Swamps and other types of wetlands are vitally important for the environment.

10 I oppose construction of the new dam. It poses unacceptable risks to the environment, including the loss of breeding habitat for a number of critically endangered birds. The dam proposal means the loss of prime agricultural land, which will all be flooded. That land is a food bowl for the region. Damming the river will also lead to water shortages further down the river. thereby negatively impacting the wetlands which are vital for migratory birds and other wildlife.

Which of the following best expresses the main idea of the text?

A The writer opposes construction of the new dam.

B The dam proposal means the loss of prime agricultural land.

C The dam poses unacceptable risks to the environment.

D The dam proposal means the land will all be flooded.

☞ Answers and explanations on pages 197-198

- An argument text presents someone's **point of view** or makes a **claim**.
- An argument uses **supporting evidence** to **convince** others to accept a point of view or claim.
- An argument can be **strengthened or supported** with **further evidence or extra information**.

Example

Astronaut crews undertake intensive training together to prepare for the physical, emotional and mental challenges they might encounter on a journey into space. Training can involve climbing in deep caves or climbing mountains, training underwater, running in a centrifuge or undertaking weightlessness drills and other team-building activities in stressful situations. Training together helps ensure a successful mission into space.

Which statement most **strengthens** the argument?

A   Astronauts train as a group so they become good friends.

B   A good rapport with the rest of the crew is essential so there will be no arguments.

C   Weightlessness drills prepare astronauts for the zero-gravity of space.

D   Working effectively in the cramped spacecraft requires teamwork.

Steps to work out the answer

1   **Identify the argument.** The creator of the text wants people to accept that astronaut crews undertake intensive training and team-building activities before they go on any journey into space because that helps to ensure a successful mission.

2   **Look for further evidence** that supports the argument.

3   **Judge** which statement most **strengthens** the argument.

D is correct. The statement that most strengthens the argument is that It takes teamwork to work effectively in a cramped spacecraft. This statement strengthens the reason crews undertake group training in stressful situations.

Incorrect answers

A is incorrect. It might be true that being good friends helps astronauts cope with the physical, emotional and mental challenges they might encounter on a journey into space but it does not best support the argument because being friends can't ensure a successful mission.

B is incorrect. It would be true that arguing with other crew members on a mission into space would not be helpful but this statement is not the one that most strengthens the argument in the text.

C is incorrect. Weightlessness drills are an example of the training crews would do but this statement does not support the argument the creator is making about team-building.

Checklist

Can you:

1   *identify the argument?*

2   *assess the impact of further evidence?*

Real Test 2

10 min

1 A government wildlife spokesperson said: 'Native reptiles are protected by law but sometimes, for people's safety, venomous snakes need to be removed from a property. Anyone who applies for a licence to catch and release reptiles in these circumstances needs to be suitably qualified.'

Which statement **strengthens** the spokesperson's claim?

A Reptiles are a natural part of a healthy ecosystem.

B If you find a snake in your garden, leave it alone and don't attempt to remove it yourself.

C A licensed reptile handler must have completed a reptile handling course and have two years experience handling venomous snakes.

D Snakes usually prefer to retreat rather than attack but they might attack if provoked.

2 A health expert said: 'Physical exercise such as brisk walking is good for making our bodies fitter and healthier but it is also good for our brains. Increased blood flow when we exercise brings more oxygen to the brain to help it do its work.'

Which statement **strengthens** the health expert's claim?

A The brain uses about 20% of the body's oxygen supply and even more if you are using it to concentrate.

B Regular exercise improves sleep and mood and helps reduce anxiety.

C Exercise is good preventative medicine.

D Exercise promotes the release of hormones that make us feel happier.

3 Davy said: 'I'm selling my old tent. I've written an advertisement. I hope I can sell it quickly. So far I've said: For sale. Fantastic secondhand, two-person tent. Waterproof. Has all its poles, ties and pegs. No rips or tears. Only ten years old. Make an offer.'

What else could Davy add to **strengthen** his claims about his tent?

A Just needs a good clean.   B not too heavy

C barely used   D Won't last so be quick!

4 Matika said: 'Dad's podiatrist said that to avoid foot problems now and later in life it's important for everyone to take proper care of their feet. She told Dad to exfoliate his feet and moisturise them, keep his toenails clipped and choose well-fitted shoes and good-quality, natural socks like bamboo.'

Which statement most **strengthens** the podiatrist's claim?

A Let your feet breathe by not wearing socks and shoes all the time.

B If you don't take care of your feet, your muscles, bones and joints can weaken.

C Dry your feet thoroughly after you wash them.

D An ingrown toenail is when the edge of a toenail grows into the skin next to the nail.

☞ **Answers and explanations on pages 198–199**

Real Test 2

5 Harry Houdini is one of the most famous magicians of all time. He was an escapologist, performing stunts in which he freed himself from handcuffs, straightjackets, chains and ropes to escape from locked jail cells and water-filled tanks.

Which statement best **supports** the argument above?

A One of Houdini's most famous stunts was called the Water Torture Cell.

B Houdini's performances were described as death defying.

C Houdini died of an infection from a ruptured appendix.

D Houdini's performances kept audiences around the world on the edges of their seats.

6 A local politician said: 'Balloons should be banned because they are a danger to wildlife. They can float and travel hundreds of kilometres, then deflate and fall into oceans and waterways. Marine animals and birds mistake them for food and swallow them. The balloons wrap around other items in the animal's stomach and cause blockages. The animal then becomes dehydrated, starves and dies.'

Which statement most **strengthens** the politician's argument?

A Balloons are a threat to wildlife.

B Bright and colourful balloons are fun.

C Wildlife can become entangled in the strings on balloons.

D A bubble machine is a good alternative to party balloons.

7 **Ali:** 'Pets can make us physically and mentally healthier. One benefit of pet ownership is increased physical activity. Dog owners, especially, get more regular exercise. Another benefit is a more positive outlook. Just looking at a pet can help us relax.'

Which one of these statements most **strengthens** Ali's argument?

A Some people are allergic to dog or cat fur.

B There are many cats and dogs available for adoption.

C Australia has one of the highest rates of pet ownership in the world.

D Research shows that people who own a pet make fewer visits to the doctor.

8 Jade and Finn are working together to design a robot that could be used to rescue people after an earthquake.

Finn: 'We should make our robot tall and strong. It should move like a human.'

Jade: 'There's a lot of rubble after an earthquake so I'd like to try a more flexible shape. I think we should model our robot on the way cockroaches move.'

Which one of these statements most **strengthens** Jade's argument?

A Robot researchers are looking to nature for inspiration for how robots can move.

B Robots are being developed to rescue humans after disasters.

C Cockroaches can squeeze into tiny places by redistributing their exoskeleton sections.

D Cockroaches can hold their breath for five to seven minutes.

☞ **Answers and explanations on pages 198-199**

Real Test 2

THINKING SKILLS—CRITICAL THINKING
Critical thinking—Assessing the impact of further evidence to strengthen an argument

9 The student council met with the principal to argue that the arts should be included in the annual school sports carnival. They argued that the school should honour the vision of the Olympic Games. They told the principal that the arts were central to the ancient Olympics.

Which one of these statements most **strengthens** the student council's argument?
A The founder of the modern Olympics had included plans for the arts as well as athletics.
B The original vision of the Olympics has been lost.
C Arts competitions could include music, painting, sculpture and writing.
D The ancient Olympics included trumpet competitions.

10 A spokesperson for a wildlife-rescue organisation was interviewed on television: 'Koalas and their habitat are under threat. But in order to help koalas we need exact information about where they live. We urgently need funds so that we can train koala detection dogs. Please donate what you can to this vital project.'

Which one of these statements most **strengthens** the spokesperson's argument?
A Koalas face threats from land clearing, bushfires and disease.
B By successfully training dogs, we can work faster and more accurately to protect koalas.
C Dogs are trained to trail the scent of wildlife fur or scat.
D Highly active dogs rescued from shelters are good candidates to train as wildlife detectors.

☞ **Answers and explanations on pages 198-199**

Key Points

THINKING SKILLS
Critical thinking—Assessing the impact of further evidence to weaken an argument

`10 MIN`

- An argument text presents someone's **point of view** or makes a **claim**.
- The argument's creator uses **supporting evidence** to **convince** others to accept their point of view or claim.
- An argument can be **weakened** by any statement that **calls into question or undermines** any of the information or claims in the argument.

Example

Arnie's chess teacher has petitioned the Department of Education to make learning the game of chess part of the mandatory curriculum in government schools. She says all children should learn chess because it teaches the skills of strategising and problem solving which are useful in all aspects of life.

Which statement **weakens** the chess teacher's argument?

A   Playing chess can teach children to be creative thinkers in real-life situations.
B   It's difficult to find people to teach children chess because it's a game that takes a lot of time and patience.
C   Many games improve the skills of strategising and problem solving, including outdoor games, like hockey which also make you fitter and healthier.
D   Learning chess teaches children to focus their attention and avoid distractions.

Steps to work out the answer

1   **Identify the argument**: that chess should be taught in schools because it teaches the skills of strategising and problem solving.
2   **Judge** which of the statements **weakens** the argument. Remember that any statement which undermines or calls into question any of the claims in the argument will weaken the argument.

C is correct. The argument is that all children should learn chess in school because it teaches the skills of strategising and problem solving. The statement that children can learn these skills playing hockey and other outdoor games, while also getting fitter and healthier, undermines the chess teacher's argument that it should be mandatory for chess to be taught in schools to teach those skills.

Incorrect answers

A is incorrect. The statement that 'playing chess can teach children to be creative thinkers in real-life situations' strengthens the argument to make chess mandatory in schools.

B is incorrect. The statement that 'it's difficult to find people to teach children chess because it takes a lot of time and patience' might be true but it does not weaken the argument about making the teaching of chess mandatory in schools.

D is incorrect. The claim that 'learning chess teaches children to focus their attention and avoid distractions' supports the argument rather than weakens it.

Checklist

Can you:
1   *identify the argument?*
2   *assess the impact of further evidence to weaken an argument?*

Real Test 3

THINKING SKILLS
Critical thinking—Assessing the impact of further evidence to weaken an argument

10 MIN

1 **Hilda:** 'The healthiest fruit, full of vitamins and minerals, is the banana. If you were stranded on a tropical island you could survive on bananas.'

Which of the following statements, if true, **weakens** Hilda's argument?

A You could survive in the short term because bananas have many vitamins and minerals.

B Bananas are deficient in protein so would not provide adequate nutrition for long-term survival.

C Bananas contain essential minerals such as potassium, magnesium and manganese.

D It's important to consult your doctor before becoming stranded on a tropical island.

2 Cauliflower is a vegetable that belongs to the same family of vegetables as broccoli, Brussels sprouts and cabbage. Its name comes from Latin and means cabbage (*caulis*) and flower (*flos*). Cauliflower contains a variety of minerals as well as phytonutrients and fibre. Eating cauliflower is good for your health.

Which one of these statements, if true, **weakens** the argument above?

A Some researchers believe that cauliflower could have anticancer benefits.

B Cauliflower is healthiest if eaten raw or steamed rather than boiled.

C In a small number of people, cauliflower can cause abdominal discomfort.

D Cauliflowers can be white, green, purple or orange.

3 **Jess:** 'I've just started playing table tennis. It's so much fun. At the moment I'm not a great player but I am developing agility and coordination and learning how to combine strokes. You have to develop quick reflexes to be good at table tennis because the ball moves so quickly. I'm getting fitter too. You should come with me and learn to play it.'

Cody: 'No. I'd be hopeless at table tennis. My reflexes are too slow.'

Which of these statements, if true, **weakens** Cody's argument?

A You can develop agility and coordination and how to combine strokes.

B The ball moves quickly in table tennis.

C You need to be fit to be good at table tennis.

D You can develop quick reflexes to improve at table tennis.

☞ **Answers and explanations on pages 199–200**

Real Test 3

4 Jeffrey: 'Our team captain, Willem, is a role model for the rest of the team. He is one of the best players on the team and he always tries his hardest. He works to bring everyone on the team together so we play as a team and support each other. He is respectful and expects everyone on the team to respect each other and our coach. He sets a good example by being a good sport.'

Which of these statements, if true, **weakens** Jeffrey's argument?

A Willem argued with the referee after the last match.

B Willem is proud of the team's achievements and tells them so.

C Willem makes quick decisions on the field.

D Willem offers extra practice sessions to players who want support.

5 Ashleigh suffers from moderate hay fever and takes an antihistamine for the symptoms. One of the potential side effects of her particular antihistamine is drowsiness. Ashleigh says being sleepy is better than the misery of constantly sneezing.

Which of these statements, if true, **weakens** Ashleigh's argument?

A Ashleigh finds it very easy to go to sleep when she has hay fever.

B Ashleigh's symptoms are difficult to control without medication.

C Antihistamines work by preventing the symptoms of an allergic reaction.

D Ashleigh works as a forklift operator and needs to be mentally alert at work.

6 Ruby said: 'Cats make the best pets. They are soft and cuddly, they don't need a lot of space and the way they chase things is cute.'

Which of these statements, if true, most **weakens** Ruby's argument?

A Studies estimate that each roaming pet cat kills 115 native animals per year.

B Cats love to chase things that move.

C It's thought that cats were first used to help farmers protect crops from mice.

D Cats are independent and easy to care for.

7 Tom: 'Shark nets are mesh fishing nets suspended in the water off beaches. They are used in a few places around the world to reduce the likelihood of humans being bitten by sharks.

They cost millions of dollars a year but they are important because they keep swimmers safe from sharks.'

Which of these statements, if true, most **weakens** Tom's argument?

A The nets rely on sharks swimming into them and becoming entangled.

B Around 40% of sharks are caught on the 'wrong side' (beach side) of nets.

C Seabirds, whales, dolphins, turtles and even crocodiles are also caught and killed by shark nets.

D Shark nets are checked every two to three days (weather permitting) for maintenance.

☞ **Answers and explanations on pages 199-200**

Real Test 3

8 Nina's parents want her to write a letter to her grandmother and post it to her. But Nina argues that an email would be better. She says emails are faster than regular post.

Which of these statements, if true, **weakens** Nina's argument?

A Photos can be printed and included in a letter.

B Videos can be shared in an email.

C It is exciting to anticipate and receive a letter in the post.

D Sending emails back and forth is more instant, like a conversation.

9 **Melani:** 'My favourite snake is the green tree snake. What's yours?'

Cooper: 'None! All snakes are awful! They bite!'

Which of these statements, if true, most **weakens** Cooper's argument?

A Snakes play an important role in many different ecosystems.

B Snakes will normally only bite when provoked or hurt.

C Snake numbers are declining.

D Snakes do not chew their food.

10 An environmentalist says: 'Not only do floods cause loss of life and property but they are also bad for the environment. They uproot trees, wreak havoc on the landscape and wash away important topsoil.'

Which of these statements, if true, **weakens** the environmentalist's claim?

A Flood waters carry sediment into the Great Barrier Reef, impacting the coral's ability to photosynthesise.

B During and after floods, many plants die in waterlogged soil.

C Floods spread invasive weeds to new areas.

D Floods replenish groundwater.

☞ **Answers and explanations on pages 199–200**

MATHEMATICAL REASONING
Whole numbers and money

- **The place value of a number** is based on the following sequence of numbers:
millions ... hundred thousands ... ten thousands ... thousands ... hundreds ... tens ... units.

  Example: 42060 in words is
  A forty-two thousand and sixty.
  B four thousand and sixty.
  C four hundred and twenty-six.
  D forty-two thousand six hundred.
  E four hundred and twenty thousand.
  The correct answer is **A**, as there are no hundreds and no units.

- **Numbers can be rounded** to the nearest units, tens, hundreds, etc. to give an approximation for the number.
  Digits 0, 1, 2, 3 or 4 round down while 5, 6, 7, 8 or 9 round up.

  Example: Celeste rounds the number 525842 to the nearest thousand. Which of these is the approximation?
  A 525   B 536   C 525000   D 525800   E 526000
  The correct answer is **E**. Look at the digit in the hundreds place. As it is 8 the number rounds up to 526000.

- When **adding**, words such as **sum** and **total** are used.

  Example: Over four days, Nathan recorded the weight of sausages he sold in his shop:
  18 kg, 23 kg, 19 kg and 25 kg. What was the total weight of sausages Nathan sold?
  A 75 kg   B 80 kg   C 85 kg   D 90 kg   E 95 kg
  The correct answer is **C**. As total means to add, then 18 + 23 + 19 + 25 = 85. Nathan sold 85 kg.

  Tip: Numbers are easier to add when written under each other.

- **Difference** and **exceed** are words used to mean that we have to **subtract**.

  Example: Twins Lyn and Lee are 139 cm and 143 cm respectively. What is the difference between their heights?
  A 282 cm   B 4 cm   C 5 cm   D 6 cm   E 3 cm
  The answer is **B**. In this question, we subtract one number from the other: 143 – 139 = 4. The difference in the twins' heights is 4 cm.

  Tip: Numbers are easier to subtract when written under each other.

- When we multiply, we can use the words **times** and **product**.

  Example: What is the product of five and nine?
  A four   B five   C fourteen   D forty-five   E fifty-four
  The correct answer is **D**. To find the product, we multiply the numbers: 5 × 9 = 45. This means the product of 5 and 9 is 45.

  Tip: Practise your times tables up to ten.

MATHEMATICAL REASONING
Whole numbers and money

- **To divide two numbers** is to find their **quotient**.

  Example: The quotient of sixty and three is
  A twenty.   **B** two.   **C** fifty-seven.   **D** sixty-three.   **E** eighteen.
  The correct answer is **A**, as 60 ÷ 3 = 20. The quotient is 20.

  Tip: It helps to remember that dividing is the opposite of multiplying.

- **When we divide**, there may be a **remainder**.

  Example: When thirty jelly beans are shared equally between four boys, how many are left over?
  A one   **B** two   **C** three   **D** four   **E** none of these
  The correct answer is **B**. This question is asking for the remainder. As 30 ÷ 4 = 7 remainder 2, there are 2 jelly beans left over.

- **When the remainder is 0**, we say that this second number is a **factor** of the first.

  Example: Which of the following is **not** a factor of 24?
  A 7   **B** 6   **C** 4   **D** 3   **E** 8
  The correct answer is **A**, as 24 ÷ 7 = 3 remainder 3. This means 7 is not a factor of 24.

- **If a number has only two factors**, the number is **prime**.

  Example: Which of the following is a prime number?
  A 10   **B** 6   **C** 8   **D** 5   **E** 39
  The correct answer is **D**, as the factors of 5 are 5 and 1, whereas each of the other answers has more than two factors.

  Tip: Except for 0 and 1, any non-prime number is called **composite**.

- **In a numerical expression**, there is an **order of operations** that has to be followed. This order is: brackets, then multiplication/division, then addition/subtraction.

  Example: $4 + 2 \times 3 =$
  A 10   **B** 18   **C** 24   **D** 20   **E** 12
  The correct answer is **A**, as the multiplying has to occur first, before the adding. This means $4 + 2 \times 3 = 4 + 6 = 10$.

- **An average is found** by finding the sum and then dividing by the number being added.

  Example: Dominique recorded the number of emails she received over four days as 6, 3, 7 and 4. The average number of emails Dominique received each day was
  A 20   **B** 2   **C** 4   **D** 5   **E** 17
  The correct answer is **D**, as the average = $(6 + 3 + 7 + 4) ÷ 4 = 20 ÷ 4 = 5$. Dominique received an average of 5 emails per day.

- **When paying cash in Australia,** the total price for items is rounded to the **nearest 5 cents**. This means 1c and 2c round down, 3c, 4c, 6c, 7c round to 5c, and 8c and 9c round up.

  Example: Eddie buys a carton of eggs priced at $3.27. How much change will he receive from a $5 note?

  A $1.70   **B** $1.75   **C** $1.85   **D** $2.75   **E** $2.80

  The correct answer is **B**. The $3.27 price rounds down to $3.25. From 25c you need 75c to make up to $4 and then another $1 to make $5. This means Eddie received change of $1.75.

- **The number line can be extended** to the left to include **negative numbers**. These numbers are used for temperatures, in finance and in many other areas.

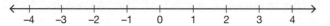

  Example: At 6 am the temperature at Perisher Valley was −5 °C. By midday it had risen by 12 °C. What was the temperature at midday?

  A −17 °C   **B** −7 °C   **C** 5 °C   **D** 6 °C   **E** 7 °C

  The correct answer is **E**. Starting at −5, it takes 5 to reach 0. As 12 − 5 = 7, the temperature rises by another 7 degrees. This means the temperature at midday is 7 °C.

Checklist

Can you:

1. *use an understanding of place value to change numerals into words?*
2. *recognise the terms used to add, subtract, multiply and divide?*
3. *find the remainder when a division occurs between two numbers?*
4. *find the factors of a number?*
5. *identify prime numbers?*
6. *use the rules for order of operations when calculating?*
7. *find the average of a sequence of numbers?*
8. *round to the nearest 5 cents to calculate change?*
9. *use a number line involving negative numbers?*

1 Lilybet rounds each of these numbers to the nearest 100. Which number changes the most?

115	183	238	277	326
A	B	C	D	E

2 Which number is six hundred more than 265 893?

A 865 893

B 271 893

C 266 493

D 265 953

E 265 999

3 Meghan uses these number cards to make three-digit numbers.

What is the difference between the largest and smallest three-digit numbers she can make?

27	37	567	594	604
A	B	C	D	E

4 Harry buys six apples at the supermarket. The total cost of the apples is $2.38. He inserts $5 into the self-serve checkout. The machine gives him the smallest number of coins possible. How many coins does he receive as change?

3	4	5	6	7
A	B	C	D	E

5 Edrick has 246 stickers and Clint has 120. Edrick gives Clint enough stickers so that they both have the same number. How many stickers does Edrick give Clint?

24	32	63	126	166
A	B	C	D	E

6 Evelyn is playing a board game with some friends. She has a pile of money which totals $1200. She decides to buy four houses at $130 each and a hotel. She has $430 remaining. What was the cost of the hotel?

$150	$250	$380	$350	$520
A	B	C	D	E

7 On a number line, which two numbers are 79 units from 152?

A 63 and 221

B 73 and 221

C 73 and 231

D 83 and 221

E 83 and 231

8 At the supermarket, strawberries are on sale for three punnets for $6 or $2.50 each. Kate bought eight punnets. What is the smallest amount of money she can spend?

A $14.00

B $17.00

C $17.50

D $18.00

E $20.00

9 The temperature in Glen Innes at 8 pm was 4 °C. By midnight it had dropped 5 degrees, and then by 6 am another 2 degrees. What was the temperature at 6 am?

6 °C	0 °C	−2 °C	−3 °C	−4 °C
A	B	C	D	E

10 It was Thomas's birthday and five of his friends took him out for dinner. The total cost of the dinner was $360. The bill was shared equally between Thomas's friends. How much did each person pay?

$50	$55	$60	$66	$72
A	B	C	D	E

☞ **Answers and explanations on pages 200–201**

Real Test 2

MATHEMATICAL REASONING
Whole numbers and money

10 MIN

1 On the weekend Idris picked lots of oranges from the tree in his backyard. He gave four oranges to each of his six friends. If he still had 18 oranges, how many did he pick from his tree?

32	42	46	48	52
A	B	C	D	E

2 William bought four bananas at 80 cents each. He handed over $5 to pay for the bananas and received his change in 20-cent coins. How many coins was he given in change?

4	7	9	11	13
A	B	C	D	E

3 Edna and Wilma are sisters and both collect teapots. Edna has 36 teapots. Wilma has 18 more teapots than her sister. How many teapots do the sisters have altogether?

54	80	84	90	108
A	B	C	D	E

4 Jordie has been given a $200 gift card for his birthday. He buys a pair of jeans for $120 and two shirts which cost $35 each. How much money remains on the gift card?

$10	$43	$45	$55	$80
A	B	C	D	E

5 What is the smallest positive number that is a multiple of 5 but leaves a remainder of 1 when divided by 6?

5	10	16	25	36
A	B	C	D	E

6 Amelia subtracted the sum of 12 and 6 from the product of 12 and 6. What is Amelia's answer?

0	36	44	48	54
A	B	C	D	E

7 What is the difference in the value of the 8 and the 6 in the number 18 364?

200	7040	7400	7940	17 040
A	B	C	D	E

8 Charlotte and Evelyn both buy some jewellery. Charlotte bought a bracelet which cost $120. Evelyn spent twice as much as Charlotte when she bought a necklace. What was the total amount of money spent?

$60	$180	$240	$300	$360
A	B	C	D	E

9 Oscar buys a salad roll and a bottle of water and pays $5. Leo buys two salad rolls and a bottle of water and pays $8. How much will Harry pay if he buys a salad roll and two bottles of water?

$6	$6.50	$7	$8.50	$9
A	B	C	D	E

10 A footy tipping competition was held between four friends. At the end of the season Charlotte had scored 40 points. Scarlett had twice as many points as Billie and 30 points more than Charlotte. Doneta scored 50 points more than Billie.

Here are three statements about the competition.

1. Scarlett won the tipping competition.
2. Billy came third.
3. Doneta scored more points than Charlotte and Billy together.

Which of these statements is/are correct?

A statement 1 only
B statement 2 only
C statement 3 only
D statements 1 and 2 only
E statements 2 and 3 only

☞ **Answers and explanations on page 201**

MATHEMATICAL REASONING
Fractions and decimals

10 MIN

- Some fractions look different but are actually the same. They are called **equivalent fractions**. Here is a list of fractions that are equivalent: $\frac{1}{2}, \frac{2}{4}, \frac{3}{6}, \frac{5}{10}, \frac{20}{40}$, and so on.

  Example: Which of the following is the same as $\frac{2}{3}$?

  A $\frac{5}{20}$ B $\frac{15}{20}$ C $\frac{4}{9}$ D $\frac{6}{9}$ E $\frac{12}{13}$

  The correct answer is **D**, as $\frac{6}{9} = \frac{2 \times 3}{3 \times 3} = \frac{2}{3}$.

  💡 *Tip:* Find a number that divides into the top (numerator) and bottom (denominator) numbers.

- **Fractions can be added or subtracted** by first rewriting them so they have the same denominator.

  Example: The sum of $\frac{1}{2}$ and $\frac{3}{4}$ is

  A $1\frac{1}{4}$.   B $1\frac{1}{2}$.   C $1\frac{3}{4}$.   D 2.   E $\frac{4}{6}$.

  The correct answer is **A**, as $\frac{1}{2} = \frac{2}{4}$, and then $\frac{2}{4} + \frac{3}{4} = \frac{5}{4} = 1\frac{1}{4}$.

- **To find a fraction of a quantity** it is usually easier to use division (and multiplication).

  Example: Ashley is walking an 18-km trail in a national park. By lunchtime he has completed $\frac{2}{3}$ of the distance. How far has Ashley already walked?

  A 10 km   B 12 km   C 14 km   D 15 km   E 16 km

  The correct answer is **B**. First find $\frac{1}{3}$ of the distance using $18 \div 3 = 6$ and then multiply by 2 to get $\frac{2}{3}$. This is 6×2, which is 12 km.

- **The place value of numbers** is extended to cater for fractions and decimals.

  … tens   ones (units)   tenths   hundredths   thousandths   ten-thousandths   …

  Example: Hermann wrote the number 51.478. How many times larger is the place value of the 4 than the 8?

  A 20 times   B 50 times   C 200 times   D 500 times   E 2000 times

  The correct answer is **B**. The 4 is 4-tenths, or $\frac{4}{10}$, or $\frac{400}{1000}$. The 8 is 8-thousandths, or $\frac{8}{1000}$. As $400 \div 8$ is 50, then it is 50 times bigger.

- **Decimals can be compared** easily if they have the same number of decimal places.

  Example: Which of the following is ordered from smallest to highest?

  A 0.2, 0.7, 0.04   B 1.2, 0.13, 0.045   C 0.03, 0.3, 0.301
  D 0.605, 0.65, 0.56   E 0.4, 0.05, 0.006

  The correct answer is **C**, by seeing 0.030, 0.300 and 0.301.

  💡 *Tip:* Zeros on the end of a decimal do not change its size.

● **When adding or subtracting decimals**, take care with the place values.

Example: 4.7 – 0.32 =

A 1.5   B 4.48   C 4.42   D 4.38   E 0.15

The correct answer is **D**, as 4.70 – 0.32 = 4.38.

💡 *Tip:* When adding or subtracting decimals, it may be helpful to write one under the other.

Checklist

Can you:

1 *recognise equivalent fractions?*
2 *add and subtract fractions?*
3 *find a fraction of a quantity?*
4 *determine the place value of digits in a decimal?*
5 *compare and order decimals?*
6 *add and subtract decimals?*

Real
Test 3

MATHEMATICAL REASONING
Fractions and decimals

10 MIN

1 Shannon needs to shade four-fifths of the rectangle. She has already started:

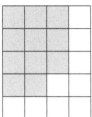

How many more squares have to be shaded?

3	4	5	6	7
A	B	C	D	E

2 What fraction of the circle is left unshaded?

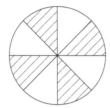

$\frac{1}{2}$	$\frac{1}{3}$	$\frac{1}{4}$	$\frac{1}{5}$	$\frac{3}{8}$
A	B	C	D	E

3 Rowan buys a bag of lollies that contains 24 jelly beans. On Saturday, he eats half of them and then he eats half of the remainder on Tuesday. How many jelly beans remain?

2	6	10	12	18
A	B	C	D	E

4 Which of the following lists are arranged from smallest to largest?

A 0.2, 0.6, 1.2, 1.4
B 0.4, 3, 0.47, 6.5
C 1.05, 1.25, 1.09, 1.99
D 0.63, 0.603, 0.64, 0.643
E 0.5, 0.06, 0.007

5 A shape is made up of 12 equal rectangles. Anonna has shaded one-third of the shape:

She wants to shade more rectangles so that three-quarters of the shape is shaded.

How many **more** rectangles does she need to shade?

3	4	5	6	7
A	B	C	D	E

6 Angelo has read one-fifth of his book. From tonight he plans to read one-tenth of the book each night. How many nights will he need to finish the book?

1	2	5	8	9
A	B	C	D	E

7 If $\frac{2}{3}$ of a number is 24, what is twice the number?

32	36	48	60	72
A	B	C	D	E

8 Harold located $\frac{1}{3}$ and 1 on a number line:

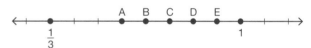

Which of these points is the location of $\frac{3}{4}$?

A	B	C	D	E
A	B	C	D	E

9 Zoey writes the whole numbers from 1 to 24. What fraction of these numbers are **not** multiples of 4?

$\frac{1}{6}$	$\frac{1}{4}$	$\frac{2}{3}$	$\frac{3}{4}$	$\frac{5}{6}$
A	B	C	D	E

10 Which of these is arranged from smallest to largest?

A 0.2, $\frac{1}{2}$, 0.31, 0.08, $\frac{3}{10}$

B 0.08, 0.2, $\frac{1}{2}$, $\frac{3}{10}$, 0.31

C $\frac{3}{10}$, 0.2, $\frac{1}{2}$, 0.31, 0.08

D 0.08, 0.2, $\frac{3}{10}$, $\frac{1}{2}$, 0.31

E 0.08, 0.2, $\frac{3}{10}$, 0.31, $\frac{1}{2}$

☞ **Answers and explanations on pages 201–202**

Real Test 4

MATHEMATICAL REASONING
Fractions and decimals

10 MIN

1 If two-thirds of the shape is to be shaded, how many squares will remain unshaded?

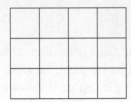

1	2	3	4	6
A	B	C	D	E

2 What is the difference between 1.6 and 2?

1.4	0.4	3.6	1.8	0.04
A	B	C	D	E

3 When Uncle Peter's pizza is delivered, it consists of eight slices. If he eats three-quarters of the pizza, how many slices remain?

6	1	4	2	3
A	B	C	D	E

4 Jack is one-quarter the age of his father and one-third the age of his mother. If Jack's mother is 36, how old is his father?

48	12	40	32	60
A	B	C	D	E

5 The diagram shows a large rectangle made up of small identical squares:

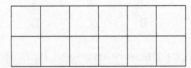

Alyssa shades $\frac{1}{4}$ of the squares. Hanna then shades $\frac{2}{3}$ of the remaining unshaded squares. What fraction of the rectangle remains unshaded?

$\frac{1}{6}$	$\frac{1}{4}$	$\frac{1}{3}$	$\frac{1}{2}$	$\frac{2}{3}$
A	B	C	D	E

6 Adam has made a large batch of cupcakes. He gives $\frac{1}{4}$ to his parents and $\frac{1}{8}$ of them to each of his friends. He still has $\frac{1}{8}$ of the cupcakes remaining. How many friends does Adam give the cupcakes to?

4	2	1	3	5
A	B	C	D	E

7 A large square is divided into two equal rectangles. One of the rectangles is divided into two equal squares. Part of the original square is now shaded:

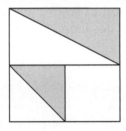

What fraction of the large square is shaded?

$\frac{1}{8}$	$\frac{1}{4}$	$\frac{3}{8}$	$\frac{1}{2}$	$\frac{5}{8}$
A	B	C	D	E

8 There are 20 balls in a bag. $\frac{7}{10}$ of the balls are red. The other balls are green, yellow or blue. If there are equal numbers of green and yellow balls, how many blue balls could be in the bag?

1	2	3	6	14
A	B	C	D	E

9 Emma picked lemons from her tree and sold $\frac{7}{10}$ of them. She still had a dozen lemons remaining. If she sold her lemons at 4 for $3, how much money would she make?

$10	$12	$15	$18	$21
A	B	C	D	E

☞ **Answers and explanations on pages 202-203**

Real
Test 4

MATHEMATICAL REASONING
Fractions and decimals

10 Which of the following squares has the largest fraction of its area shaded?

A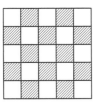

B

C

D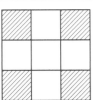

E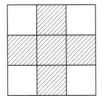

☞ **Answers and explanations on pages 202-203**

- When you are asked to write a story in your test, you can write any kind of story you like. It can be **true or imaginary, funny or serious**. There is no single right way to respond. However, you must write on the topic or question you are given. So read the question carefully.

- Whatever kind of story you choose, you should aim to write in **an entertaining and interesting way**. However, the markers know you don't have much time so they won't expect a perfect, polished story. They know it takes more than 20 minutes to write a really good story.

- Even if you are very good at writing stories, remember you will have a lot less time than you usually have. So **practice with a time limit** is very useful.

- There are many different kinds of **stimulus material** used in these tests. For example, you might be given a picture, a story title, or the first or last sentence of a story. Usually the stimulus will allow you to answer in many different ways.

- A common story question is to ask you to **imagine a situation** and to write about it. For example, you might be asked to imagine you are a different kind of person, an animal or an object, and to write about what your life is like. We will look at these *Imagine if ...* stories in this session.

- For these *Imagine if ...* stories you have to really **use your imagination**, but the question is very open so you have plenty of opportunity to show your ideas. It is usually best to choose a topic that you know something about, so you can quickly come up with some good ideas.

- Other questions lead you directly to a **narrative story** (e.g. about people and what they do, or what happens to them). Your own experiences are very useful when writing these narrative stories—especially in test conditions. We will look at this kind of story in Week 3.

- On the next page is an example of an *Imagine if...* story written in response to a test question, though not under test conditions. In your test, you **might not have time** to produce a polished piece of writing like this. However, if you are **well prepared** you will be able to aim for a similar standard.

Sample

WRITING
'Imagine if ...' story

10 min

Question

Imagine you are a person living in a different time period. It might be in the past or in the future. Write about your life. You can choose to write about one moment, one hour, one day, one year or your whole life.

Response

Structure

Language

Title—make one up if none is given

My Diary   23 January 2522

First words—grab the reader's atention

Today's my tenth birthday and Mum has promised me a really phantasmagorical party this afternoon. She says I'll never guess where we are going. I think it might be Mars. My friend Ellie went there for her birthday party last year.

Interesting, imaginative detail

Introduction to story (orientation)—who or what you imagine yourself to be, and when or where you are

When I woke up, our house servant, KX99, gave me breakfast. KX99 is an android from Jupiter. Breakfast was a Coco Pops capsule—a special treat.

Ideas from your **own life experiences**

I went into the mindblaster machine to do my lessons. Today I learnt all about the 21st century. I am so glad I did not live back then. People had to stay on Earth the whole time. How boring! After my lessons I had all morning to go and play with my new little brother, Horatio. He's having some repairs done but I am allowed to play with him for a few hours each day.

Correct spelling and grammar

Body of your story (events, experiences, thoughts and feelings)

Now it's almost two o'clock and time for the party. I wonder where everyone is. Wham, whiz, pow! What's happening? I'm having trouble writing this diary but it's lucky I don't have to use pen and paper to write my ideas down (like people 500 years ago).

Expressive words to talk about people, things and what they do

This must be the birthday surprise. I'm in the timezapper and flashing back through time, and there's Ellie and the others as well. Whoosh! We're going backwards—2422, 2322, 2222, 2122 …

Good use of **punctuation**

Conclusion—(often a comment)

I can't believe it. We're in the 21st century—2022. No-one in the class has timezapped for their party before. Mm. I wonder what kind of party food capsules they had in 2022.

Practice Tasks

- These tasks will give you some ideas about how to start writing quickly and get a good, interesting 'Imagine if ...' story done in the short time you have in the test.

- You will have to look back at *My Diary* on page 35 to answer some questions and then do some writing yourself. Your writing will be based on the same question, as there are so many ways to answer the question. However, write about something different from the story on page 35. You might still want to write about the future but be sure to use your own ideas.

- Here is the question again. Look at it now before you start the tasks.

Practice question

Imagine you are a person living in a different time period. It might be in the past or in the future. Write about your life. You can choose to write about one moment, one hour, one day, one year or your whole life.

- The first thing to do is to quickly **brainstorm some ideas**. You don't need to write these down but you do need to think about a few different ideas. For this question, your brainstorm might include these ideas:

  ○ caveman days

  ○ life on a convict ship

  ○ gold-rush days.

- *Tip:* Think back to experiences you have had (holidays, excursions, and so on), books you have read, or films and television programs you have watched. These could all give you ideas to start off with.

- Choose a topic you know something about—you'll be able to start writing more quickly and have more ideas about a familiar topic. The *My Diary* writer liked reading science-fiction stories and watching space programs on television. This gave her lots of ideas for a story about a day 500 years from now.

- You also have to decide what kind of story to write—will it be funny, happy, sad, mysterious, realistic or fantasy? 'Imagine if ...' stories generally give you the chance to write all of these kinds of stories. **Write the kind of story you are best at.**

- In a test you do not have time to do a detailed plan of your story before starting writing, but it is important to spend a few minutes working out a **very rough plan** of how your story will develop.

Practice Tasks

- 'Imagine if ...' stories often use the following general structure. There are other ways to structure your story but this can help you get going quickly in a test.
  - ○ **Introduction**: who or what you imagine yourself (or someone else) to be and when or where you are
  - ○ **Body**: what happened, what things were like, how you thought or felt
  - ○ **Conclusion**: something to finish off your imaginative account (perhaps a comment, a joke or a warning)

  Here is the plan for *My Diary*.

Introduction	diary—birthday—500 years in future—party
Body	my day—breakfast—android servant
	school lessons
	baby brother
Conclusion	time travel back to 21st century

Task 1

Think about the Practice question on page 36. Jot down two or three story ideas. Remember to write about a topic you know something about or have interesting ideas about.

_____

_____

_____

Task 2

Now choose one of your story ideas to continue with. Do a rough plan for your idea. Use the headings below. Give yourself about two minutes.

- 💡 *Tip:* In your test, only write enough in your plan to get you going. If you are sure in your head about what you are going to write, don't waste time writing down a plan. Just start!

Orientation _____

Body _____

_____

_____

_____

Resolution _____

_____

- The introduction (or **orientation**) to your story should **capture the readers' attention** and make them interested in reading further. It usually also tells readers **who or what** you are imagining yourself (or someone else) to be and, if important, **where and when** the story takes place.

- You should only write a **couple of sentences** and then quickly get to the main part of the story. In the test you won't have time to give too much detail.

🔆 *Tip:* Try to write a first sentence that captures your readers' interest but don't spend too much time on it. It is better to get started than to spend valuable minutes trying to compose the best first sentence you've ever written.

Task 3

Read the first paragraph of *My Diary* and answer the questions.

Who is the story about? _____

When is the story set? _____

Where is the story set? _____

What is going on? _____

Task 4

Now write the introduction for the Practice question using your rough plan. Make it as interesting as you can but don't write too much—you are only setting up the story for the reader. Give yourself about five minutes.

_____

_____

_____

_____

_____

_____

_____

_____

☞ **Answers on page 203**

Practice Tasks

WRITING
'Imagine if …' story—Writing the introduction

- The body of *Imagine if …* stories is made up of **interesting events and experiences**, and **your thoughts and feelings**.

- These events and experiences might be interesting because they are funny or surprising, or because they make us **wonder about these situations**. For example, the events in *My Diary* make us think about what it will be like in 2522. Will people be eating capsules instead of food? Will they be travelling through time?

- In this kind of story you are likely to get great ideas once you start writing. So although it is good to have a plan, you might not depend on it as much as in other kinds of writing. **If you get an interesting idea as you write, use it!**

- Your own **everyday experiences can be very useful** even though you are imagining another time, place, person or situation. In *My Diary*, for example, the writer used her love of Coco Pops and her friendship with Ellie.

- Try to use **vivid, interesting, precise words** to describe people, things and actions. Even if your story does not work exactly as you want it to, you will still get marks for expressing your ideas well.

Task 5

What idea did you find the most interesting in *My Diary*? Tick your choice.

going to Mars for a birthday party	☐
having an android for a servant	☐
eating a Coco Pops capsule for breakfast	☐
doing lessons in a mindblaster machine (whatever that is!)	☐
repairs being done on a baby	☐
ideas going straight to writing without using a pen and paper	☐
travelling through time	☐

Task 6

1 Write the words used in *My Diary* to describe
  a the party (paragraph 1). _____
  b the servant (paragraph 2). _____
  c the sounds the timezapper makes (paragraphs 4 and 5). _____

2 Which words did the writer make up? _____

☞ **Answers on page 203**

Practice Tasks

Task 7

Now continue writing your story on the next page. Try to include words and sentences that create vivid, interesting images. Give yourself about ten minutes.

💡 *Tip:* Similes can help you create vivid word pictures. Look at the following examples:

> as fast as a comet
>
> as black as a black hole
>
> as boring as watching my sister's dancing concert

Remember: Get into the habit of checking your spelling and grammar as you write. Quickly correct mistakes as you see them. You might not get time to look back and do a final check.

Practice Tasks

WRITING
'Imagine if ...' story—Writing the conclusion

- In the 'Imagine if ...' kind of story, the conclusion will usually be quite short. You will probably write it when you can't think of much more to say or when you know your time is running out. However, you should try to think of an interesting way to end your story.

- One of the easiest ways to end is with a comment of some kind (e.g. a warning, a lesson or a funny comment). In *My Diary* the writer ends by wondering about party food in the 21st century.

Tip: Don't just keep going on and on. Keep your eye on the time and be ready to write a quick ending if needed.

Task 8

Write an ending for your story. Give yourself about five minutes.

_____

_____

_____

_____

_____

_____

_____

_____

_____

_____

Note: If you like, you can work on your story some more, improving what you have written so far and writing it out again on your own paper. Use the checklist below to review your writing.

Checklist for writing an 'Imagine if ...' story

Have you:

1 *started your story with a few sentences to capture the readers' attention and tell them what your story is about (who, what, when, where)?*
2 *included interesting, imaginative events and experiences?*
3 *given your story an ending of some kind?*
4 *used some vivid, interesting language to describe the people, things and actions in your story?*
5 *checked your grammar, punctuation and spelling?*

Remember: In the test, you won't have time to revise thoroughly and make big changes. You may have time to change a few words but you will really be aiming to do a good piece of writing in one draft.

Choose **one** of the writing tests below to do now. Use your own paper.

If you like, you can do both tests. However, it would be better to do them on different days. For extra practice, you could use the tests again, writing in different ways each time.

Set yourself a time limit of 20 minutes. Use the checklist on page 41 to give it a quick review.

Test 1

Imagine you are an imaginary pet—a kind of animal never seen or heard of before. Describe what kind of pet you are. If you can, think up a name for the kind of animal you are.

Write about what you would do all day and how you would get on with your owners (e.g. how you could make them happy, how you would communicate with them, etc.). You might write about the best part of your day or some of the problems you have with other pets in the neighbourhood.

OR

Test 2

Imagine a day without any of the usual chores and problems—a day in which you can do exactly what you like. Write a story about your day, starting with waking up. Think about what you would eat, where you would go, who you would see and what you would do.

What's next?

Week 2

This is what we cover this week:

Day 1   **Reading:** Poetry

Day 2   **Thinking Skills:**

   ◎ Critical thinking—Drawing a conclusion

   ◎ Critical thinking—Identifying an assumption

   ◎ Critical thinking—Checking reasoning to detect errors

Day 3   **Mathematical Reasoning:**   ◎ Patterns and algebra

                                           ◎ Length and area

Day 4   **Writing:** 'What would you do if ...?' opinion

- In your test you will be asked to answer questions about **poems**. Some poems are funny and other poems are serious but all express ideas and feelings about human experiences.

- Poetry can be more difficult to understand than other kinds of writing. **Words are used in unusual ways and with different meanings**. Even punctuation is used differently.

- Poetry is usually written to be read out loud but of course you can't do this in a test. However, it can help to **'say it aloud' in your head** and imagine the rhythm and beat of the poem.

- Always **read the poem right through before answering** the questions (unless you run out of time). However, you will probably need to read it right through more than once to really understand it.

- Think about the **overall meaning** of the poem as you read—don't just focus on a line at a time. Ask yourself what it is saying about the subject.

- In general, when asked a question about one line of the poem, you will need to **read the lines before and after** that line to get the right answer.

- You might be asked about:
  - the **meaning of a word, a line, a stanza (verse) or the whole poem**—poets sometimes choose words that are not often used in everyday conversation or use everyday words in unusual ways
  - the poet's use of **imagery and symbols**—how the poet has created an image in our minds about how something looks, sounds, tastes, feels, smells or moves (e.g. the 'jaws of a cave' might be used to describe a cave entrance or opening). Note: You probably won't be asked to identify a particular kind of imagery but you may be asked to interpret it
  - the poet's use of **personification**—where the poet gives an animal or the natural environment a human characteristic (e.g. The dry land begged the skies for rain.)
  - the poet's use of **alliteration**—the repetition of consonant sounds in words near each other (e.g. the repetition of the 's' sound in 'slid silently and softly')
  - the kind of **character** adopted by the poet to write the poem (e.g. a farmer, mother, child, old person or lonely person)
  - **how the poet feels** or would feel about something.

Practice Task 1

READING
Poetry

10 MIN

Use this first practice task as a guide. Try to answer the questions wihtout looking at the answers. Then look at the answers for tips about how to get the answer right. Don't worry if you don't get every answer right. Try to do it in 10 minutes but don't worry too much about this. The point is to help you understand the kinds of questions you will find in the test and how to answer them.

Corroboree

Hot day dies, cook time comes.
Now between the sunset and the sleep-time
Time of playabout.
The hunters paint black bodies by firelight with
5   designs of meaning
To dance corroboree.
Now didgeridoo compels with haunting drone
    eager feet to stamp,
Click-sticks click in rhythm to swaying bodies
10 Dancing corroboree.
Like spirit things in from the great surrounding dark
Ghost-gums dimly seen stand at the edge of light
Watching corroboree.
15 Eerie the scene in leaping firelight,
Eerie the sounds in that wild setting,
As naked dancers weave stories of the tribe
Into corroboree.

Oodgeroo Noonuccal

From *A First Australian Poetry Book*, compiled by June Factor, Oxford University Press, 1983; reproduced with permission

1 What time of day is the poem about?
  A early morning   **B** late at night
  C early evening   **D** early afternoon

2 What effect does the music of the didgeridoo have?
  A It makes people want to dance.
  B It makes people sleepy.
  C It scares people.
  D It makes them want to paint their bodies.

3 What are like 'spirit things' (line 11)?
  A trees
  B ghosts
  C dancers
  D those watching

4 In lines 16–17, what does the poet mean that the dancers 'weave stories of the tribe / Into corroboree'?
  A They make up new stories.
  B They express traditional stories by their dancing.
  C They make decorations from threads and wool to suit the stories.
  D They recite stories at the same time as they dance.

5 The second half of the poem conveys strongly
  A the energy of the corroboree.
  B the magical atmosphere of the corroboree.
  C the unearthly atmosphere of the corroboree.
  D the rhythmical music of the corroboree.

☞ **Answers and explanations on page 203**

Practice Task 2

READING
Poetry

10 MIN

Read the poem carefully and answer the questions. Circle the correct answer for each question. Try to keep to the time limit. This is a short poem so you should do it in less than 10 minutes. When you finish, check the answers. If you did not choose a right answer or if you were unsure about it, read the answer explanation.

The Beach

The beach is a quarter of golden fruit,
A soft ripe melon
Sliced to a half-moon curve,
Having a thick green rind
5   Of jungle growth;
And the sea devours it
With its sharp,
Sharp white teeth.

William Hart-Smith

From *A First Australian Poetry Book*, compiled by June Factor, Oxford University Press, 1983; reproduced with permission

---

1 What does the poet compare the beach to?
  A a melon   **B** fruits of all kinds   **C** the moon   **D** a mouth

2 What does the poet mean us to imagine the sea to be?
  A a jungle   **B** the moon   **C** a mouth   **D** teeth

2 What does the poet compare the waves to?
  A teeth   **B** the rind of the melon
  C jungle growth   **D** ripe fruit

4 What is the 'thick green rind' (line 4)?
  A the trees and bushes that grow behind the beach sand
  B the shallow sea at the edge of the beach
  C the seaweed at the edge of the beach
  D the birds that gather on the beach

5 What does the word 'devours' (line 6) mean, as it is used in the poem?
  A crashes   **B** wrecks   **C** washes   **D** eats

☞ **Answers and explanations on page 204**

Practice Task 3

Read the poem carefully and answer the questions. Circle the correct answer for each question. This is a longer poem than the last one but you should still try to finish it in 10 minutes.

The Ant Explorer

Once a little sugar ant made up his mind to roam—
To fare away far away, far away from home.
He had eaten all his breakfast, and he had his ma's consent
To see what he should chance to see and here's the way he went—
5   Up and down a fern frond, round and round a stone,
Down a gloomy gully where he loathed to be alone,
Up a mighty mountain range, seven inches high,
Through the fearful forest grass that nearly hid the sky,
Out along a bracken bridge, bending in the moss,
10   'Twas a dry, deserted desert, and a trackless land to tread,
Till he reached a dreadful desert that was feet and feet across.
He wished that he was home again and tucked-up tight in bed.
His little legs were wobbly, his strength was nearly spent,
And so he turned around again and here's the way he went—
15   Back away from desert lands feet and feet across,
Back along the bracken bridge bending in the moss,
Through the fearful forest grass shutting out the sky,
Up a mighty mountain range seven inches high,
Down a gloomy gully, where he loathed to be alone,
15   Up and down a fern frond and round and round a stone.
A dreary ant, a weary ant, resolved no more to roam,
He staggered up the garden path and popped back home.
CJ Dennis

Practice Task 3

1 The poem talks about the ant as though it is a human being. This is to
   A help us understand what it might be like to be an ant.
   B make us laugh at the actions of the ant.
   C focus on a particular ant.
   D contrast an ant's life to a human's life.

2 As used in the poem, what is 'consent' (line 3) closest in meaning to?
   A confidence
   B permission
   C encouragement
   D none of the above

3 What do you think the 'gloomy gully' is in line 6?
   A a small dip in the ground
   B a deep valley
   C the shadow of the ferns
   D a dark cave

4 Lines 10–11 help us understand
   A how far the ant is wandering from home.
   B how tired the ant must be.
   C how big the desert is.
   D how the stretch of ground looks to the ant.

5 The poem is effective because
   A most of us have at some time watched an ant struggling through the dirt.
   B most of us find the ant such an interesting creature.
   C it teaches us about ant behaviour.
   D the poet loves ants.

☞ **Answers and explanations on pages 204-205**

Real Test

10 MIN

Now test your reading skills within a strict time limit. Don't work beyond the time limit. If you can finish in less than 10 minutes, that is even better. Circle the correct answer for each question and then check your answers. If you get an answer wrong, read the explanation carefully and check the poem again.

The People Upstairs

The people upstairs all practise ballet
Their living room is a bowling alley
Their bedroom is full of conducted tours.
Their radio is louder than yours,
5   They celebrate week-ends all the week.
When they take a shower, your ceilings leak.
They try to get their parties to mix
By supplying their guests with pogo sticks,
And when their orgy at last abates,
10 They go to the bathroom on roller skates.
I might love the people upstairs more wondrous
If instead of above us, they just lived under us.

Ogden Nash

❶ The poet
  A wants to move.
  B wants the people upstairs to move.
  C wants to meet the people upstairs.
  D wants the people upstairs to invite him to their parties.

❷ Who are the people upstairs?
  A dancers
  B rollerskaters
  C people who have parties every night
  D none of the above

❸ Which word means the same as 'abates' as used in the poem?
  A increases
  B relaxes
  C abandons
  D lessens

❹ When the people upstairs have a party, the poet thinks they must give their guests
  A rollerskates.
  B pogo sticks.
  C conducted tours of their home.
  D bowling balls.

❺ Which statement best sums up the poet's attitude to the people upstairs?
  A He is frustrated by their noise.
  B He finds it amusing to imagine what they could be doing.
  C both A and B
  D none of the above

☞ **Answers and explanations on page 205**

- In order to **draw a conclusion**, you need to **read and assess** all of the information and evidence provided.
- A conclusion can only be **true** if it is **supported by evidence**.
- A conclusion can be **eliminated** if there is **evidence that refutes it**.

Example

Hakan's friends started a hobby club. Thirty other students joined immediately. The club couldn't decide on a name so they decided to hold a vote. The choices were Dream Team, Alliance or Heatwave. Every member of the club got to vote on their two favourite names. They could not vote for the same name twice. A name would only be chosen if everyone used one of their votes to vote for it. Otherwise a new set of names would be suggested and a new vote held.

Each of the suggested names—Dream Team, Alliance and Heatwave—received at least one vote.

Knowing **one** of the following would allow us to know the result of the vote. Which one is it?
A   Every club member voted for either Heatwave or Alliance or both.
B   Dream team was the most popular vote.
C   No club member voted for Dream Team and Heatwave.
D   Only two people voted for Heatwave.

Steps to work out the answer
1   Read the **information** in the text.
2   Read the suggested **conclusions**.
3   **Judge** which conclusion must be true based on the **evidence** in the text.

C is correct. If no club member voted for both Dream Team and Heatwave, everyone must have voted for Dream Team and Alliance OR Heatwave and Alliance. This means you can work out the result of the vote. Everyone voted for Alliance so Alliance won the vote.

Incorrect answers

A is incorrect. The fact that every club member voted for either Heatwave or Alliance or both does not help you conclusively work out the result of the vote.

B is incorrect. The fact that Dream Team was the most popular vote does not help you work out the result because, in the style of voting described, the most popular name might not have been the winner.

D is incorrect. The fact that only two people voted for Heatwave does not give you enough information about the voting preferences to help you determine the result of the overall vote.

Checklist
Can you:
1   *read a text and draw a conclusion from the evidence presented?*
2   *assess whether conclusions are supported by evidence?*
3   *assess whether a conclusion can be eliminated because there is evidence that refutes it?*
4   *assess when conclusions are neither proven nor disproved because the evidence is incomplete or unavailable?*

Real Test 1

THINKING SKILLS
Critical thinking—Drawing a conclusion

10 MIN

1 Mia, Yoshi and Mahesh collect stamps. Mia collects stamps from Australia, Greece, Thailand, the United Kingdom and Singapore. Yoshi collects stamps from Thailand, Australia and Japan. Mahesh collects stamps from France, the United Kingdom, Thailand, Australia and New Zealand.

Stamps from which countries does Mia collect that neither Yoshi nor Mahesh collect?
A France and New Zealand
B the United Kingdom and Thailand
C Singapore and Thailand
D Greece and Singapore

2 **Rasha:** 'I love scary stories and thrillers because they are suspenseful and exciting and I prefer real-life stories about creepy humans because they are scarier than stories about monsters or aliens.'

David: 'I like fantasy stories. I don't like scary stories. I get a feeling of dread the whole way through them because I know something bad will happen and I hate that feeling.'

Evie: 'I like the suspense of horror stories but my favourite stories are survivalist or adventure stories which are plausible enough to be true, which makes them really exciting.'

Alan: 'I think fantasy and science fiction are the only genres capable of creating really exciting plots.'

John: 'I like stories that could be true. Then I can empathise with the characters.'

Which of the children like stories that John should also like?
A Evie and David   B Alan and Rasha   C Rasha and Evie   D David and Alan

3 At the horseriding school, the instructor said to her stable hands: 'We have three people booked tomorrow for a cross-country ride. We'll choose horses from our four best-behaved cross-country horses: Cinnamon, Oakie, Sugar and Phantom. Cinnamon has a sore fetlock so we might not be able to take her out. We'll check her in the morning. If Cinnamon can't go out then Oakie will go in her place. If Cinnamon can go out then we'll take Phantom and not Sugar.'

So, if Oakie goes out in Cinnamon's place, which of the other horses will go on the ride?
A Sugar only
B Phantom only
C Sugar and Phantom
D Phantom and Oakie

☞ **Answers and explanations on pages 205-206**

Real Test 1

4 Sixty per cent of dust inside the home comes from outside the home. This includes air pollution blown in by the wind as well as soil and other matter carried in on shoes. Dust emanates from our clothing, pet dander and the goods we bring indoors with us, as well as our own skin. Certain types of dust are particularly bad for your health and it is estimated that around 20% of people have an allergy to dust or dust-related allergens such as dust mites, pollen, pet dander and skin particles.

Which of the following is the main conclusion that can be drawn from information in the text?
A House dust comes from everywhere and can cause problems for people's health.
B Asbestos dust is sometimes created when renovating old homes.
C People should take their shoes off at the door to avoid tracking unhealthy dust particles into their homes.
D Any tiny particles that go into the air eventually settle on surfaces as dust.

5 When grandma was having physiotherapy after recovering from pneumonia, the physiotherapist told her that to have even a chance of recovering her muscle strength during the following six weeks she must do her exercises at least every second day.

If the physiotherapist is correct, which statement is also true?
A All the elderly people recovering from pneumonia and doing exercises every second day will fully regain their muscle strength within six weeks.
B None of the elderly people recovering from pneumonia who do less exercise than every second day will regain their muscle strength within six weeks.
C Some of the elderly people who've had pneumonia but who exercise less than every second day will regain full muscle strength within six weeks.
D Only the elderly who don't exercise every second day will regain full muscle strength within six weeks.

6 Wei wanted to buy a drone but to have enough money to buy a drone, she would first need to sell her remote car for the best price. Her mother told her: 'To have any chance of getting the best price for the car, you will need to clean it and make sure the battery is charged and the car is working properly.'

Based on the above information, which conclusion **cannot** be true?
A Wei did not clean the remote car but it sold for the best price.
B Wei sold her remote car and bought a new drone.
C Wei sold her remote car but did not have enough money to buy a new drone.
D Wei cleaned the remote car and made sure it was working properly but it did not sell.

☞ **Answers and explanations on pages 205-206**

Real Test 1

7 Chloe, Levi and Na are all keen gardeners. Chloe grows beans, tomatoes, lettuce, spinach and lavender. Levi grows passionfruit, lavender and spinach. Na grows tomatoes, basil, spinach, roses and lavender.

Which plants does Chloe grow that neither Levi nor Na grows?

A beans and tomatoes
B beans and lettuce
C lettuce and spinach
D roses and passionfruit

8 Sofia was learning to rock climb and was impatient to progress to the next level. Her instructor told her: 'To have even a chance of progressing to the next level you will need to have had at least 10 hours of climbing practice.'

If Sofia's instructor is correct, which one of these statements must be true?

A Only the climbers who have had less than 10 hours practice will progress to the next level.
B All the climbers who have had 10 hours practice will progress to the next level.
C Some of the climbers who have had less than 10 hours practice will progress to the next level.
D None of the climbers who have had less than 10 hours practice will progress to the next level.

9 Max was deciding between having a pinata or a clown for his birthday party. His father told him: 'If you don't have a pinata then you can have a clown. But if you do have a pinata, then we'll go to the skate park instead of having the party at home.'

If Max does not have a clown for his party, what will he have?

A a skating party at home
B a pinata at home
C a pinata at the skate park
D a clown at the skate park

10 The drama club wanted to decide on the genre of their next performance. They decided to have a vote. Members could vote for a musical, a comedy or a historical drama. Everyone had to cast two votes but they could not vote for the same genre twice. A genre would only win if everyone voted for it. If there was no winner, then the drama teacher would make the final decision. Each genre received at least one vote.

Knowing **one** of the following would allow us to know the result of the vote. Which one is it?

A Only two people voted for a historical drama.
B Every student voted for either historical drama or comedy, or both.
C Musical was the most popular vote.
D No student voted for both musical and historical drama.

☞ **Answers and explanations on pages 205-206**

Key Points

10 min

- An **assumption** is information that is **not stated** in a text.
- It is something extra that is **assumed or taken for granted** by the creator, reader or listener of the text in order to draw a conclusion.
- Be careful! **Assumptions are not always right** and can lead to **incorrect conclusions**.

Example

Noah: 'My neighbours cut down the big gum tree in their backyard!'
Lucia: 'They must not like nature!'

Which assumption has Lucia made in order to draw her conclusion?

A   Anyone who cuts down a gum tree does not like nature.
B   Anyone who cuts down a tree wants a swimming pool.
C   Noah's neighbours do not like nature.
D   The gum tree was diseased.

Steps to work out the answer

1   **Identify the conclusion**: Noah's neighbours must not like nature.
2   **Identify the evidence given to support this conclusion**: Noah's neighbours cut down a gum tree.
3   Ask yourself: What important point (not stated in this evidence) would **need to be assumed for the conclusion to hold**?

A is correct. Lucia's conclusion is that Noah's neighbours must not like nature. She based this conclusion on the evidence that Noah's neighbours cut down a gum tree. So, for her conclusion to hold, it must be assumed that anyone who cuts down a gum tree does not like nature:

EVIDENCE + ASSUMPTION = CONCLUSION

Noah's neighbours cut down a gum tree + anyone who cuts down a gum tree does not like nature = Noah's neighbours must not like nature.

Remember: Assumptions are not always right. For example, it would not be right that anyone who cuts down a gum tree does not like nature, but that is what Lucia must have assumed in order to draw the conclusion she did. Assumptions can be based on the reader or listener's own background, knowledge and prejudices. When assumptions are not right, they can lead to incorrect conclusions.

Incorrect answers

B is incorrect because it does not support Lucia's conclusion. She could have assumed that anyone who cuts down a tree wants a swimming pool but that assumption would not lead to the conclusion that Noah's neighbours do not like nature.
C is incorrect because it is Lucia's conclusion, not her assumption.
D is incorrect because it does not support Lucia's conclusion. She could have assumed that the gum tree was diseased but this assumption would not lead to the conclusion that Noah's neighbours do not like nature.

Checklist

Can you:

1   *identify a conclusion?*
2   *identify the reasoning or evidence given to support this conclusion?*
3   *identify something that was not stated in the evidence that would need to be assumed or taken for granted if this conclusion is to hold?*

Real Test 2

10 min

1 Ella's teacher, Mr Lin, caught Ella dropping rubbish in the playground. He told Ella she had to spend the rest of lunchtime picking up papers.

Ella: 'There's nothing wrong with dropping rubbish. Everyone else does it!'

Which assumption has Ella made in order to draw her conclusion?

A Mr Lin is unfair.

B It's okay to do something if everyone else does it.

C Other students should not drop rubbish.

D Teachers should collect the rubbish.

2 Ying scored four goals in the netball game on Saturday.

Josh: 'Ying is a good goal shooter.'

Which assumption has Josh made in order to draw his conclusion?

A Ying loves playing netball.

B Ying scored four goals on Saturday.

C Anyone who scores four goals is a good goal shooter.

D Ying is a good goal shooter.

3 The principal at Lee's school said that if students did not wear the proper school uniform, it would hurt the reputation of the school.

Lee: 'We should wear the proper school uniform.'

Which assumption has Lee made in order to draw his conclusion?

A Lee likes wearing the school uniform.

B Students should wear the proper school uniform.

C Any student who does not wear the proper school uniform will hurt the reputation of the school.

D Students should not do something that would hurt the reputation of the school.

4 **Jun:** 'I can't come to the movies with you. I'm going to stay home and finish a project.'

Lily: 'You must really love working on the project.'

Which assumption has Lily made in order to draw her conclusion?

A Jun has not finished his project.

B Anyone who stays home to work on a project must not like the movie.

C Jun loves working on the project.

D Anyone who stays home to work on a project must love working on the project.

5 **Gemma:** 'If Dad scratches the new car one more time, Mum will get really upset.'

Ben: 'Dad must not scratch the car again!'

Which assumption has Ben made in order to draw his conclusion?

A Dad should not do something that would upset Mum.

B Dad keeps scratching the car.

C Dad does not like the car.

D Mum will be upset if Dad scratches the car again.

☞ **Answers and explanations on pages 206-207**

Real Test 2

THINKING SKILLS
Critical thinking—Identifying an assumption

6 **Stella:** 'Annabel is one of the top triathletes in Australia. She uses a nutritionist to help with her diet.'
Isaah: 'Annabel's diet enables her to perform so well.'

Which assumption has Isaah made in order to draw his conclusion?
A An adequate diet is essential for everyone's health.
B The nutritionist must be an expert in diet and athletic performance.
C The nutritionist ensures that Annabel's diet is perfect for her.
D Triathletes like Annabel need to eat a lot of food to give them energy to perform well.

7 **Liam:** 'I have to go home straight after school. Mum asked me to help her make a hat for Halyna's party at preschool. Everyone has to dress as their favourite book character. Halyna loves the Mad Hatter from Alice in Wonderland.'
Fern: 'Halyna will look terrific in a Mad Hatter hat.'

Which assumption did Fern make in order to draw her conclusion?
A Liam has to leave school early.
B Liam likes to help his mum do things for Halyna.
C Liam will make a Mad Hatter hat for Halyna.
D Liam is clever at craft and making things.

8 **Tilda:** 'We're taking Nero to a birthday party for dogs on Saturday. It's for Campbell's dog, Otis. Otis will be one year old. The party is at a cafe in Hornsby. Campbell has booked the garden area of the cafe.'
Patrick: 'Campbell will have all sorts of tasty doggy treats for the dogs to eat.'

Which assumption has Patrick made in order to draw his conclusion?
A Parties always have appropriate food for the guests.
B Otis the dog is turning one and it's a big event.
C Campbell loves Otis very much and likes to spoil him.
D The cafe in Hornsby is pet friendly.

9 **Adrien:** 'A huge tree limb fell off the tree in our front yard on Saturday. It nearly fell on the car.'
Chad: 'That fierce storm on Tuesday must have damaged the limb.'

Which assumption has Chad made in order to draw his conclusion?
A The storm damaged the tree limb and made it fall.
B Adrien was lucky the tree limb did not fall on the car.
C Storms often damage trees.
D It can take days for a damaged tree limb to fall down after a storm.

10 **Gabbi:** 'Even though I did not get into the team last year and I was devastated about failing I'm going to try out for the volleyball team again this year because I have been practising.'
Octavia: 'Gabbi must think she's improved enough to make it onto the team this year because she was really upset last year when she tried out and failed.'

Which assumption has Octavia made in order to draw her conclusion?
A Gabbi doesn't mind trying out and failing.
B Gabbi must think her volleyball has improved since last year.
C Gabbi must have practised very hard to improve so much.
D Gabbi would only try out if she felt she would make it onto the team.

☞ **Answers and explanations on pages 206–207**

THINKING SKILLS
*Critical thinking—Checking reasoning
to detect errors*

- A reasoning error is a **mistake or weakness in an argument**.
- A reasoning error is something that **has not been thought of**, or that **has been assumed**, when drawing a conclusion.

Example

> Only those chess club members who attended every coaching session last term will be allowed to play in the tournament.

Aarav: 'I attended every coaching session last term so I'll definitely be playing in the tournament.'

Uma: 'I missed a coaching session last term so I won't be able to play in the tournament.'

If the information in the box is true, whose reasoning is correct?

A Aarav only

B Uma only

C Both Aarav and Uma

D Neither Aarav nor Uma

Steps to work out the answer

1 **Identify the conclusion** made by each child.

2 **Identify the evidence** given to support each child's conclusion.

3 For each child's conclusion, ask yourself: Does the conclusion follow from the evidence? If it doesn't follow from the evidence, why doesn't it? There must be a **flaw or error in the argument**. What has been assumed or not thought of?

B is correct. Only Uma's reasoning is correct. We know that only chess club members who attended every coaching session last term will be allowed to play in the tournament. So, since Uma missed a coaching session last term, she will not be allowed to play in the tournament.

Incorrect answers

A is incorrect because Aarav's reasoning is incorrect. Even though he attended every coaching session last term, Aarav has not thought that there may be other reasons why some chess players are unable to play in the tournament. So it is a flaw in his reasoning to say that he will **definitely** be playing.

C and D are incorrect by a process of elimination.

Checklist

Can you:

1 identify a conclusion?

2 identify the reasoning or evidence given to support this conclusion?

3 detect any reasoning errors or flaws in the argument?

10 MIN

---

1 The tour guide on Pluto always warns guests leaving the compound to beware of the great Pluto beast. It has purple scales and walks upright on three legs. Its legs are relatively short but its feet are large. Each foot can be up to 60 cm long.

Ria: 'Look at those tracks! They are in sets of three and quite large so they must be from a Pluto beast!'

Faisal: 'No, they can't be Pluto beast tracks. Each footprint is only about 30 cm.'

If the information in the box is true, whose reasoning is correct?

A Ria

B Faisal

C Both Ria and Faisal

D Neither Ria nor Faisal

---

2 Ms Street loves windy days. Whenever it's windy when she has lunchtime playground duty, it always puts her in a good mood. And when Ms Street is in a good mood, she always gives us an early mark.

Ilja: 'If it's windy at lunchtime today while she is on duty, she's sure to give an early mark this afternoon!'

Livvy: 'She gave us an early mark last Friday—it must have been windy.'

If the information in the box is true, whose reasoning is correct?

A Ilja only   B Livvy only   C Ilja and Livvy   D Neither Ilja nor Livvy

---

3 Jim's teacher said that any student who does not return their permission slip by Monday will not be allowed to go on the excursion to the zoo on Tuesday.

Jim: 'I've returned my permission slip already. I'll definitely be allowed to go on the excursion to the zoo.'

Which one of the following sentences shows the mistake Jim has made?

A Jim did not return his permission slip in time.

B There may be another reason Jim is not allowed to go to the zoo.

C We do not know how many students can go to the zoo.

D The excursion to the zoo might be changed to Wednesday.

---

4 To have any chance of passing the clarinet exam, you must practise for at least fifteen minutes five times a week.'

Ava: 'I practise clarinet five times a week for at least fifteen minutes, sometimes more. I'll definitely pass the exam.'

Hank: 'I practise clarinet every day, even if only for a few minutes. But at least five days a week I practice for fifteen minutes. I might pass the exam.'

If the information in the box is true, whose reasoning is correct?

A Ava only   B Hank only   C Ava and Hank   D Neither Ava nor Hank

---

☞ **Answers and explanations on pages 207–208**

5 Loren's mother is in the department store. She is looking for the dress Loren wants for her birthday. Loren saw it in the department store. She told her mother the dress is blue with crocodiles.

Sales assistant: 'Here's a blue dress. And it has crocodiles around the hem—it must be the one she wants!'

Which one of the following sentences shows the mistake the sales assistant has made?

A Loren might now prefer a green dress.

B Loren might have seen the dress in a different store.

C There might be more than one dress that is blue with crocodiles.

D Even if the dress is blue, it might not have crocodiles.

6 Only those people who have collected ten tokens are allowed to register for entry to the competition.

Eddie: 'Nathan has ten tokens so he'll definitely enter the competition.'

Serena: 'Lance has not collected ten tokens so he definitely won't be able to enter the competition.'

Who reasoning is correct?

A Eddie only

B Serena only

C Both Eddie and Serena

D Neither Eddie nor Serena

7 When making frosting for the coconut and lime slice you need to use enough butter so that the frosting will set. If the mixture is too runny, add more icing sugar to stiffen it. If it's too thick to spread, add more lime juice.

Max: 'My frosting is too runny. I must have used too much lime juice.'

Sacha: 'My mixture is too runny I need to add more icing sugar.'

Ricki: 'My mixture spreads well but won't set I'll need to mix in some butter.'

Keisha: 'My mixture spreads well so I will have to add more lime juice.'

Whose reasoning in incorrect?

A Max

B Sacha

C Ricki

D Keisha

☞ **Answers and explanations on pages 207-208**

Real Test 3

8 **Leesa:** 'My Granddad's car is linked to his smart phone by bluetooth. To operate the phone as a car key, the phone must be on and the bluetooth enabled. The car unlocks automatically when he approaches it if he has his phone on him and it locks automatically when he walks away from it because the car can no longer detect the bluetooth signal.'

Eric: 'So if the car doesn't automatically lock when your Granddad walks away from it, he could have left his phone in the car so the connection is still detectable.'

Will: 'If the car doesn't open when he approaches it, your Grandad's phone must not be switched on or connected to bluetooth or maybe he doesn't have his phone with him.'

Whose reasoning is correct?

A Eric only

B Will only

C Both Eric and Will

D Neither Eric nor Will

9 When camping near water, remember that just because you can't see a crocodile does not mean there is not one close by—especially if you are in an area known to be a crocodile habitat such as along the coast of North Queensland. Crocodiles can stay underwater for over an hour so be cautious. Camp well away from the water's edge. Don't use small watercraft because crocodiles have been known to take people from small vessels. And remember that crocodiles are most active at dusk, during the night and at dawn.

Cody: 'If it's not a known crocodile habitat and it's during the day, I'll be safe to kayak out in deeper water as long as I stay away from the water's edge.'

Hanna: 'Just because crocodiles are most active at night and at dawn and dusk, it doesn't mean they are not active during the day and if it's a known crocodile habitat there could be crocodiles there even if you can't see them.'

Whose reasoning is correct?

A Cody only

B Hanna only

C Both Cody and Hanna

D Neither Cody nor Hanna

10 All tortoises are turtles but not all turtles are tortoises. Tortoises live on the land and have elephant-like feet made for walking rather than flipper-like limbs. Sea turtles come onto land to lay eggs.'

Charlie: 'Tortoises must be turtles that live on land.'

Sam: 'I can't see its feet but that turtle must be a tortoise. It's laying eggs.'

If the information in the box is true, whose reasoning is correct?

A Charlie only

B Sam only

C Both Charlie and Sam

D Neither Charlie nor Sam

☞ **Answers and explanations on pages 207–208**

MATHEMATICAL REASONING
Patterns and algebra

10 MIN

- **A number sequence has a rule** that can be used to find the missing number(s).

- A number sequence can involve the **addition or subtraction** of a constant value.

  Example: The next number in the sequence 16, 24, 32, 40, _____ is

  A 8   B 48   C 50   D 52   E 56

  The correct answer is **B**, as the numbers are going up by 8.

- In some sequences, the number is found by **multiplying or dividing**.

  Example: Complete the sequence 1, 3, 9, 27, _____.

  A 54   B 3   C 30   D 81   E 84

  The correct answer is **D**, as the numbers are multiplied by 3, and $27 \times 3 = 81$.

- Some sequences may be formed using special number groups, such as **square numbers**.

  Example: Complete the sequence 1, 4, 9, 16, 25, _____.

  A 7   B 11   C 36   D 44   E 49

  The correct answer is **C**, as the numbers are the squares of 1, 2, 3, 4, 5 and 6.

  💡 *Tip:* Practise saying the square numbers up to 12^2.

- A sequence could be developed by **using existing numbers** in the sequence.

  Example: Complete the sequence 1, 1, 2, 3, 5, 8, 13, 21, _____.

  💡 *Tip:* These are called Fibonacci numbers.

  A 34   B 29   C 26   D 22   E 35

  The correct answer is **A**, as $1 + 1 = 2$, $1 + 2 = 3$, $2 + 3 = 5$, and so on to $13 + 21 = 34$.

- The sequence may be contained within a **table**.

  Example:

1	3	6	8
5	11		26

  The number missing in the table is which of the following?

  A 21   B 22   C 18   D 17   E 20

  The correct answer is **E**, as **$1 \times 3 + 2 = 5$**, **$3 \times 3 + 2 = 11$** and **$8 \times 3 + 2 = 26$**. The number in the top row is multiplied by 3 and then another 2 is added. This means the missing number is $6 \times 3 + 2 = 20$.

- The missing number in the sequence may have to be found **using a calculation**.

  Example: Which calculation would give the missing term in the following sequence?

  32, 26, 20, _____, 8.

  A $4 + 3 \times 2$ B $4 \times (2 + 5)$ C $16 - 2 \times 2$ D $20 \div 4 + 3 \times 3$ E $20 - 6 \times 4$

  The correct answer is **D**, as the missing number in the sequence is 14. By checking each alternative we can see that $20 \div 4 + 3 \times 3 = 5 + 9 = 14$.

  💡 *Tip:* Do not forget the order of operations rule.

MATHEMATICAL REASONING
Patterns and algebra

- **A number sentence contains numbers and mathematical operations**. To find a missing number, use the inverse operations. The inverse operation of addition is subtraction, and the inverse operation of multiplication is division.

  Example: What is the missing number in the number sentence: $36 + \boxed{?} = 80 - 23$.

  A 7   **B** 19   **C** 21   **D** 29   **E** 31

  The correct answer is **C**. First $80 - 23$ is $80 - 20 - 3$ which is 57. This means $36 + \boxed{?} = 57$. The missing number is $57 - 36$ which is $57 - 30 - 6 = 21$.

- **Number puzzles are solved** by working out a number rule from the existing numbers and using it to find the missing number(s).

  Example: What is the missing number in this puzzle?

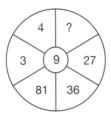

  A 7   **B** 9   **C** 18   **D** 20   **E** 72

  The correct answer is **B**. Looking diagonally across the circle, $36 \div 9$ is 4 and $27 \div 9$ is 3. This means the missing number is $81 \div 9$ which is 9.

Checklist

Can you:

1. complete a number sequence using a rule involving adding or subtracting?
2. complete a number sequence using a rule involving multiplying or dividing?
3. complete a number sequence using square numbers?
4. complete a number sequence using a rule involving the existing numbers in the sequence?
5. find the missing number in a table by first finding the rule?
6. complete a calculation to find the missing number in a sequence?
7. use a number sentence to find the value of the missing number?
8. complete a number puzzle by first finding a rule?

Real Test 1

MATHEMATICAL REASONING
Patterns and algebra

1

2	10
3	14
4	X
5	22
6	26

The value of X is
A 4
B 8
C 18
D 20
E 16

2 Look at the following sequence of sums.
1 + 3, 3 + 5, 5 + 7, _____, 9 + 11.
The missing sum will add to

12	14	16	18	20
A	B	C	D	E

3 Look at the following sequence.
1, 3, 6, 10, _____, _____, 28, 36.
The missing numbers are
A 15 and 21   B 14 and 20   C 14 and 21
D 15 and 22   E 14 and 15

4 The numbers 1 to 6 are placed on the puzzle so that the sum of the three numbers on each straight line is the same.

Which of these could be the sum of each of the straight lines?

3	4	6	8	9
A	B	C	D	E

5 In this diagram,
7 + 5 = 12.

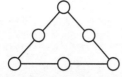

Here is a new pattern which works in the same way.

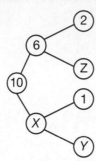

What is the value of Y × Z?

8	12	14	16	20
A	B	C	D	E

6 Oscar is arranging some blocks in a line to make a pattern. He starts with three grey blocks followed by two purple blocks. He repeats this a number of times.

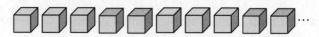

When finished, Oscar has used 24 grey blocks in the pattern. How many purple blocks has Oscar used?

15	16	18	24	36
A	B	C	D	E

7 Lachlan uses the rule 'Double and then subtract 4' to make a sequence of numbers. The fifth number in the sequence is 20. What is the third number in the sequence?

68	10	12	56	8
A	B	C	D	E

8 Here are the first four terms of a sequence: 4, 8, 16, 32 … What is the difference between the fourth term and seventh term?

24	28	124	224	228
A	B	C	D	E

9 The letters P and Q each represent a different digit.

$$\begin{array}{r} PQ \\ \times\ \ \ 6 \\ \hline QQQ \end{array}$$

What digit is represented by P?

7	6	5	4	3
A	B	C	D	E

10 Here is a number sentence.
38 + 7 × ⬚ = 75 − 9
Find the missing number.

3	4	5	6	7
A	B	C	D	E

☞ **Answers and explanations on pages 208-209**

Real Test 2

MATHEMATICAL REASONING
Patterns and algebra

1 A series of squares is formed using matches as shown below.

The number of matches used to make five squares is

19	20	17	16	15
A	B	C	D	E

2 The top row of a chessboard has eight squares. A grain of wheat is placed on the first square, two on the second, four on the third, eight on the fourth, and so on.

How many would be placed on the eighth square?

32	64	128	256	512
A	B	C	D	E

3

5	7	10	13	20
11	15	21		41

The missing number in the table is

26	27	28	29	24
A	B	C	D	E

4

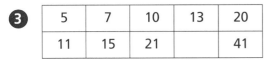

The diagram shows the first four triangular numbers. These numbers are 1, 3, 6, 10. The next triangular number is

11	12	14	15	16
A	B	C	D	E

5 The numbers 1 to 7 are placed on the puzzle so that the sum of the three numbers on each straight line is the same.

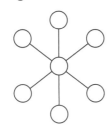

What is the sum of each of the straight lines?

3	4	6	12	15
A	B	C	D	E

6 In the circles below, Abbey is going to write the numbers from 6 to 14 once each.

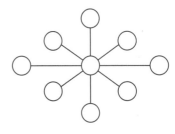

The three numbers in each line must add to 30. What number must Abbey write in the middle circle?

8	9	10	11	12
A	B	C	D	E

7 In this diagram, $4 \times 5 = 20$.

Here is a new pattern which works in the same way.

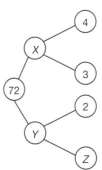

What is the value of $X + Y + Z$?

12	15	16	20	21
A	B	C	D	E

☞ **Answers and explanations on page 209**

Real Test 2

8 Cassie made a pattern by placing shapes in a line. She started with 4 triangles, followed by 3 squares and then 2 rectangles. She repeated this sequence many times. When she was finished, she had used 36 triangles. How many squares had she used?

15	18	21	24	27
A	B	C	D	E

9 A sequence of numbers is written using the rule 'Each number is 8 less than double the previous number'. If the third number in the sequence is 32, what is the sum of the first and second numbers?

28	34	36	40	52
A	B	C	D	E

10 In a sequence of numbers, 63 is the third term, 70 is the fourth term and 84 is the sixth term. What is the difference between the eighth term and the 14th term?

6	7	28	35	42
A	B	C	D	E

☞ **Answers and explanations on page 209**

MATHEMATICAL REASONING
Length and area

10 MIN

- An understanding of **distance** is important but you cannot take your ruler into the examination room. Remember: Most sheets of paper are around 30 cm in length. This is the length of your ruler. Your index finger is around 5 cm in length. These facts will help you with questions that involve an estimation of length.

  Example: The length of the line _____ is close to
  A   2 cm   B   7 cm   C   15 cm   D   22 cm   E   30 cm

  The correct answer is **B**. Stretching your finger along the line helps in the estimate.

  💡 *Tip:* Know the length of everyday objects.

- The **perimeter** is the distance around the outside of a shape.

  Example: The shape is made up of six squares with sides 1 cm each.

  The perimeter of the shape is
  A   6 cm   B   12 cm   C   15 cm   D   20 cm   E   18 cm

  The correct answer is **B** and is found by counting.

  💡 *Tip:* Number each side length when counted.

- The **area** is the space contained within a shape.

  Example: Which of the following has the greatest area?

  A   B   C   D   E

  The correct answer is **D** and is found by counting the number of squares.

- When the dimensions of a shape are measured in centimetres (cm), the area is expressed in **square centimetres** (cm²).

  Example: Natalia uses centimetre-squared paper to draw a rectangle measuring 8 cm by 6 cm.
  What is the area of the rectangle?

  14 cm²   28 cm²   48 cm²   54 cm²   64 cm²
   A   B   C   D   E

  The correct answer is **C**. There are 6 rows of 8 squares.
  As $6 \times 8 = 8 \times 6 = 48$, the area is 48 cm².

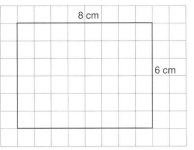

8 cm

6 cm

Not to scale

MATHEMATICAL REASONING
Length and area

- Rectangles can be split into two identical triangles. This means the **area of each triangle** is half the area of the original rectangle. This can be used to find the area of a triangle drawn on a grid.

Example: A triangle is drawn on centimetre-squared paper. What is the area of the shaded triangle?

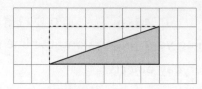

A 3 cm²   **B** 4 cm²   **C** 5 cm²   **D** 6 cm²   **E** 8 cm²

The correct answer is **D**. The rectangle shown has dimensions 6 cm by 2 cm. As 6 × 2 is 12, the area of the rectangle would be 12 cm². As half of 12 is 6, the area of the shaded triangle is 6 cm².

- A question may involve **both perimeter and area**.

Example: The area of a square is 25 square centimetres. The perimeter is
A 5 cm   **B** 10 cm   **C** 20 cm   **D** 30 cm   **E** 16 cm

The correct answer is **C**. As 5 × 5 = 25, the length of each side of the square is 5 cm. As the square has four equal sides and 4 × 5 = 20, the perimeter is 20 cm.

💡 *Tip:* Drawing a diagram can help.

Real Test 3

MATHEMATICAL REASONING
Length and area

10 MIN

1 The diagram shows a normal school ruler.

The perimeter of a normal school ruler is closest to

60 cm	30 cm	34 cm	66 cm	120 cm
A	**B**	**C**	**D**	**E**

2 A sequence is formed by adding squares.

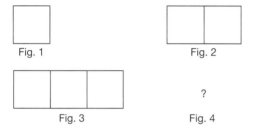

If the perimeter of figure 3 is 8 units, the perimeter of figure 4 would be

A 10 units   B 11 units   C 12 units
D 14 units   E 16 units

3 A rectangle has a perimeter of 12 cm and the length of one of the sides is 4 cm. The length of the other side is

8 cm	2 cm	4 cm	3 cm	6 cm
A	**B**	**C**	**D**	**E**

4 A rectangle has a perimeter of 28 cm. The length is 2 cm longer than the width. What is the area of the rectangle?

24 cm²	36 cm²	48 cm²	56 cm²	60 cm²
A	**B**	**C**	**D**	**E**

5 Eleanor drew this shape on centimetre-squared paper:

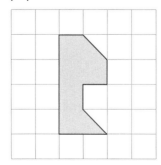

What is the area of the shape?

$4\frac{1}{2}$ cm²	5 cm²	$5\frac{1}{2}$ cm²	6 cm²	$6\frac{1}{2}$ cm²
A	**B**	**C**	**D**	**E**

6 A square piece of centimetre-squared paper is folded as shown:

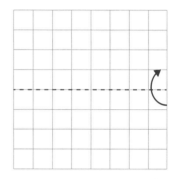

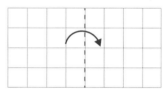

The shaded sections are now cut and thrown away:

The sheet of paper is then unfolded completely.

What is the area of paper that remains?

28 cm²	36 cm²	40 cm²	44 cm²	48 cm²
A	**B**	**C**	**D**	**E**

7 A rectangle has a perimeter of 32 cm. The length is 8 cm longer than the width. What is the area of the rectangle?

96 cm²	64 cm²	72 cm²	80 cm²	48 cm²
A	**B**	**C**	**D**	**E**

☞ **Answers and explanations on pages 209-210**

Real
Test 3

MATHEMATICAL REASONING
Length and area

8 Two shapes are drawn on centimetre-squared paper:

The shapes are cut out and joined to form a square. What is the perimeter of the square?

9 cm	11 cm	12 cm	16 cm	22 cm
A	B	C	D	E

9 A 60-cm-long piece of wire is cut into two lengths. The longer piece is three times as long as the shorter piece. What is the length of the longer piece?

15 cm	20 cm	40 cm	45 cm	48 cm
A	B	C	D	E

10 This shape is made from identical squares. The area of each square is 4 cm². What is the perimeter of the shape?

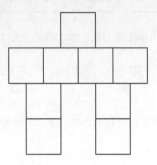

24 cm	28 cm	32 cm	36 cm	40 cm
A	B	C	D	E

☞ **Answers and explanations on pages 209-210**

Real Test 4

MATHEMATICAL REASONING
Length and area

1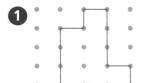

The perimeter of the shape is
A 16 units   B 8 units   C 12 units
D 10 units   E 14 units

2

12 cm

The area of the rectangle is 36 cm². The distance around the outside of the shape is
48 cm   15 cm   30 cm   18 cm   24 cm
A   B   C   D   E

3 What is the perimeter of a square with an area of 16 cm²?

16 cm   32 cm   24 cm   48 cm   64 cm
A   B   C   D   E

4 A piece of wire is cut into two equal lengths. One piece is bent in the shape of an equilateral triangle with side length 8 cm. The other piece is bent in the shape of a square. What is the length of each side of the square?
4 cm   6 cm   8 cm   12 cm   16 cm
A   B   C   D   E

5 Connor drew this shape on centimetre-squared paper:

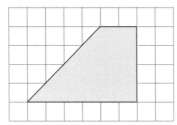

What is the area of the shape?
16 cm²   16½ cm²   17 cm²   17½ cm²   18 cm²
A   B   C   D   E

6 A square piece of centimetre-squared paper is folded as shown:

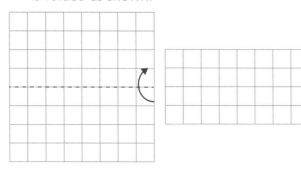

The shaded sections are now cut and thrown away:

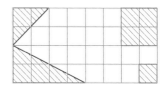

The sheet of paper is then unfolded completely.
What is the area of paper that remains?
32 cm²   36 cm²   38 cm²   40 cm²   42 cm²
A   B   C   D   E

7 George drew this rectangle on a sheet of centimetre-squared paper.

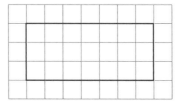

James drew a square with the same perimeter as George's rectangle. What is the difference in the areas of their two shapes?
2 cm²   4 cm²   5 cm²   6 cm²   8 cm²
A   B   C   D   E

☞ **Answers and explanations on pages 210-211**

Real Test 4

MATHEMATICAL REASONING
Length and area

8 James rode from the picnic area, past this sign to the waterfall. After a rest he rode back to the lookout.

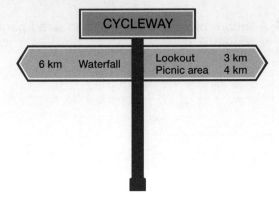

CYCLEWAY

| 6 km | Waterfall | Lookout | 3 km |
| | | Picnic area | 4 km |

How far did James ride?

| 9 km | 13 km | 17 km | 19 km | 26 km |
| A | B | C | D | E |

9 These two identical squares have an area of 36 cm². The shape of the overlap is also a square with an area of 4 cm².

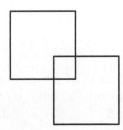

What is the perimeter of the combined shape?

| 40 cm | 42 cm | 44 cm | 46 cm | 48 cm |
| A | B | C | D | E |

10 In the diagram the big square is divided into two identical triangles and seven identical squares. The area of each small square is 4 cm². What is the total area of the shaded parts?

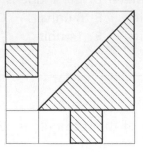

| 18 cm² | 20 cm² | 24 cm² | 26 cm² | 28 cm² |
| A | B | C | D | E |

☞ **Answers and explanations on pages 210-211**

WRITING
'What would you do if ...?' opinion

- When you are asked in the test to write your opinion on a topic or question, you always need to give reasons for your opinion and be **well organised and clear**.

- As with all test questions, you must **write on the topic or question** you are given. So read the question very, very carefully.

- In the scholarship test you will definitely be asked to write your opinion on a topic, so **practice within a time limit** is useful.

- A common kind of opinion question is to ask what you would do in a certain situation. You might be asked:
  ○ What would you do if ...?
  ○ Where would you go if ...?
  ○ What changes would you like to see ...?
  We will look at this kind of opinion question in this session.

- 'What would you do if ...?' questions can be about **real, serious topics** or **unreal, fun topics**. In either case they give you a good opportunity to use your imagination and come up with interesting and creative ideas.

- Whatever the topic, you will still need to **support your opinion with reasons**.

- Other kinds of questions give you a topic, statement or question and ask you to give your opinion on it. These are more often on real, serious topics. You might be asked:
  ○ Do you agree or disagree with ...?
  ○ Give your opinion on ...
  ○ Is ... a good or bad idea?
  ○ What (or who) do you think is ...?
  We will look at this kind of opinion question in Week 4.

- One good thing about opinion questions in these tests is that the **topic is always very general**. It will be something every student will be able to write about using their own everyday experiences. So don't worry about being asked to write about something you know very little about—and don't think you need to study specific topics before the exam.

- On the next page is an example of a 'What would you do if ...?' opinion written in response to a test question, though not under test conditions. In your test, you **might not have time** to produce a polished piece of writing like this. However, if you are **well prepared**, you will be able to aim for this standard.

Sample

WRITING
'What would you do if ...?' opinion

10 MIN

Question

If you could go anywhere you wanted to, where would you go and why? You might choose to go to another planet or to somewhere else in space. You might choose to go under the sea or to the top of the highest mountain—or anywhere at all.

Give at least two good reasons for going there.

Response

Structure

Language

Title—give your writing a title if you are not given one

Introduction to the topic, and your opinion

Body—reasons for your opinion (facts, experiences and arguments)

Topic sentences that state main reasons

Paragraphing to separate reasons

Conclusion— (often a comment)

[Travelling to Outer Space]

If I could travel anywhere in the universe, I would go into outer space to a galaxy beyond the Milky Way. I know that in the real world, I would frizzle up or freeze to death in less than a second. But in my imagination that is where I would fly. I can give you two reasons.

First I would like to experience what it is like to travel through space. I think it would be absolutely thrilling (and terrifying) to travel through the blackness and zap past enormous planets and stars and whiz through comets and asteroids. I would especially like to experience the trip back to planet Earth and see that shining blue ball get closer and closer and closer.

Second I would really like to know whether any aliens exist out there. I think if there are any extraterrestrials, they are probably living in another galaxy so that is why I want to travel that far. I think if they were in our galaxy, we would have heard from them by now. I think that seeing an alien would be the most exciting thing that could possibly happen to me. Of course, I would be terrified as well.

So that is where I would go—into space where no-one has ever gone before. You never know: one day I just might.

Interesting, imaginative detail

Precise, vivid language to express ideas

Words to show the **strength of your opinion**

'Signpost' words that help your reader follow your ideas

Correct **spelling, grammar** and **punctuation**

Practice Tasks

50 MIN

- These tasks will give you some ideas about how to get writing quickly and express your opinion in the short time you have in the test.

- You will have to look back at *Travelling to Outer Space* to answer some questions and then do some opinion writing yourself. Your writing will be based on the same question, as there are so many ways to answer it. However, you should write about something different from the story on page 74. You can write about travel to outer space if you want but be sure to use your own ideas.

- Here is the question again. Look at it now before you start the tasks.

Practice question

If you could go anywhere you wanted to, where would you go and why? You might choose to go to another planet or to somewhere else in space. You might choose to go under the sea or to the top of the highest mountain—or anywhere at all.

Give at least **two** good reasons.

- It is important to take a few minutes to plan your writing but the good news is that this type of writing is easy to structure. You are basically saying to the reader: **I think … and I think this way for these reasons—X, Y and Z.**

- So your first step is to ask yourself: **What do I think about this question?** If you had plenty of time, you could carefully consider the arguments for and against choosing a particular travel destination—but you don't have much time at all. So you really have to ask yourself: **What is a reasonable answer to this question? What can I choose that I can make an argument for? What do I know enough about so that I can write something interesting?**

For this question, you could easily argue for any travel destination at all, without knowing much at all about the place. However, for some questions it might be easier to argue one way than another way. So you should think about this before you start.

Important: There is no **one** right answer!

● Your next step is to ask yourself: **What are two or three good reasons I can use to support my opinion?** (You won't have time for more than two or three.) Then quickly write down your reasons in a rough plan. Don't waste time on your conclusion when you are planning—just think about it when you get to it.

Here is the plan for *Travelling to Outer Space.*

Introduction	outer space—another galaxy
Reasons	1 want to travel through space
	2 want to find out if aliens exist

Task 1

Do a brief plan for your response to the Practice question in the space below. There is space for three arguments but two is enough if they are good arguments. Give yourself about two minutes.

💡 *Tip:* Do your plan as quickly as you can. Write in note form, not whole sentences.

Introduction (opinion) _____

_____

_____

Reasons

1 _____

_____

_____

_____

2 _____

_____

_____

_____

3 _____

_____

_____

Practice Tasks

WRITING
'What would you do if ...?' opinion—Getting started

- The important thing is to **make your opinion perfectly clear** at the very start. So in the **introduction** clearly state your answer to the question, as the writer of *Travelling to Outer Space* did.

- You might want to begin your opinion sentence with phrases such as:

> I think …
> I believe …
> In my opinion …
> It is my opinion that …

- It can be a good idea to write a sentence to summarise the arguments you are going to make. This gives the reader a kind of **'map' to follow** as they read. For example, the writer of *Travelling to Outer Space* could have written this sentence: *I would like to travel to another galaxy to experience space travel, to find out about aliens and to see the earth from space.* This sentence would have given a good summary map of the text. However, a map is not absolutely necessary, especially if you are writing a short piece.

Task 2

Write your introduction for the Practice question now. Give yourself about five minutes.

_____

_____

_____

_____

_____

_____

_____

_____

_____

_____

> It isn't possible to cover in detail all the types of questions you could get in the test but the advice here is useful for most 'What would you do if …?' opinion questions. For example, look at this question: *Which three books would you take to a desert island and why?*
>
> You can still use the advice here but instead of one paragraph for each reason, you would write one paragraph for each book you choose.

- When you write your opinion, the main part of your writing will be the **reasons for your opinion**. Your reasons might be facts or examples, or just sensible arguments for thinking the way you do. If you don't give any reasons for your overall opinion, your writing won't be very convincing.

- You should break up your reasons into **paragraphs—one main reason per paragraph**. This helps the reader follow your ideas.

- A common way to write your 'reason paragraphs' is to write one sentence that states the reason in a general way. This is called a **topic sentence**. For example, in *Travelling to Outer Space* the student wrote in paragraph 2: *First I would like to experience what it is like to travel through space.*

- After the topic sentence, write one or two **sentences to support or develop the reason**. For example, in paragraph 2 the student wrote: *I think it would be absolutely thrilling (and terrifying) to travel through the blackness …* This shows the writer has really thought about their opinion and so makes it more convincing.

Task 3

1 Look back at *Travelling to Outer Space.* Underline the topic sentence in paragraph 2.

2 Write one phrase to show what every sentence in paragraph 2 is about. _____

- As with all the writing for your test, you should aim to use **vivid, expressive language**. Try to avoid common words such as *cool, nice, like, amazing* and *good*. These words give only a very general picture of what you are trying to say.

  Try instead to be **precise**. For example, in *Travelling to Outer Space* the writer uses the words *thrilling* and *terrifying* to describe what it would be like to fly through space.

- You can help your reader follow your ideas by giving them **'signposts'**—words and phrases that show them how your ideas are connected. Here are some useful signpost words:

firstly	first of all	secondly	thirdly	next
one reason	another reason	for example	in fact	

- Your opinion will be more powerful and interesting if you use **words that show how strongly you feel or how certain you are about your opinions**. There are many words to help you do this. Some examples are:

very	might	especially	really	so many	every
all	most	almost all	so much	definitely	certainly
simply	surely	completely	totally	absolutely	probably
perhaps	must	extremely	could		

☞ **Answers on page 211**

Task 4

Write the body of your opinion piece now, giving two or three reasons for your opinion. Give yourself about ten minutes.

_____

_____

_____

_____

_____

_____

_____

_____

_____

_____

_____

_____

_____

_____

_____

_____

_____

_____

_____

_____

Remember: Check your grammar, spelling and punctuation as you go. You might not have much time to check it at the end.

Practice Tasks

WRITING
*'What would you do if ...?' opinion—
Writing the conclusion*

- A good conclusion helps to make your opinion more convincing and rounds off the whole text. You may not have time to write very much but if you can, try to state your overall opinion again (varying your words if possible), and to write something interesting or powerful to 'wrap up' all your ideas.

- Some ways to start your conclusion are:

> So …   In conclusion …   To sum up …   In summary …

Task 5

Write your conclusion now. Give yourself about three minutes only.

_____

_____

_____

_____

_____

_____

_____

Note: If you like, you can work on your writing some more, improving what you have written so far and writing it out again on your own paper. Use the checklist below to review your writing.

Checklist for writing a 'What would you do if ...?' opinion text

Have you:

1 *introduced the topic or question and given your overall opinion?*
2 *given two or three good reasons for your opinion?*
3 *used interesting, creative ideas to explain your reasons?*
4 *developed your reasons with facts, examples or logical arguments?*
5 *used signpost words to help the reader follow your ideas?*
6 *written a short conclusion?*
7 *checked your grammar, punctuation and spelling?*

Remember: In the test, you won't have time to revise thoroughly and make big changes. You may have time to change a few words but you will really be aiming to do a good piece of writing in one draft.

Real Test

Choose **one** of the writing tests below to do now. Use your own paper.

If you like, you can do both tests. However, it would be better to do them on different days. For extra practice you could use the tests again, writing in different ways each time.

Set yourself a time limit of 20 minutes. Use the checklist on page 80 to give it a quick review.

Test 1

NEW COMPETITION

BEST PLACE TO LIVE?
WHAT DO YOU THINK?

*Prizes to be won
—all ages*

Write your entry for the competition. Give your opinion on the best place to live. You can choose the place you live now, or somewhere you have lived before or visited.

Be sure to give your reasons. Why is it a good place to live? What makes it special?

OR

Test 2

If a creature from outer space landed in your schoolyard, would you run away and hide? Or would you go up and introduce yourself? Think carefully. There are good reasons to take both these actions. If you want, you could argue for a different action altogether.

Write what you would do and why. Give at least **two** good reasons.

Let's start to revise!

Week 3

This is what we cover this week:

Day 1 **Reading:** Factual texts

Day 2 **Thinking Skills:**

- ◎ Problem solving—Word problems
- ◎ Problem solving—Position, order and direction
- ◎ Problem solving—Numerical reasoning

Day 3 **Mathematical Reasoning:** ◎ Volume, capacity, mass and time

                                                  ◎ 2D and 3D shapes

Day 4 **Writing:** Narrative story

10 MIN

- In your test, you will be asked to answer questions about extracts from **factual texts**. These could be, for example, information websites, travel brochures or newspaper reports.

- Factual texts are texts that focus on **information**. This does not mean they only contain facts. They might also include **ideas** and **opinions**.

- In the NSW Opportunity Class Placement Test you will be asked to do a **cloze activity** instead of answering multiple-choice questions. In the ACER Scholarship tests you will probably still be asked to answer multiple-choice questions (as you were with Literary texts and Poetry in this book).

- A cloze activity is where you have to match words, phrases or sentences to a blank space in a text so the text makes sense. You might be familiar with this type of activity. In the Opportunity Class Placement Test you will need to **match sentences**.

> This part of the book will give you practice with this type of question format but remember: Always check the latest advice about the test you are going to sit.

- With cloze, the best approach under test conditions is to **read the whole text quickly and then skim the missing sentences**. Then look through the sentences one by one and roughly work out where they should go. You might change your mind on these as you firm up your ideas. You may easily see where one or two go so start with these, crossing them off to eliminate them and then keep going. When you are happy with all your answers, write them in.

- In the Opportunity Class Placement Test and here in the following Practice Tasks you will be given **one extra sentence** which does not belong in the text.

- It is important to read the sentences around the missing sentence and sometimes the whole paragraph and those before and after it to get the answer right. You will have to look at **linking words and phrase**s such as 'however', 'as a result' and 'because'. You should also pay attention to words such as 'this', 'these' and 'another' which we frequently use to link ideas when we write.

- Whichever test you are sitting, the cloze activities, which follow are good preparation for tackling questions on **factual texts**.

Use this first practice task as a guide. It is shorter than this section in the actual test with fewer missing sentences but it will give you a good idea of what is required. Read the text carefully then read the sentences A–E and work out which one fits each space.

Note: There is **one** extra answer which you do not need to use.

Then look at the answers to get explanations about why each answer was right. Don't worry too much about the time limit but try to improve your speed over the next practice tasks.

Dugongs—and their close relatives, the manatees—have always been part of the Aboriginal Dreaming. Hunting dugongs and sharing their meat is part of many important ceremonies in northern coastal Australia. **1** _____ .

This gentle, unique creature is not well known and is seldom seen. **2** _____ . They are also found in other parts of the Indo-Pacific region. They live for about 70 years and grow to three metres long and 400 kilograms in weight. The female first falls pregnant between 10 and 17 years of age. Its baby is born after 13 months and it suckles for two years, with a new calf born every three to five years. Mother and baby stay close together, the calf sometimes riding on its mother's back or being clasped by a flipper while suckling.

Dugongs look a little similar to seals or dolphins. **3** _____ . They grow small tusks, though these are usually only visible in adult males and older females. Their whale-like tail moves up and down, and they use their flippers for balance and to turn. Because their nostrils are on top of their wide snout, they breathe by surfacing only a very small part of their large, round head. They hear well and communicate by squeaks, chirps and barks.

4 _____ . They are quite defenceless, swim in shallow water and cannot see well. Dugongs are protected from commercial hunting but Aboriginal and Torres Strait Islander traditional hunting is allowed to continue.

From 'Mermaids and other endangered sea creatures' by Hazel Dittebrandt, *The Helix*, no. 66, June/July 1999; reproduced with permission

---

Choose from the sentences below **(A–E)** the one that fits each gap. Remember: There is **one** extra sentence you will not need to use.

A Because they graze on seagrass, they are sometimes called sea cows.
B About 85 000 dugongs live in the northern Australian coastal waters from Perth to Brisbane.
C However, dugongs are in serious danger of becoming extinct.
D They reach adult size between 4 and 17 years of age.
E Their huge size provides food for many isolated communities.

☞ **Answers and explanations on page 211**

Practice Task 2

READING
Factual texts

10 min

Again, read the text right through and then read the missing sentences and work out which one goes in each space. Remember: There is one spare sentence which you won't need to use. When you finish, check the answers. This text is a little longer than the last one and this time you will have to match six missing sentences. Try to work more quickly this time and keep to the time limit. You will have to work very quickly in the real test.

For several centuries fishermen from Macassar, now part of Indonesia, sailed to the north coast of Australia. There they gathered and processed trepang, the sea slug which abounds in the shallow waters around the coast. The Macassans sold the dried trepang to merchants in Timor. **1** _____ . They also bartered with the Aboriginal people, trading metalware in the form of knives, axes and fish-hooks for supplies of tortoiseshell and pearl shell.

No one knows for sure when the trade began but the Spanish captain Luis Vaes de Torres reported seeing what he called Malay vessels near the Gulf of Carpentaria in 1606. **2** _____ . Each prau carried about thirty men and several dugout canoes for use in the more shallow waters. Some of these canoes were traded with the Aborigines, who learned from the design and constructed their own canoes from local trees.

The Macassans were annual visitors and often returned to the same trepanging spots. **3** _____ . These campsites gave easy access to the trepang and offered some protection from the Aborigines if relationships deteriorated. The relationships between the Macassans and the Aboriginal people with whom they came in contact varied enormously. **4** _____ . When relationships were good, however, Aboriginal men often helped to collect, cook, dry and smoke trepang for the Macassans, and some Macassan captains formed liaisons with Aboriginal women. There are also oral records of Aboriginal men travelling around the Australian coast by prau and even going as far as Macassar and back. **5** _____ . Gifts, commodities and language were exchanged and the influence of the Macassan presence in the north can be seen in some of the Aboriginal art, rituals and stories of the region. **6** _____ .

From *Too Many Captain Cooks* by Alan Tucker © Alan Tucker 1994. First published by Omnibus Books, an imprint of Scholastic Australia Pty Ltd, 1994; reproduced with permission of Scholastic Australia Pty Ltd

Choose from the sentences below **(A–G)** the one that fits each gap. Remember: There is **one** extra sentence you will not need.

A They shifted base several times each season and usually camped on offshore islands or the tips of peninsulas.

B The annual visits had reciprocal benefits.

C There are records of several violent clashes between the two groups.

D These peoples, in turn, transported it to Canton (now Guangzhou), where it was considered a great delicacy.

E These vessels, known as praus, brought up to a thousand Macassans to Australia during the northern dry season from April to October.

F The visitors were never seen as a threat to the land.

G Sea slugs (also called sea cucumbers) are echinoderms from the class Holothuroidea.

☞ **Answers and explanations on pages 211–212**

Practice Task 3

Again, read the text right through then read the missing sentences **A–G** and choose your answers. Remember: There is **one** spare sentence which you won't need to use. Work as quickly as you can and aim to finish in **under** 10 minutes. When you finish, check the answers and read the answer explanations if necessary.

Leonardo da Vinci lived in Italy from 1452 to 1519, during a historical period we call the Italian Renaissance. This was a period when art and culture were highly valued and when many wealthy people hired artists to make statues, paint pictures and decorate churches, homes and public buildings. Leonardo began his artistic life as a garzone—a studio boy—and then an apprentice in the workshop of Andrea del Verrocchio, a well-known painter at the time. **1** _____. Leonardo worked alongside a number of artists who are still revered worldwide, such as Perugino and Botticelli.

Leonardo painted the most famous painting in the world—The Mona Lisa, now in the Louvre Museum in Paris. Most people who see this painting believe there is something mysterious about the woman's smile. They argue about whether she really is smiling and wonder what she is thinking. Leonardo also painted the picture that is perhaps the second most famous in the world—The Last Supper. This painting shows Jesus with his twelve disciples the night before he died. **2** _____. Fortunately, it has now been restored so we can still enjoy its beauty.

Leonardo was an extremely clever and talented man—a real genius. Not only was he a painter, he was also a scientist, architect, mathematician, engineer and inventor. His approach to science was observational rather than experimental. **3** _____. His notebooks are crammed with extraordinary drawings of all kinds of things. He made notes on anatomy, astronomy, botany, engineering and a range of other scientific and technical subjects. Interestingly, most of the writing in his notes is backwards. The writing only becomes legible when it is held up to a mirror. It is thought that because he was left-handed it was probably easier for him to write from right to left. **4** _____.

Leonardo was especially interested in the human body. As an artist he was given permission to dissect human corpses to find out how the body worked. His drawings of human anatomy were incredibly detailed. He did not only draw bones, muscles and sinews. **5** _____. Furthermore, he made significant observations and discoveries for that time about the human heart and heart disease.

Leonardo was hundreds of years ahead of his time with his inventions. He invented weapons, armoured fighting vehicles, a parachute and various flying machines. He studied the flight of birds, bats and even insects for 20 years in an attempt to devise a way for man to fly. **6** _____. At one point he had to flee Milan and go to live in Venice. There he found employment as an engineer and invented a system of barricades to prevent attacks on the city and a scheme to change the flow of a major river to prevent floods.

**Practice
Task 3**

Choose from the sentences below **(A–G)** the one that fits each gap. Remember: There is **one** extra sentence you will not need.

A   He described and drew in extreme detail as a way of determining how things worked.

B   He also used a variety of shorthand and symbols.

C   This system was a common path to becoming an artist at this time.

D   He spent his last three years in France and was buried in Chateau d'Amboise.

E   It was done on the wall of a church and so has faded and flaked over the centuries.

F   He also observed and recorded the effects of age and even human emotion on the human body.

G   His engineering skills were valued during his lifetime.

☞ **Answers and explanations on page 212**

Read the text right through then read the missing sentences A–G and choose your answers.
Remember: There is one spare sentence which you won't need to use. Work as quickly as you can and
stop at 10 minutes. If possible, aim to finish in 8 minutes. You will have to work very quickly in your
actual test. When you finish, check the answers and read the answer explanations if necessary.

Can you imagine a world without money? Or a world without even the idea of money? Well,
thousands of years ago money was not used at all. Instead, humans had the 'barter' system. This
meant if people wanted something they weren't able to make or produce themselves, they had to
find someone who could produce it. **1** _____ . If they didn't like what was offered, they
couldn't get the goods they wanted! It wasn't only goods that were bartered, it was services too:
making wheels, tanning leather, herding cattle.

This type of exchange was relied upon by all early civilisations. The earliest evidence of such
bartering is from the Phoenicians around 6000 BCE and the Babylonians, both Mesopotamian
societies in what is now the Middle East. There are still cultures within modern society who rely on
this type of exchange. **2** _____ . Interestingly, bartering has made a bit of a comeback
in recent years with modern technologies helping out. Now we have online swap markets and
auctions, for example.

In ancient times, however, when bartering was still the main mechanism for buying and selling,
certain things came to be used as money because practically everyone would take these things in
exchange. **3** _____ . For example, cows, tobacco, grains, skins, salt and beads were all
used as money at some time. It is difficult for us to imagine buying a horse, for example, with jars
of salt but that is exactly what happened. Salt, in fact, was so valuable that Roman soldiers were
paid in it. This practice gave us the word 'salary'. **4** _____ . Later on, people made coins,
which had a consistent purity and weight, and represented certain amounts of various objects.
So a certain number of coins represented a cow, or 50 pounds of tobacco, and so on.

Today, of course, we have notes and coins issued by the government, and everyone accepts this as
money. **5** _____ . You might sometimes find a friend who you can do a direct trade
with—perhaps one skateboard or game for another. But mostly this is impossible. Money also
allows us to save. It would be difficult to save up lots of cows until you wanted to spend them.
Where on earth would you put them while you saved? **6** _____ . If you have ever done
jobs around the house to earn money to buy something like a bicycle, you will have learnt the
value of what you were saving for by how much work you had to do.

Adapted from *The Big Book of Tell Me Why* by Arkady Leokum, Barnes & Noble Books, New York, 1965

Choose from the sentences below **(A–G)** the one that fits each gap. Remember: There is **one** extra
sentence you will not need.

A Eventually all these kinds of money were replaced by pieces of metal, especially gold and silver.
B They were always needed.
C Then they had to offer that person something in exchange.
D However, it is not something a modern society or economy has totally relied upon.
E Money makes it possible to trade in our modern world.
F Just as with most systems, there are pluses and minuses associated with bartering.
G Money is also a measure of value.

☞ **Answers and explanations on pages 212-213**

THINKING SKILLS
Problem solving—Word problems

10 min

- Many problems are written ones where the words need to be interpreted. **Read** all problems **carefully** and make sure you **understand** what is required.

- Word problems might involve reasoning about totally unfamiliar topics. Use **common sense**.

- **Be careful with the wording** of questions. For example, if a question asks which option **must** be true it does not mean that the incorrect options are necessarily false. It just means that we cannot be certain that they are true.

- Remember you **only** need to **answer the question**. You don't need to sort out all the information. Be careful to answer the question that is asked.

Example 1

Evie took three jelly beans from a jar that held only red and black jelly beans. She ate the jelly beans, one after the other. The first one she ate was black and the last one was red.

Which **must** be true?
A   Evie ate one black and two red jelly beans.
B   Evie ate one red and two black jelly beans.
C   Evie ate a black jelly bean after a red jelly bean.
D   Evie ate a red jelly bean after a black jelly bean.

Steps to answer the question
1   Read the question carefully and note what is required for the question. In this case we need to find the option that **must** be true.
2   Think about what is happening in the question.
3   Consider each of the possibilities.

D is correct. In this case Evie ate a black jelly bean, a second jelly bean that was either red or black, then a third jelly bean that was red. Now, if the second jelly bean Evie ate was red then she ate that red one after the first black one. If the second jelly bean was black then the last jelly bean Evie ate, which was red, was eaten after that second black one. So, whatever colour the second jelly bean was, Evie at some stage ate a red one after a black one.

The jelly beans must have been either one black and two red or one red and two black. So either the statement in A or the statement in B will be true, but there is not enough information to determine which of A or B **must** have been correct.

Evie cannot have eaten a black jelly bean after a red one, so C is not correct.

Example 2

Ali, Imran, Mel, Sara and Thomas have these five offices in a row at their workplace.

Ali is somewhere between Thomas and Mel.

Imran is somewhere between Ali and Sara.

Mel is somewhere between Sara and Imran.

Which is **not** true?

A Mel is next to Ali.

B Ali is next to Thomas.

C Imran is next to Mel.

D Mel is next to Sara.

Steps to answer the question

1 Read the question carefully and determine what is required. In this case we need to find the statement that is **not** true.

2 Use the given information to determine what you can.

3 Remember you are looking for what is not true, not what is true.

A is correct. Ali, Imran and Mel all have offices between other people, so they must have the middle three offices in some order. So Thomas and Sara have the two outside offices. Now Mel is between Sara and Imran and Imran is between Sara and Ali. The order must be Sara, Mel, Imran, Ali and Thomas (from right to left or from left to right). Mel is not next to Ali, so the statement that is not true is Mel is next to Ali. A is the statement that is not true.

Ali must be next to Thomas, Imran is next to Mel and Mel is next to Sara. The statements in the other options are all true so these are not the correct answers.

> ☼ *Tip:* If a person is 'somewhere' between two others it does not necessarily mean that person must be next to the others. There may be other people between the two others as well.

Checklist

Can you:

1 *read questions carefully and understand what is required?*

2 *consider the options and judge whether they logically follow from the given information?*

3 *take care to make sure that you answer the question that has been asked?*

Real Test 1

THINKING SKILLS
Problem solving—Word problems

1 Maddy, Lily and Zara are sisters.

If Zara is younger than Lily and Maddy is older than Zara, which one of the following statements must be correct?
- **A** Maddie is the oldest.
- **B** Lily is the oldest.
- **C** Zara is the youngest.
- **D** Lily and Maddy are twins.

2 Five children—Kylie, Lauren, Dylan, Emily and Angus—are riding their bikes. Each of the bicycles is a different colour, either red, blue, green, pink or yellow.

It is known that:
- Angus's bike is either red or green
- neither Lauren's nor Emily's bike is red or blue
- the pink bicycle belongs to Kylie.

What colour is Dylan's bike?
- **A** red
- **B** blue
- **C** green
- **D** yellow

3 A cupboard has three shelves. Cups are kept on one shelf, plates on another and cookbooks on the third. If the plates are above the cookbooks and the cups are below the plates, which **must** be true?
- **A** Plates are on the top shelf.
- **B** Cookbooks are on the bottom shelf.
- **C** Cups are on the middle shelf.
- **D** Cookbooks are on the middle shelf.

4 Annabel, Khalid, Marlee, Salim, Theresa and Victor all live in the same street. Annabel and Khalid are the same age. Theresa is older than Salim but younger than Khalid. Annabel is older than Marlee but younger than Victor.

Which might **not** be true?
- **A** Victor is the oldest.
- **B** Marlee is the youngest.
- **C** Annabel and Khalid are equal second oldest.
- **D** Salim is younger than Annabel.

5 Logan has to choose a different sport each term of the school year. The choices are:

Term 1	Term 2	Term 3	Term 4
cricket	tennis	soccer	tennis
swimming	soccer	hockey	swimming
basketball	basketball	baseball	baseball

Logan chose swimming, basketball, soccer and tennis. Which **must** be correct?
- **A** Logan chose swimming in term 1.
- **B** Logan chose basketball in term 2.
- **C** Logan chose soccer in term 3.
- **D** Logan chose tennis in term 4.

6 Bailey, Nicholas, Louis and Timothy are brothers. Bailey is older than Timothy but younger than Nicholas. Louis is younger than Nicholas.

Which **must** be true?
- **A** Louis is the youngest.
- **B** Timothy is the youngest.
- **C** Bailey is the second oldest.
- **D** Nicholas is the oldest.

☞ **Answers and explanations on pages 213-214**

Real Test 1

THINKING SKILLS
Problem solving—Word problems

7 Georgia has to choose one shape from each box to complete a design.

Box 1	Box 2	Box 3	Box 4
octagon	rectangle	square	kite
square	trapezium	circle	parallelogram
hexagon	circle	kite	triangle
rectangle	triangle	rhombus	hexagon

Which four shapes **cannot** be the ones Georgia chooses?

A rectangle, square, kite, circle

B triangle, hexagon, octagon, circle

C kite, triangle, trapezium, hexagon

D parallelogram, hexagon, rectangle, octagon

8 Some boys and girls are playing with a frisbee. A girl threw the frisbee to another child who then threw it to a boy.

Which **must** be correct?

A A girl sent the frisbee to a girl.
B A boy sent the frisbee to a boy.

C A girl sent the frisbee to a boy.
D A boy sent the frisbee to a girl.

9 Four boxes are stacked together. One box holds toys, one has clothes, a third has shoes and the other has papers. Two are on the bottom and the other two stacked on top of those.

Sharon knows that:

● the boxes holding clothes and toys are diagonally opposite each other

● the box holding shoes is on the bottom.

Which of the following must Sharon also know?

A The box holding toys is on top of the box holding shoes.

B The boxes holding papers and clothes are beside each other.

C The box holding clothes is on the bottom.

D The box holding papers is on the top.

10 In a classroom, six children are sitting in a row, one person at each desk.

It is known that:

● Irene is next to both Tayla and George

● Julian is at one end

● Dana is not next to either Harry or George.

Which **must** be true?

A Dana is next to Tayla.
B Harry is next to Julian.

C Julian is next to George.
D Tayla is next to Harry.

☞ **Answers and explanations on pages 213-214**

10 min

- In some problems you might need to work through and place people or objects in **order**.
- Read the question carefully and make sure you understand what is required. You need to be able to read and **sort** written information and that given in tables.
- Often things might need to be placed in **numerical** order or in a **grid**. They might be organised from **right to left** (or left to right). **Compass directions** might also be used.

left ← → right

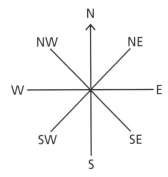

Example 1

Children at a kindergarten have been asked to use four different colours to paint a train. These are the colours they can choose from:

Engine	Carriage 1	Carriage 2	Carriage 3
red	green	yellow	blue
blue	red	purple	green
grey	pink	orange	yellow

Zach wants to use blue, yellow and purple. If he uses those colours, which of these statements is true?

A He can use red for the engine.
B He can use pink for carriage 1.
C He can use orange for carriage 2.
D He can use green for carriage 3.

Steps to work out the answer

1 Read the question carefully and make sure you understand what is required. In this case one colour must be chosen from each of the columns in the table.
2 Look at the table and find the colours that Zach wants to use.
3 Eliminate the options that cannot be true.

B is correct. Only carriage 2 can be purple, so if Zach uses purple, it must be for carriage 2. This means that Zach cannot use orange for carriage 2. **C is not correct**. Either carriage 2 or carriage 3 can be yellow. If Zach uses purple for carriage 2, and if he also uses yellow, it must be for carriage 3. So Zach cannot use green for carriage 3. **D is not correct**. Either the engine or carriage 3 can be blue. If Zach uses yellow for carriage 3, and if he also uses blue, it must be for the engine. So Zach cannot use red for the engine. **A is not correct**.

So Zach uses blue for the engine, purple for carriage 2 and yellow for carriage 3. He can use any of green, red or pink for carriage 1. The true statement is that he can use pink for carriage 1. B is correct.

Example 2

Jono has a frame with spaces for 16 photographs. He has filled the spaces with eight photos of his daughter, Emma, and eight of his son, Lachlan. Every row, every column and both diagonals have two photos of Emma and two of Lachlan. Row 4 has photos of Lachlan at each end and there is another photo of him at B3.

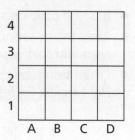

Which statement is **not** correct?

A   There is a photo of Lachlan at A2.

B   There is a photo of Emma at D2.

C   Column B and Column C have photos of Lachlan in the same rows.

D   Row 1 and Row 3 have photos of Emma in the same columns.

Steps to answer the question

1   Read the question carefully and make sure you know what is required. In this case we want to know which statement is not correct so we must take time to consider each option and not rush to put the first answer that **is** correct.

2   In order to work out whether the statements are correct we need to fill in the positions of all the photos.

3   Then we need to consider each option to see if it is correct or not.

	A	B	C	D
4	L	E	E	L
3	E	L	L	E
2	L	E	E	L
1	E	L	L	E

B is correct. We are told that the top row has photos of Lachlan at A4 and D4, so there must be photos of Emma at B4 and C4. There are photos of Lachlan at A4 and B3, so the other photos in that diagonal must be of Emma. Column C then has photos of Emma at C4 and C2 so C1 and C3 must have photos of Lachlan. Row 3 can then be completed followed by column D, the other diagonal and the remaining rows.

There is a photo of Lachlan at A2. There is also a photo of Lachlan at D2, so the statement 'There is a photo of Emma at D2' is incorrect. Columns B and C are the same. Rows 1 and 3 are the same. The answer to the question is B.

Checklist

Can you:

1   *read questions carefully and understand what is required?*

2   *work through the given information to find the answer?*

3   *use tables and grids?*

4   *understand and use directions such as left and right?*

5   *use compass directions?*

Real Test 2

THINKING SKILLS
Problem solving—Position, order and direction

10 MIN

1 Four people are sitting around a square table, one person on each side. Meg is on Ryan's left and Elizabeth is on Vincent's right.

Which statement is correct?
A Elizabeth is on Meg's left.
C Meg is on Vincent's left.
B Ryan is on Vincent's right.
D Meg is opposite Elizabeth.

2 Jill chooses one marble from each of four buckets to play a game. The marbles she chooses are different colours.

Bucket 1	Bucket 2	Bucket 3	Bucket 4
blue	orange	black	red
green	black	red	yellow
yellow	green	blue	grey
white	grey	brown	pink

Three of the marbles she has chosen are green, red and brown.

What colour **cannot** the fourth marble be?
A orange
B blue
C pink
D white

3 Alice has this set of drawers. She keeps pins and needles in one drawer and buttons in another. The other drawers hold material, thread, scissors, bobbins, elastic, ribbons and patterns (one type of thing in each drawer).

Alice knows that pins and needles, thread and scissors are all in the top row. She also knows that the material is directly above the patterns and right of the ribbons. The patterns are left of the buttons.
Which **must** be correct?
A The pins and needles are in the centre of the top row.
B The patterns are in the centre of the bottom row.
C The ribbons are furthest right in the middle row.
D The buttons are furthest left in the bottom row.

left ⬚⬚⬚ right

4 Five students—Abdul, Eli, Frances, Polly and Sophie—filled the top five positions in an exam. Eli got a lower mark than Frances but a higher mark than Polly. Frances got a lower mark than Abdul but a higher mark than Sophie.

Which **must** be correct?
A Polly came fourth.
B Eli came third.
C Frances came second.
D Sophie came fifth.

5 Six horses—Carter, Diva, Flowerpot, Magic, Patra and Wyatt—have stables all in a row. The stables of Patra and Wyatt are furthest apart. There is one stable between those of Flowerpot and Magic. Diva's stable is next to Patra's. The two middle stables belong to Flowerpot and Carter.

Which horse occupies the stable next to Wyatt?
A Carter
B Diva
C Flowerpot
D Magic

☞ **Answers and explanations on pages 214-215**

Real Test 2

6 One week at school some special activities are happening. Student can choose one activity on each of four days. The possible activities are:

Day 1	Day 2	Day 3	Day 4
pottery	board games	card games	bowling
chess	bocce	table tennis	drama
French cricket	photography	painting	Scrabble
board games	drama	chess	photography

Maria wants to do drama, play board games and try pottery. Which of these will she **not** be able to also do?

A painting   B photography   C chess   D table tennis

7 John, Mitchell, Erin and Phoebe are seated at a picnic table. John and one of the others are sitting on one side of the table facing the beach and the other two are on the opposite side of the table facing the park. Phoebe is sitting diagonally opposite Erin.

Which must be correct?
A Phoebe is sitting next to John.   B Mitchell is facing the park.
C Erin is directly opposite Mitchell.   D John is directly opposite Phoebe.

8 There are four houses in a row painted in different colours. One is grey, one is green, one is white and the other is yellow. The grey house is to the left of the green house. The white house is to the right of the yellow house. The yellow house is to the right of the grey house.

Which **must** be correct?
A The grey house is furthest left.   B The yellow house is furthest left.
C The green house is furthest right.   D The white house is furthest right.

9 Apwood, Geneva, Joyville, Lakeland, Rogan, Turpentine, Verbena and Yenton are eight towns. Verbena is north of Rogan and south-east of Geneva. Yenton is west of Joyville and north-west of Rogan. Apwood is south of Turpentine and north of Verbena. Lakeland is north of Joyville and east of Turpentine.

Which town is south-west of Joyville?
A Apwood   B Geneva   C Rogan   D Turpentine

10 Six friends, including Jackie and Jess, are sitting down to a meal at a rectangular table. Three people are seated along each side of the table. Nathan and Mary are sitting as far apart as possible. Geri is seated directly opposite Mary. Daisy is next to Nathan.

Which **must** be true?
A Daisy is directly opposite Jess.
B Nathan is directly opposite Jackie.
C Jess is next to Mary.
D Jackie is next to Jess.

☞ **Answers and explanations on pages 214-215**

THINKING SKILLS
Problem solving—Numerical reasoning

10 MIN

- Problems requiring numerical reasoning usually do not require any special mathematical knowledge. They often involve only **simple addition or subtraction**.
- Read the question **carefully** and make sure you understand exactly what is required.
- Use your reasoning skills to solve the problem. You might work **forwards or backwards** through the given information.
- **Diagrams and tables** can be used as an aid.
- Sometimes you may be able to use the given options to see **which one works**.
- Often it is possible to **check** that your solution is correct.

Example 1

Victoria has these four cards:

She places three of the cards face down on the table.

The first and last card of these three add to 5 and the first and second add to 8.

Which card was **not** placed face down on the table?

A 2   **B** 3   **C** 4   **D** 5

Steps to answer the question

1. Read the question carefully and make sure you understand what is required. In this case three of the four cards are used and you have to determine which card is not used.

2. Use the given information to first work out which cards must be used.

C is correct. We are told that the first and third card add to 5. Of the given cards only 2 + 3 = 5, so one of the first and third cards must be 2 and the other must be 3. Now the first and second cards add to 8. Of the given cards only 3 + 5 = 8, so one of the first and second cards must be 3 and the other must be 5. So the first card must be 3, the third card must be 5 and the second card must be 2. This means that the card not placed face down on the table must be 4.

Example 2

Seven friends compete in a competition and receive points from 0 to 6 in each of three rounds. The person who comes first gets 6 points, second place earns 5 points and so on. The winner is the person who has the most points at the end of the three rounds.

These are the points earned in the first two rounds.

Points	Round 1	Round 2
6	Mary	Thomas
5	Archie	Anne
4	Anne	Liam
3	Thomas	Archie
2	Liam	Mary
1	Jason	Ellen
0	Ellen	Jason

Thomas came second in the last round and second altogether.

Who won the competition?

A Anne   **B** Archie   **C** Liam   **D** Mary

Steps to work out the answer

1 Read the question carefully and make sure you understand what is required. In this case we need to find the person who can have the most points after three rounds.
2 Look at the table and find the total points that each person already has.
3 Find the person who can finish with more points than Thomas.

A is correct. As Thomas came second in the third round, he would have scored 5 points in that round. His total would be 3 + 6 + 5 = 14. Because Thomas came second, the winner of the competition must have scored more than 14 points in total. So far, Anne has scored 9 points, Archie has scored 8 points, Liam has scored 6 points and Mary has scored 8 points. If Anne comes first in round 3, she will get another 6 points and have a total of 15. No-one else can reach 15 points, so Anne must have won the competition.

☀ *Tip:* When checking options to find the correct answer always check all the options even if you think you have found the right answer. That works as a check!

Checklist

Can you:

1 *read questions carefully and determine what is required?*
2 *work through the given information to find the answer?*
3 *use tables or diagrams if they can be helpful?*
4 *work backwards when required?*
5 *check that your answer is correct?*

Real Test 3

THINKING SKILLS
Problem solving—Numerical reasoning

1 Trent is laying tiles in a pattern. His pattern uses 5 green, 3 grey and 4 white tiles. Trent has 31 more green tiles, 21 more grey tiles and 19 more white tiles.

How many more times can Trent complete his pattern?

A 4   B 5   C 6   D 7

2 Five cars are parked in a row. The red car is two places from the white car. The blue car is last. The white car is next to the silver car. The black car is not next to the red car, which is not first.

Which car is in the second spot?

A black   B red   C silver   D white

3 Some people took part in a trivia quiz over three rounds. They collected points in each round:

Name	Emma	Max	Joe	Sara	Zane	Rose
Round 1	18	15	17	16	19	20
Round 2	15	16	17	18	20	19
Round 3	18	17	19	20	16	15

One person scored two more total points than Emma but two less than Zane.

Who was that?

A Max   B Joe   C Sara   D Rose

4 One hundred balloons were to be used in a display. These are the numbers of each colour:

Colour	red	white	blue	green	yellow
Number	24	15	22	21	18

The sponsor of the event decided that he didn't want to use blue balloons. As a result, 8 more white, 7 more yellow, 5 more green and 2 more red balloons were used.

Two colours then had the same number of balloons. What were the two colours?

A red and green   B green and yellow   C red and yellow   D yellow and white

5 Fiona is making a necklace by putting beads on a string. She has a pattern of 10 beads of three different colours that she keeps repeating. After the last pattern she has used 35 pink, 14 blue and 21 white beads altogether. Fiona has another 30 white, 27 blue and 43 pink beads.

How many more patterns can Fiona complete?

A 7   B 8   C 9   D 10

6 In a school exam, the top four marks out of 100 were 97, 96, 94 and 91. The marks were those of Toby, Samuel, Shea and Lucy in some order. Shea got a higher mark than Samuel. Toby got a lower mark than Lucy whose mark was lower than Shea's.

Which **must** be true?

A Toby got 91 marks.   B Samuel got 94 marks.
C Lucy got 96 marks.   D Shea got 97 marks.

☞ **Answers and explanations on pages 216-217**

Real Test 3

THINKING SKILLS
Problem solving—Numerical reasoning

7 Gaby is playing with some blocks. The blocks are red, yellow and blue and she is using 15 of one colour, 12 of another and 10 of the third.

If Gaby uses more yellow than blue blocks and fewer blue blocks than red ones, which must be correct?

A Gaby is using 15 red blocks.   **B** Gaby is using 15 yellow blocks.
C Gaby is using just 10 blue blocks.   **D** Gaby is using exactly 12 yellow blocks.

8 Six boys—Elton, Jayden, Lachlan, Mohammad, Sean and Wes—were the only runners in a race. Jayden finished ahead of Lachlan. Wes finished after Sean. Elton finished between Lachlan and Jayden who both finished between Sean and Wes.

If Mohammad finished first, who finished in 5th place?

A Elton   **B** Jayden   **C** Lachlan   **D** Wes

9 Five friends competed in two races. The results in the first race were:

Position	1st	2nd	3rd	4th	5th
Name	Ben	Kevin	Jake	Roger	Adam
Time (min)	46	48	49	54	56

In the second race Ben had a fall. The results were:

Position	1st	2nd	3rd	4th	5th
Name	Kevin	Jake	Roger	Adam	Ben
Time (min)	39	41	44	47	59

Who improved his time the most?

A Kevin   **B** Jake   **C** Roger   **D** Adam

10 In a competition, competitors were marked on their speed and accuracy. Both of these were marked out of 10 and the total score, which determined the position in the competition, was the sum of those two marks.

Here are the results:

Speed		Accuracy	
Molly	10	Stella	9
Amelia	9	Kate	8
Tilly	8	Molly	7
Kate	7	Ivy	6
Ivy	7	Tilly	6
Stella	5	Amelia	5

Which is **not** correct?

A Molly came first.   **B** Stella came second.   **C** Tilly came equal third.   **D** Ivy came last.

☞ **Answers and explanations on pages 216-217**

MATHEMATICAL REASONING
Volume, capacity, mass and time

10 min

- **The volume is the amount of space in a 3D shape.**

  Example: Erica used identical cubes to make this 3D model. Each cube has a volume of 2 cm³. What is the volume of the model?

  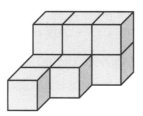

  A 7 cm³   **B** 9 cm³   **C** 14 cm³   **D** 18 cm³   **E** 54 cm³

  The correct answer is **D**. There are 9 cubes in the model. As 9 × 2 is 18, the volume is 18 cm³.

- **When a 3D solid is filled it is said to have a capacity.** There are 1000 millilitres (mL) in 1 litre (L).

  Example: A bottle contains a litre of water. If Jason pours 200 mL from the bottle into each of three glasses, how much water remains?

  A 400 mL   **B** 500 mL   **C** 600 mL   **D** 797 mL   **E** 800 mL

  The correct answer is **A**. As 1 L is 1000 mL, and 200 × 3 is 600 then 1000 − 600 = 400 which means there is 400 mL remaining.

- **The mass of a range of common objects** should be known. The mass of an apple is around 200 g, that of a loaf of bread about 800 g, and a Year 4 student could be around 30 kg.

  Example A normal hen's egg would have a mass of about

  A 6 g   **B** 60 g   **C** 600 g   **D** 6 kg   **E** 60 kg

  The correct answer is **B**. It is lighter than an apple but certainly heavier than 6 g.

  💡 *Tip:* Know the mass of everyday objects—practise with your set of scales at home.

- **A unit of mass is the kilogram,** which is the same as 1000 grams (g).

  Example: Shaun has a mass of 32 kg which is increasing by 500 g per month. What will his mass be in six months?

  A 32.5 kg   **B** 34 kg   **C** 36.5 kg   **D** 29 kg   **E** 35 kg

  The correct answer is **E**. The working is 32 + 0.5 × 6 = 32 + 3 = 35. This means Shaun's mass will be 35 kg.

  💡 *Tip:* Kilo means 1000. Here 500 g has been written as 0.5 kg.

- **The number of days in each month** can be remembered by the following verse: 30 days has September, April, June and November. All the rest have 31 days, except February alone which has 28 days, or 29 days in any leap year.

  Example: Melanie receives her class project on 14 August and it is due three weeks later. On what day is the project due?

  A 31 August   **B** 2 September   **C** 3 September   **D** 4 September   **E** 5 September

  The answer is **D**. It takes 17 days to get to the end of August, and then 4 more days after that. This means the project is due on 4 September.

Key Points

MATHEMATICAL REASONING
Volume, capacity, mass and time

- The number of minutes between **different times** on a digital clock can be calculated.

  Example: The amount of time from 11:47 am to 3:15 pm is
  A 188 min **B** 198 min **C** 208 min **D** 218 min **E** 212 min
  The correct answer is **C**. From 11:47 to midday is 13 min, then 180 min (3 hours) to 3 pm, then 15 min. The amount of time is 13 + 180 + 15 = 208 min.

- Students need to recognise the time using both **digital and analog** clocks.

  Example: The analog clock is seven minutes slow:

  The correct time on the digital clock is

  A ⟦**5:45**⟧ B ⟦**5:31**⟧ C ⟦**5:47**⟧ D ⟦**5:33**⟧ E ⟦**5:35**⟧

  The correct answer is **A**. The time on the analog clock is 5:38 and is seven minutes slow. As 38 + 7 = 45, the correct time is 5:45.

  🔆 *Tip:* Remember how to change between 12- and 24-hour time.

Checklist

Can you:
1 *find the volume of a solid made from identical cubes?*
2 *solve problems involving containers of different capacities?*
3 *estimate the mass of common objects?*
4 *use the conversion between kilograms and grams in a problem?*
5 *use a calendar to find the number of days between dates?*
6 *read analog and digital clocks?*

Real Test 1

MATHEMATICAL REASONING
Volume, capacity, mass and time

10 MIN

1 If 25 April is a Tuesday, which day of the week is 11 May?
- **A** Wednesday
- **B** Sunday
- **C** Friday
- **D** Saturday
- **E** Thursday

2 Laura's project is due on 15 June. If she has had three weeks to complete it, when was the project given to her by her teacher?
- **A** 24 May
- **B** 25 May
- **C** 26 May
- **D** 27 May
- **E** 28 May

3

NOVEMBER

S	M	T	W	T	F	S
		1	2	3	4	5
6	7	8	9	10	11	12
13	14	15	16	17	18	19
20	21	22	23	24	25	26
27	28	29	30			

Bill, Bob and Ben used the calendar to plan a game of golf. Bill was overseas until the 13th, Bob could only play on Saturdays, and Ben was flying to Canada for a fortnight on the last Thursday of the month. On what day will the group play golf?
- **A** 19 November
- **B** 26 November
- **C** 25 November
- **D** 12 November
- **E** 5 November

4 If a coin has a mass of 50 g and a medallion weighs 80 g, what is the mass of two coins and three medallions?

130 g	260 g	340 g	240 g	103 g
A	B	C	D	E

5 Fran pours out 420 grams from a 1-kg bag of sugar. How much is left in the packet?

420 g	80 g	580 g	680 g	480 g
A	B	C	D	E

6 Simon went to bed at ten to nine. He got out of bed the next morning at 6:45 am. How long was Simon in bed?
- **A** 9 h 5 min
- **B** 9 h 55 min
- **C** 10 h 5 min
- **D** 10 h 55 min
- **E** 14 h 5 min

7 Water is to be poured from Container Q into Container P so that they have the same amount. How much water needs to be poured from Q into P?

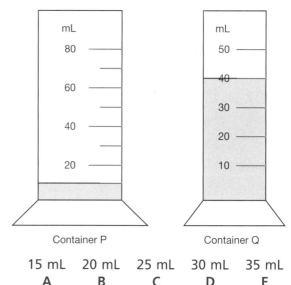

Container P   Container Q

15 mL	20 mL	25 mL	30 mL	35 mL
A	B	C	D	E

8 A fish tank when full of water has a mass of 32 kg. When the tank is half full of water the mass is 20 kg. What is the mass of the fish tank without water?
- **A** 6 kg
- **B** 8 kg
- **C** 10 kg
- **D** 12 kg
- **E** 16 kg

☞ **Answers and explanations on page 217**

MATHEMATICAL REASONING
Volume, capacity, mass and time

9 Bruce has three cylinders each with a mass of *X* kg, where *X* is a whole number. He has an 11-kg mass, an 18-kg mass and a set of scales. What number is represented by *X*?

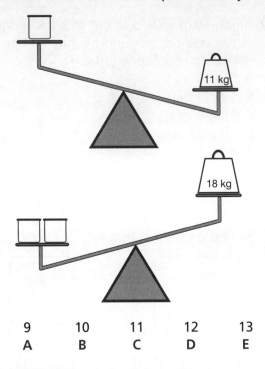

9	10	11	12	13
A	B	C	D	E

10 From 7 am to 9 am weekdays, trams leave a station every 10 min. If one tram leaves at 7:00, how many trams have left the station by 9 am?

6	9	10	12	13
A	B	C	D	E

☞ **Answers and explanations on page 217**

Real Test 2

MATHEMATICAL REASONING
Volume, capacity, mass and time

10 MIN

1

SEPTEMBER						
S	M	T	W	T	F	S
					1	2
3	4	5	6	7	8	9
10	11	12	13	14	15	16
17	18	19	20	21	22	23
24	25	26	27	28	29	30

During the month of September, Adam jogged 6 km every Sunday afternoon. How far did he jog during September?

12 km	24 km	30 km	36 km	5 km
A	B	C	D	E

2 If 5 March is a Tuesday, what day of the week is 28 March?
A Tuesday   B Wednesday   C Thursday
D Friday   E Monday

3 A movie starts at 6:14 pm and finishes at 8:36 pm. The running time for the movie is
A 222 min   B 132 min
C 128 min   D 142 min
E 216 min

4

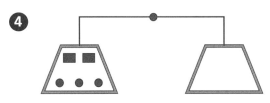

Two blocks and three discs are placed on one side of a set of scales. If the mass of a block equals the mass of three discs, how many discs are required on the other side to balance the set of scales?

3	6	9	12	8
A	B	C	D	E

5 6.8 kg is removed from a 40-kg bag of fertiliser for use on the garden. The amount remaining in the bag is

46.8 kg	34.2 kg	33.8 kg	33.2 kg	2.2 kg
A	B	C	D	E

6 On a hot day Annabelle switches her air-conditioner on at a quarter to one in the afternoon. She turns it off at 5:30 the next morning. How long is the air-conditioner switched on?
A 4 h 15 min   B 14 h 15 min
C 14 h 45 min   D 16 h 15 min
E 16 h 45 min

7 Two containers of water are shown. Ariana needs 1 L of water in a bucket. She pours all the water from Container X and some of the water from Container Y. How much water remains in Container Y?

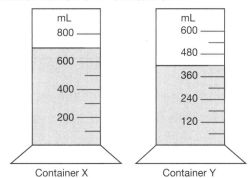

Container X   Container Y

120 mL	160 mL	180 mL	220 mL	240 mL
A	B	C	D	E

8 Jacob needs to buy 4 kg of rice. His supermarket sells two different bags: a 500-g bag of rice for $2 or a 2.5-kg bag for $9. What is the smallest amount Jacob can pay?

$14	$15	$16	$18	$19
A	B	C	D	E

9 Oliver is renovating his bathroom. Each box of floor tiles has a mass of 24 kg and each box of wall tiles has a mass of 12 kg. There are 6 tiles in each box. What is the total mass of 10 floor tiles and 8 wall tiles?

56 kg	58 kg	60 kg	62 kg	64 kg
A	B	C	D	E

10 A 2-litre jug is one-quarter full of juice. Aleesha pours 200 mL of juice from the jug into each of two glasses. How much juice will it take to refill the jug so it is full?

120 mL	250 mL	1200 mL	1800 mL	1900 mL
A	B	C	D	E

☞ **Answers and explanations on page 218**

MATHEMATICAL REASONING
2D and 3D shapes

- **A large shape may contain smaller shapes** of different sizes.

  Example: How many triangles are in the diagram?

  A 9   **B** 12   **C** 13   **D** 14   **E** 10

  The correct answer is **C**, by counting the triangles (9 small, 3 medium, 1 large).

   Tip: Look for all sizes of triangles.

  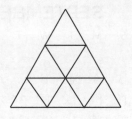

- Some shapes are named according to the number of sides: **triangle** (3), **quadrilateral** (4), **pentagon** (5), **hexagon** (6), **octagon** (8) and **decagon** (10).

- A horizontal line and a vertical line form a **right angle**. A protractor measures the right angle as 90°.

  Example: Florence wrote the letter E on a sheet of paper using four straight lines. How many right angles can be counted on the letter?

  A 1   **B** 2   **C** 3   **D** 4   **E** 5

  The correct answer is **D**. There are four right angles marked as dots on the letter.

- A **solid** has three dimensions and can have **edges, vertices (corners)** and **faces**.

  Example: How many edges has a square-based pyramid?

  A 4   **B** 6   **C** 5   **D** 10   **E** 8

  The correct answer is **E**, by counting the four edges leading from the apex and the four edges on the base.

- A **prism** is named after the shape of its base.

  Example: How many faces has an octagonal prism?

  Tip: There are octagons on both ends of the prism.

  A 6   **B** 8   **C** 9   **D** 10   **E** 16

  The correct answer is **D**, by counting the octagons on each end and the eight side faces.

- The **net** of a prism is the flat shape that is folded to form the prism.

  Example: The letters A to F are written on the squares of a net of a cube. When the cube is formed, what letter is opposite F?

  A A   **B** B   **C** C   **D** D   **E** E

  The correct answer is **A**, as A will be opposite F.

  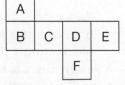

Checklist

Can you:

1 *name plane shapes according to the number of sides?*

2 *name prisms by checking the number of edges on its base?*

3 *count the number of faces, edges and vertices (corners) of a solid?*

Real Test 3

MATHEMATICAL REASONING
2D and 3D shapes

10 MIN

1 Count the number of rectangles in the shape:

2	4	5	7	9
A	B	C	D	E

2 How many faces has a hexagonal prism?

8	10	12	16	14
A	B	C	D	E

3 Which of the following is **not** correct about a cube?
A It has six faces.
B It has eight corners.
C It is a solid.
D It has 10 edges.
E All faces are squares.

4 A special solid is formed when the bases of two identical square-based pyramids are glued together. How many faces will the new solid have?

8	10	12	14	16
A	B	C	D	E

5 Emma used identical cubes to make this solid. How many cubes cannot be seen from this orientation?

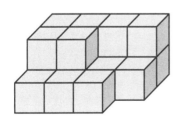

1	2	3	4	5
A	B	C	D	E

6 Isla drew these five shapes on grid paper. Which shape(s) contain at least one right angle?

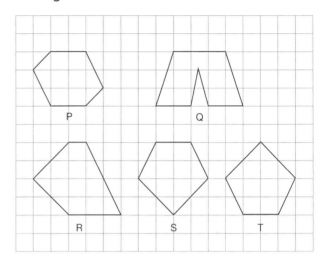

A P only
B R and T only
C S and T only
D R, S and T only
E none of the shapes

7 Logan built this model using identical cubes. He picks up the object and looks at it from all directions. What is the total number of cube faces he can count?

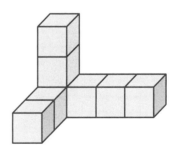

A 32
B 34
C 42
D 49
E 54

☞ **Answers and explanations on pages 218-219**

Real
Test 3

MATHEMATICAL REASONING
2D and 3D shapes

8 Here are three shapes. The shapes are joined together with no overlap. What type of shape is formed?

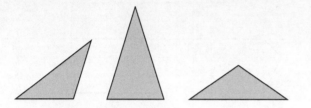

A regular pentagon
B equilateral triangle
C square
D parallelogram
E regular hexagon

9 How many small cubes have been removed from the original solid?

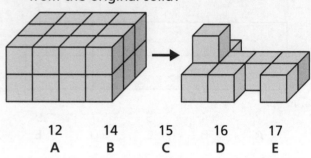

| 12 | 14 | 15 | 16 | 17 |
| A | B | C | D | E |

10 Here is the net of an open box. The box is formed and placed on a table with the top open. Which face is at the bottom of the box?

	P	Q	
		R	S	T

| P | Q | R | S | T |
| A | B | C | D | E |

☞ **Answers and explanations on pages 218-219**

Real Test 4

MATHEMATICAL REASONING
2D and 3D shapes

10 MIN

1 The rectangle has been divided into identical squares:

How many squares of any size can be found in the diagram?

8	10	11	12	9
A	B	C	D	E

2 The diagram shows a large and a small shape:

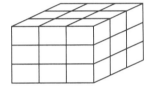 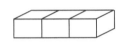

How many of the smaller shapes fit into the larger shape?

3	9	12	27	6
A	B	C	D	E

3 This net is used to build a solid:

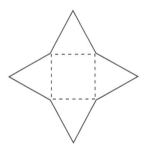

How many edges will the new solid have?

4	5	8	12	6
A	B	C	D	E

4 Here are some letters written using straight lines:

A   E   F   H   K   T   V

Jayden picked **two** of the letters.

What is the most number of right angles he can count in his two letters?

3	4	5	6	8
A	B	C	D	E

5 Kahlia uses 11 small cubes to make this solid. She paints the solid red. How many small cubes have only three faces painted red?

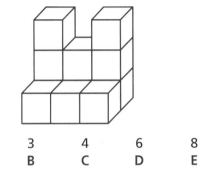

2	3	4	6	8
A	B	C	D	E

6 Alyssa drew this shape. Which of these is closest to the sum of the angles inside the shape?

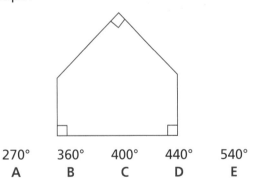

270°	360°	400°	440°	540°
A	B	C	D	E

7 Ella built this model using identical cubes. She picks up the object and looks at it from all directions. How many faces of the cubes cannot be seen?

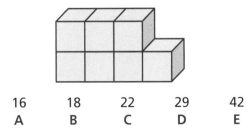

16	18	22	29	42
A	B	C	D	E

☞ **Answers and explanations on page 219**

Real Test 4

MATHEMATICAL REASONING
2D and 3D shapes

8 The prism is made of an equal number of white cubes and grey cubes. There are 32 cube faces on the prism:

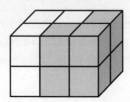

The prism is split into two new shapes. The grey shape is picked up and viewed from all sides. How many faces of cubes can be counted?

12	14	18	22	24
A	**B**	**C**	**D**	**E**

9 Jannah has a regular hexagon. She makes one straight-line cut to divide the hexagon into two shapes. Which of these can she make?

P: a pentagon and a triangle

Q: two quadrilaterals

R: a pentagon and a quadrilateral

A P only

B Q only

C P and Q only

D P and R only

E P, Q and R

10 Which figure can Tom **not** make using these two shapes?

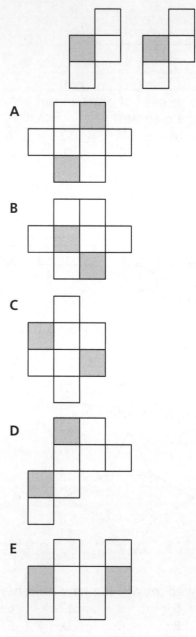

A

B

C

D

E

☞ **Answers and explanations on page 219**

- You have done some work already on writing stories (in Week 1), so you know many important things about writing a story in your test and have had some practice.

- Remember that you can always choose what kind of story you write as long as you do as the question asks. Your story can be **true or imaginary, funny or serious**.

- Whatever kind of story you write, you should aim to write in an **entertaining and interesting way**. However, the markers understand you only have 20 minutes and so won't expect an absolutely perfect story.

- Even if you find it quite easy to write stories, you need to remember that you will have a lot less time than you usually have. So it is a good idea to **practise writing stories within a time limit**.

- You might be given a picture, a story title, the first or last sentence of a story, or just a group of words as the **stimulus material** to write about.

- You have already practised writing stories where you have to imagine you are in a different situation of some kind. These 'Imagine if …' stories are quite common in tests and give you a great opportunity to show how **imaginative and creative** you can be.

- In this session, we will practise writing stories that follow a typical **narrative** structure. Probably most of the stories you write are narratives about people (and something interesting or unusual that happens to them), and that is the kind of story we will look at here.

- Your own experiences are useful for writing narratives, especially in test conditions. You don't have much time to think up brilliant, imaginary characters and settings. So it is a good idea to think about your life and about things that have happened to you before you go into the test. You might be able to write a story, for example, about your family, your class or your school, a favourite possession or a place you go for holidays. You might use an experience of winning or losing a competition, getting or losing a pet, having a new baby in the house or finding a new friend.

- On the next page is an example of a narrative story written in response to a test question, though not under test conditions. In your test, you **might not have time** to produce a polished piece of writing like this. However, if you are **well prepared**, you will be able to aim for this standard.

Question

Write a true or imaginary story based on what you can see in the picture.

Response

Structure

Title—make one up if none is given

First words grab the reader's atention

Introduction (orientation)—who, what, when, where, why

Body—unusual or interesting thing that happens (also called the complication)

Conclusion—how things turn out, e.g. a problem is solved, a task is done (also called the resolution)

Language

Descriptive language

Use of **dialogue** (not always needed)

Time words

Expressive words to talk about people, things and what they do

Good use of **punctuation**

Correct **spelling and grammar**

The Day I Almost Lost Ted

It was council clean-up time and my mum had told me to throw out the things I did not want. On my bed was my old, ratty teddy bear. I knew the kids at my new school wouldn't have teddy bears on their pillows. 'I'm too old for teddies,' I told myself as I tossed Ted onto the junkpile outside.

That night there was a terrible storm and I realised what a mistake I'd made. I was so scared without Ted that the next morning I decided to go and get him back.

But he wasn't there. The old lady next door told me Jimmy Kent had taken him. I ran to Jimmy's house and asked him to give Ted back. 'Mum wouldn't let me keep him so I threw him on someone else's pile,' Jimmy said.

I raced frantically down our road searching each junkpile for Ted and finally saw him on the one outside my own house. I also saw Matt, the meanest, toughest kid at school. He was eyeing off my teddy with a peculiar look on his face. 'Oh no,' I thought. 'I'm never going to be able to walk in that school again.'

But Matt said something very surprising. 'You have a teddy bear as well? I thought I was the only one. You're not throwing him out, are you?'

'Of course not,' I said. 'He just got caught up with some other things.'

Matt smiled. After that, Matt and I became best friends and Matt wasn't so mean and tough any more—at least not to me.

By H McLean; reproduced with permission

Practice Tasks

WRITING
Narrative story—Getting started

`50 min`

- These tasks will give you some ideas about how to start writing quickly and get a good, interesting story done in the short time you have in the test.

- You will have to look back at *The Day I Almost Lost Ted* to answer some questions and then do some writing yourself. Your writing will be based on the same question, as there are so many ways to answer it. However, you should write about something different from the story on page 112. You might still want to write about a teddy bear but be sure to use your own ideas.

- Here is the question again. Look at it now before you start the tasks.

Practice question
Write a true or imaginary story based on what you can see in the picture.

- The first thing to do is to quickly **brainstorm some ideas**. You don't need to write these down but you do need to think about a few different ideas. The student who wrote *The Day I Almost Lost Ted* also thought about these ideas:

  ○ Mum throwing out the TV

  ○ finding an old teddy on someone's junkpile

  ○ family fights about what to throw out.

  💡 *Tip:* Don't try anything too complicated or you may not finish in time.

- The easiest and quickest place to start is with **your own life**—people you know or things that have happened to you. The student who wrote *The Day I Almost Lost Ted* used his experiences. He loved his teddy but was beginning to wonder if he was too big to have one. This gave him the idea to start with and then he invented details to make a good story.

- You also have to decide what kind of story you are going to write. Will it be funny, happy, sad, mysterious, realistic or fantasy? **Write the kind of story you are best at.**

- In a test, you do not have time to make a detailed plan of your story before starting to write but it is important to spend a few minutes working out a **very rough plan** of how your story will develop.

Practice Tasks

WRITING
Narrative story—Getting started

● Many stories use the following common narrative structure. There are other ways to structure narratives but this one can help you get going quickly in a test.
  ○ **Introduction**: who or what the story is about and where and when it takes place
  ○ **Body**: something interesting or unusual that happens
  ○ **Conclusion**: what happens in the end (e.g. a problem is sorted out or a mystery is solved)

Here is the plan for *The Day I Almost Lost Ted*.

Introduction	too old for teddy—throw out
Body	storm—miss Ted—look for him but he's gone
	kid takes him but throws him out again
	tough guy from school finds him
Conclusion	tough guy has a teddy too

Task 1

Think about the Practice question on page 113. Jot down two or three story ideas. Remember: Your own experiences can be the best starting point.

_____

_____

_____

Task 2

Choose **one** of your story ideas above to continue with. Now do a rough plan for your idea. Use the headings below. Give yourself about two minutes.

💡 *Tip:* In your test, only write enough in your plan to get you going. If you are sure in your head about what you are going to write, don't waste time writing down a plan. Just start!

Introduction _____

_____

Body _____

_____

_____

_____

Conclusion _____

_____

- The introduction to your story (the **orientation**) should **capture the reader's attention** and make him or her interested in reading further. It usually also tells the reader **what or who** the story is about, and perhaps also about **where, when and why** the events are happening.

- You should only write a **couple of sentences** and then quickly get to the main part of the story. In the test you won't have time to give too much detail.

- Also think about these questions before you start:
  - ○ Will you write yourself into the story (*I watched*, we *watched*) **OR** will you be 'outside' the story (*he watched, they watched*)?
  - ○ Will you write in the present tense (*she stops suddenly*) **OR** the past tense (*she stopped suddenly*)?

Task 3

Read the first paragraph of *The Day I Almost Lost Ted. Finish the following sentence.*

The story is about a boy who decides to throw out his teddy because _____

_____

Task 4

Now write the introduction for the Practice question using your plan. Make it as interesting as you can but don't write too much—you are only setting up the story for the reader. Give yourself about five minutes.

_____

_____

_____

_____

_____

_____

_____

_____

☞ **Answers on page 219**

Practice Tasks

WRITING
Narrative story—Writing the body

- Good stories, or narratives, usually include something **interesting or unusual** that happens. This forms the body of the story (also called the story **complication**). The complication makes a story different from a simple recount of what happened—as in a diary, for example.

- The complication is usually interesting because it is funny, unusual, upsetting, spooky, exciting or sad. In a story about people and what happens to them, the complication is often about **something that goes wrong**. This makes the story interesting and dramatic.

- Because you don't have as much time in a test as you usually have to write a story, it is best to **stick to your rough plan** and try to make it work. Of course, you might get an absolutely brilliant brainwave that leads you to write something completely different from your plan! If so, that's great.

- Try to use **vivid, interesting words** to describe people, things and actions. Even if your story does not work exactly as you want it to, you will still get marks for expressing your ideas well.

- Choose **action verbs** that precisely describe what is happening. For example, don't use *went*, *walked* or *ran* if you can use a more expressive verb such as *rushed*, *slipped*, *stamped*, *slid*, *trudged*, *slithered* or *fled*. Don't use *said* if you can use more interesting verbs such as *gasped*, *moaned* or *announced*.

Task 5

What goes wrong after the boy throws his teddy bear on the junkpile in *The Day I Almost Lost Ted*? Circle the correct answer.

a   He misses his teddy.

b   His teddy disappears from the junkpile.

c   He looks for his teddy.

Tip: Don't explain everything that happens in detail. Just tell the important events.

Task 6

1 Write the words used in *The Day I Almost Lost Ted* to describe

  a   the teddy bear (paragraph 1): _____

  _____

  b   the look on Matt's face (paragraph 4): _____

  _____

2 Write the verbs used instead of

  a   threw (paragraph 1): _____

  _____

  b   looking at (paragraph 4): _____

  _____

Tip: When you choose good descriptive language, you are painting a picture in words. Try to choose words that give interesting detail.

☞ **Answers on page 219**

Task 7

Now continue writing your story. Try to include words and sentences that create vivid, interesting images of the characters and the action. Give yourself about ten minutes.

_____

_____

_____

_____

_____

_____

_____

_____

_____

_____

_____

_____

_____

_____

_____

_____

_____

_____

_____

_____

_____

_____

Remember: Quickly check your grammar, spelling and punctuation as you write.

- You have to end your story somehow (e.g. solve a problem, reveal a mystery, complete a task or explain why someone did something). The conclusion can be the most difficult part to write so think about how you will end your story when you are planning it. The conclusion is also called the **resolution**.

- Many stories finish with a **comment** of some kind—a warning, a lesson or a funny remark. This can be a good way to 'wrap up' a story and bring it to a quick conclusion. In *The Day I Almost Lost Ted* the writer comments that he and Matt are now good friends.

Task 8

Write an ending for your story. Add a comment to finish it off if you think it would improve your story. Give yourself about five minutes.

_____

_____

_____

_____

_____

_____

_____

_____

_____

Note: If you like, you can work on your story some more, improving what you have written so far and writing it out again on your own paper. Use the checklist below to review your writing.

Checklist for writing a narrative story

Have you:

1 *started your story with a few sentences to capture the reader's attention and tell them what your story is about (who, what, when, where)?*
2 *included something interesting or unusual that makes your story worth telling?*
3 *given your story an ending of some kind?*
4 *used some vivid, interesting words to describe the people, things and actions in your story?*
5 *checked your grammar, punctuation and spelling?*

Remember: In the test, you won't have time to revise thoroughly and make big changes. You may have time to change a few words but you will really be aiming to do a good piece of writing in one draft.

Choose **one** of the writing tests below to do now. Use your own paper.

If you like, you can do both tests. However, it would be better to do them on different days. For extra practice, you could use the tests again, writing in different ways each time.

Set yourself a time limit of 20 minutes. Use the checklist on page 118 to give your narrative a quick review.

Test 1

Use this picture as the basis for a story.

OR

Test 2

Write a story that begins: 'I'll never forget that Sunday.'

Only one week to go!

Week 4

This is what we cover this week:

Day 1 **Reading:** Varied short texts

Day 2 **Thinking Skills:**

- ◎ Problem solving—Shapes and objects
- ◎ Problem solving—Measurement and time
- ◎ Problem solving—Tricky problems

Day 3 **Mathematical Reasoning:** ◎ Symmetry, folding, position and scale

◎ Statistics and probability

Day 4 **Writing:** 'Agree or disagree' opinion

- In this section of the test you will be asked to **match short text extracts to questions** about them. This question type is currently only used in the NSW Opportunity Class Placement Test but preparing for this format will help you develop your reading skills and benefit you when sitting any test.

  > **Remember:** You must check the latest format of the test you are going to sit.

- You will be given a set of four short texts to read on the same general theme but with different content and style. The texts could be, for example, **personal stories, information texts or opinion texts**.

- To answer the questions, you will have to look for **main ideas, the purpose of texts or some specific detail**. You might also have to recognise something the text suggests rather than states clearly.

- The best way to approach this kind of task is to **quickly glance at the questions first** to get an idea of what you are being asked to do. Then read each text. You must read quickly, however. You won't be asked about every piece of information in the text but will only have to pick up a couple of ideas from each.

- Pay particular attention to the **first sentence** of the text. It will give you **clues** about the type of text and content.

- As you read, you might start getting some ideas about which questions relate to which texts. **Make some light marks** to show this and keep reading.

- When you have finished reading the texts, go back and read the questions one by one and **scan each text to see if it matches the question**. If you find one that matches the question, check all the other texts again to make sure they do not **also** match it.

- Sometimes you will see something in one text that is **close** to the idea in the question and quickly decide the answer but there might be another text which is much closer to the idea. You will need to **be careful in checking and rechecking your answer** all the way through the task. However, you will also have to work quickly.

**Practice
Task 1**

READING
Varied short texts

Use this first practice task as a guide. Read the questions and texts, then answer as you think best. Next look at the answers to get explanations of why they are correct. The aim is to give you practice with this specific type of question. It may be a little different from what you are familiar with in reading comprehension tests. Don't worry about time with this first task although you should aim to finish in 10 minutes. Try to improve your speed with the later practice tasks.

For questions 1–8, choose the text which you think best answers the questions. All four texts are on the theme of reading.

Which extract …

lists reasons to read a particular kind of fiction? **1** ____

suggests that reading can help us see things from a different perspective? **2** ____

refers to favourite books read as a small child? **3** ____

suggests that reading can take us away from everyday worries? **4** ____

argues that the evil characters are better in one kind of genre? **5** ____

links reading fiction to learning about real time periods and real places? **6** ____

explains the way one person learned to read? **7** ____

compares the characters in one kind of fiction to those in another? **8** ____

Extract A

I have always loved reading. I learnt to read from reading the backs of cereal packets and hair products. I would read anything! I remember sitting in the bath and reading out loud the words on the back of the shampoo bottle. I remember asking my mother about tricky words like 'thoroughly' and 'lather" but bit by bit I began to work out the words and their meanings myself. I also remember sitting at the kitchen table while my mother got my big brother off to school and reading the lists of ingredients on the back of the cornflakes packet: What's sodium, Mum? What's calcium? She would tell me to just hurry up and finish my breakfast. When I went to school, we were given readers with repetitive words in meaningless stories. I liked the pictures but there were no interesting words like 'thoroughly', 'sodium' and 'calcium'.

☞ **Answers and explanations on page 220**

Extract B

My favourite book genre is fantasy. I just can't read enough of it. Even as a very young child when books were read to me, I always preferred the ones with a touch of fantasy. I loved classic stories such as *The Lion, the Witch and the Wardrobe*, *Peter Pan*, *The Wizard of Oz* and *Alice in Wonderland*. I suppose many people would not think of these books as fantasy but of course they are. Characters walk through wardrobes, go down rabbit holes and fly away to magical lands. That's magic! That's fantasy! As I got older, I discovered Tolkien's *The Hobbit* and then *The Lord of the Rings*. That was it! I was totally hooked on other worlds and the fantastical creatures in them. I could read nothing but fantasy after that. Reading about ordinary boys and girls living in houses like mine just didn't keep me reading—even if they did get up to amazing adventures sometimes.

Extract C

Why do so many people love fantasy fiction? There are many reasons but one of the most important is that the characters go on heroic quests against unbelievable odds. It's about bravery and strength of character and never giving up. Another important reason is that there are true villains. And what villains they are! Villains can flourish in this genre like no other. And we love them—even while we quake with fear. But they have to be believable. If we can't relate to them we can't care about them or forgive them their faults. The physical worlds created by fantasy authors are another attraction. The worlds are totally unlike our own and as humans we love exploring the new and unknown. What happens in a fantasy world is only limited by the imagination of the author. There are no rules. Everything is bigger, better and more exciting.

Extract D

Why do I love reading fiction? Well, firstly I can't imagine life without it. It takes me to a different world for part of the day. I am able to forget who I am and imagine myself in this other world. Even though I love my life, I actually cannot get through a day without reading a work of fiction. Fiction helps me forget other problems, big and small. It gives my mind some time to rest until I get back to the real world. Fiction also allows me to live life in another person's shoes for a while. This helps me understand how other people might see things. I also love learning something new about the world. I love reading stories set in different places and time periods. These often set me on an internet hunt to find out exactly what was going on in that place at that time. Books mean I am never alone and certainly never bored.

Practice Task 2

Read the questions and texts, then answer as you think best. Next, look at the answers for explanations of why and how those answers are correct. Try to work quickly but, again, don't worry if you can't do it in 10 minutes.

For questions 1–8, choose the text which you think best answers the questions. All four texts are on the theme of holidays.

Which extract …

suggests things often go wrong on holidays? **1** ____

advertises holiday activities? **2** ____

describes an unpleasant holiday experience? **3** ____

encourages the reader to have an adventure on holiday? **4** ____

relates the history of holidays? **5** ____

suggests young people don't always enjoy holidays with their own families? **6** ____

shows an unusual way to get an ideal holiday? **7** ____

explains why holidays have not always been possible for ordinary workers? **8** ____

Extract A

These summer holidays we are offering a range of fun water activities for school kids. For the first time we are offering snorkelling. Learning to snorkel is pretty easy once you get over the fact you have to put your head in water and breathe. Soon you will be floating dreamily in the water and gazing below you at amazing sights below the water's surface. At Blue Bay Waters we will provide everything you need for your snorkelling adventure: masks, fins and skins. Other options these holidays are surfing lessons. We cater for all levels from the complete novice to those who have some experience but want to hone their skills. We even take five year olds to learn about beach safety, rips and tides. For the really adventurous we offer a two-day surf camp. And what's a holiday without an adventure?

Extract B

The only thing I want to do on holiday is read books but one time my best friend talked me into going horseriding with his family. The first day I was shocked to learn we were going to be on the horses for the entire morning! Up till then I had only ever been on a horse for half an hour and my horse had refused to leave the yard. Anyway they gave me a very steady old horse and off I went. By 10.30 I had fallen off three times. So not so steady after all! By lunchtime I looked like a sack of potatoes. My spine felt like jelly and I was close to tears. That night we camped by a river and the temperature dropped to minus 3. The teeth chattering (and snoring) made it impossible to sleep. The next morning they gave me an even older horse but even so it managed to throw me and I fell badly. I then got to read some books—in Tumut Hospital. Perfect.

☞ **Answers and explanations on page 220**

Practice Task 2

Extract C

Family holidays are some of the most memorable times of our lives so it's no wonder that so many movies have been made about them. If you can't go away on holiday, the next best thing is watching movies about holidays. And the best of these are the movies about holidays gone wrong. For me the oldest are still the best. Clark Griswold and his family adventures in the *National Lampoon's Vacation* movies still make me laugh out loud. It does not matter where Clark goes, he makes anything that ever goes wrong on your holiday (and they always do) a small mishap in comparison. These totally silly but hilarious movies always top any polls taken on people's favourite vacation movies. *Little Miss Sunshine* and *The Way Way Back* are other favourites. These two more serious films will strike a chord with those young people who might find it hard going on family holidays.

Extract D

The word holiday comes from an old English word *haligdag*, meaning 'holy day'. It gradually came to mean a day when ordinary working people could have a break. But where did the idea come from to go away for a holiday? Such travel could only occur in times of relative peace and stability and there was not much of this. From the fifth to the 15th century, people only travelled to find new lands, to raid the lands of enemies or to go on religious pilgrimages. For any travellers, methods of travel were limited and safety was not guaranteed. Pirates and highway robbers were a constant threat. Travel opened up in the 19th century with the expansion of railways and the arrival of steamships but holidays were still only for the very wealthy. For most, time off work meant no money and so most people stayed at home with family and friends. Holidays as we know them only took off in the 20th century but for many people around the world, the idea of going away for a holiday is still unrealistic.

Practice Task 3

Read the questions and texts, then answer as you think best. Next, look at the answers to get explanations of why they are correct. Try to work more quickly this time and finish in under 10 minutes. You will have to work very quickly in the actual test.

For questions 1–8, choose the text which you think best answers the question. All four texts are on the theme of technology.

Which extract …

compares today's entertainment technologies with those of past years? **1** ____

lists the benefits of technology for learning? **2** ____

mentions the importance of playing with small children? **3** ____

mentions the dangers of technology for children's learning? **4** ____

says technology improves children's ability to do more than one thing at a time? **5** ____

refers to parents' frustration with their children's love of electronic devices? **6** ____

admits that some applications can benefit small children? **7** ____

mentions the dangers of technology for social interaction? **8** ____

Extract A

What should we do about screens and very young children? Well, firstly, children under two should not be using electronic devices at all. We know they are attracted to them. They see you using them so why wouldn't they want them in their little hands too? But the minute you give in to this, there is no going back. Secondly, for the over twos, let your child look at your smartphones or tablets for short periods only. Use them as an occasional treat. But don't let this screen time interfere with opportunities for other play with them. Make time to play alongside your child and interact with them face to face. This is essential for their social, personal and physical development. Thirdly, look for apps that help develop vocabulary, maths, literacy and science. There is a great choice available these days. Lastly, use your own devices sensibly and be a good model for your children.

Extract B

It can be surprising, even frightening, for parents and grandparents to observe how easily toddlers learn to swipe across screens and open up apps. While we know there are great benefits in technology, there are real concerns about how this immersion in technology from an early age will affect children as they grow up. Research shows that the average child between 8 and 10 years old spends about 8 hours per day with a variety of media at school and home. Some teenagers say they send thousands of text messages a month and spend hours each week interacting with others on social media platforms. One concern is that the constant use of communication technology will lead to a lower attention span and affect children's ability to learn. Another is that children will be less able to deal with face-to-face interactions. Will they prefer to text or talk on social media instead of talking to an actual person?

☞ **Answers and explanations on pages 220-221**

Practice Task 3

Extract C

Here is my grandmother's contribution to my school project on technology and entertainment:

When I was a child we read books and listened to the radio, although we called it the wireless. The radio was like the television for us. Every morning my mother would listen to her favourite radio programs—mostly love stories. In the afternoon we listened to comedies and quiz shows. We all sat around together in the kitchen and listened. No one spoke. We had to listen carefully to hear the words. We didn't have television until I was about 12. Before that we used to go over to a neighbour's house in our pyjamas and watch TV there. All the kids from the neighbourhood would come in until their mothers called them home again. It was great fun all sitting there together laughing at cartoons. It's hard to imagine now when I compare it to how young people sit in their bedrooms on their computers and phones.

Extract D

Today I want to talk to you about the benefits of technology for children, though I can tell by the look on your faces that you can't think of any positives at all. You are probably sick and tired of dragging your offspring away from their phones or tablets day after day. Well, today you will hear how classroom technologies are opening up the world to your child every day. I'll be showing you evidence that technology helps young children learn to multitask effectively, improve their visual and spatial development, and enhance their problem-solving and decision-making skills. Is it possible? I hear you ask. But I won't stop there. You are right to have concerns so I'm going to give you some strategies to deal with your children's love of screens. There is so much you can do to help your children get the benefits of technology and avoid the negative effects.

Real
Test

READING
Varied short texts

30 MIN

Read the questions and texts, then answer as you think best. Next look at the answers for explanations of why and how they are correct. Finish at 10 minutes or, even better, before 10 minutes is up.

For questions 1–8, choose the text which best answers the question. All four texts are on the theme of sport.

Which extract …

explains how communication skills can develop in sport?　　**1** _____

mentions competitive pastimes other than sport?　　**2** ____

argues that winning and losing is not the most important thing in life?　　**3** ____

suggests that people who don't play sport are not necessarily unfit?　　**4** ____

argues that sport is the best way to experience working as a team?　　**5** ____

demonstrates the passion that supporters can feel for their team?　　**6** ____

puts forward the view that sport helps learning?　　**7** ____

explains a particular aspect of a sport and what it means for the players?　　**8** ____

Extract A

Some children are just not interested in team sports so why should they play it at school? At our school we see many reasons for participation in team sport. Most importantly, it teaches children to work as part of a team. There is no better way for children to get this experience during school days. They might work together on a school project but working physically together as part of a team is a different thing altogether. Also, sport of all kinds gives children the experience of both winning and losing. Until you have learnt to accept a loss with grace, you cannot grow into adulthood. In sport, children come to value the competition itself and not just whether they have won the game or not. Needless to say, sport of any kind provides all-important exercise for growing bodies. And there are mental spin-offs too. The more physical activity, the better the concentration in class activities.

Extract B

Some people are obsessed with sports. I'm not. In fact I get no enjoyment out of it at all—either playing it or watching it. To me it's just a game. Some people argue it's the best drama you can get but I'd rather watch one of my favourite TV series for that. It's not that I'm unfit and a couch potato. In fact I go to the gym regularly. I suppose it goes back to school days. If you can't run fast, you can't be much good at sport. And I couldn't run fast. The teachers and other kids were not too bad about it but I still felt it. So I got out of sport whenever I could and played less and less. In some ways I regret this because I lost a few friends but then I found my friends in gaming. And if you think sport is competitive, take a look at people who love playing video games!

☞ **Answers and explanations on page 221**

Extract C

Netball has grown dramatically across Australia to become one of the biggest team sports in the country played by over one million women, children and even men. More Australian girls play netball than any other sport. Because it is a team sport, young players learn valuable social and communication skills as they work with their teammates. Each player has a particular position and role in the game and players have to talk to each other throughout the game to work out a strategy and score goals. Netball is unusual in that the player must stand still once they have the ball. This means players must use a variety of passes and throws to get the ball to another player: high, low, short, long. As they learn these kinds of passes in training, they develop their hand-eye coordination and reaction times. It's a very fast-moving game so it's fantastic for developing fitness and strength.

Extract D

My team lost last year in a terrible, soul-destroying grand final where they were demolished by 105 points. It was embarrassing. It was crushing. It was awful. I felt sick for a week. I couldn't turn on the television. I couldn't speak to my friends because they went for the other team. I couldn't get interested in anything. But gradually I pulled out of it. I started to talk to others and even managed to laugh and joke about it. I realised it was just a game and that life is full of far more important things than who wins or loses a game, especially one you aren't even playing in yourself. It still hurts but I'm still a fan. I still shout at the television like a maniac and get dressed up in orange and grey when I go to the games. And well, there's always next year!

THINKING SKILLS
Problem solving—Shapes and objects

- Read the question carefully and **identify** what it requires.
- It is important to be familiar with the common **2D shapes and 3D objects**.
- Try to **visualise** the shapes or objects as you work through the questions.

Example 1

Five shapes have been arranged in this rectangle:

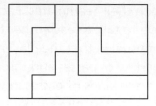

Which of the following four rectangles has the same five shapes? (They might be turned around or over.)

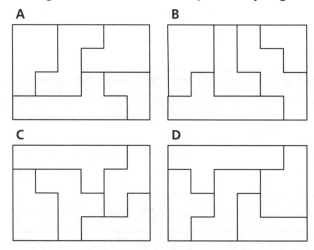

Steps to work out the answer

1. Read the question and make sure you understand what is required. Here you are looking for the two rectangles that are made up of exactly the same shaped pieces, although they might be moved around or turned over.

2. Some pieces are in all of the rectangles. Look for unusual shapes to eliminate some of the rectangles.

B is correct.

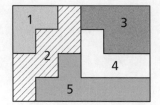
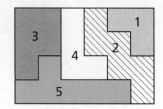

THINKING SKILLS
Problem solving—Shapes and objects

Example 2

This is a net of a normal dice:

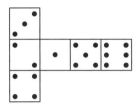

After Carla rolls the dice, 1 is on the top face and 3 is on the front face.

What number will be on the left side?

    A 2   **B** 4   **C** 5   **D** 6

Steps to work out the answer

1   Read the question carefully and make sure you are clear about what is required. Here you need to find the number on the left side of the dice when 1 is at the top and 3 is on the front face.
2   Try to envisage the dice in that position.

C is correct. If 1 is at the top, 6 will be on the bottom. If 3 is on the front face, 4 will be on the back face and 2 will be on the right side. So the number on the left side will be 5.

Tip: On normal dice the numbers on the opposite faces always add to 7.

Checklist

Can you:

1 *find what is required when working with shapes and objects?*
2 *identify the common 2D shapes and 3D objects?*
3 *visualise shapes as they would fit together?*
4 *understand how objects will look when viewed from different directions?*
5 *recognise different nets?*

THINKING SKILLS
Problem solving—Shapes and objects

1 This is the net of an unusual dice:

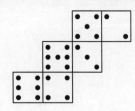

What do the numbers on each pair of opposite sides add up to?

A 7   **B** 8   **C** 9   **D** 10

2 Each of these squares is divided into five pieces:

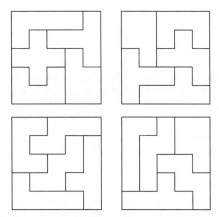

How many of the squares use exactly the same five pieces?

A 0   **B** 2   **C** 3   **D** 4

3 Charlie has a cube with symbols on the faces. On Charlie's cube the star is opposite the circle, the triangle is opposite the square and the heart is opposite the cross.

Which could be the net of Charlie's cube?

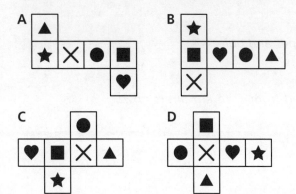

4 Four pieces like this can be placed together to form a square:

Four of which of the following pieces could be placed together to form a square?

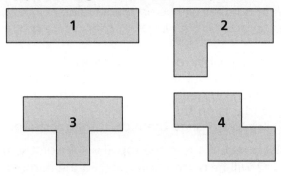

A 1, 2, 3 and 4   **B** 1, 2 and 3 only
C 1 and 2 only   **D** 1 only

5 An unusual dice used in a game has numbers not spots on its faces. (A line is shown under each number so there is no confusion between 6 and 9.) The numbers on opposite faces add to 13.

Which one of the following nets could fold to form that dice?

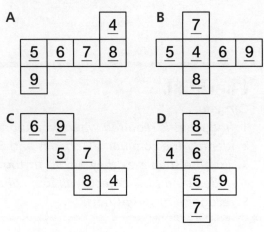

☞ **Answers and explanations on pages 221-222**

Real Test 1

THINKING SKILLS
Problem solving—Shapes and objects

6

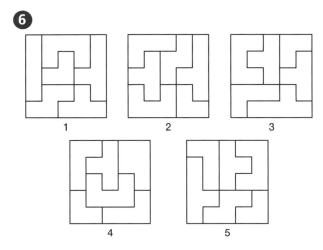

Which two squares are made up of the same five shapes? (They might be turned around or over.)

A 1 and 3   **B** 2 and 3

C 2 and 5   **D** 4 and 5

7 This is the front view of some books that are standing on a shelf:

Which of these could be a view from the top?

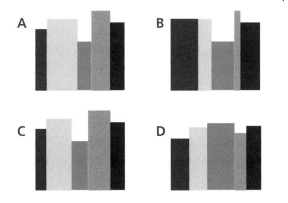

8 A piece of paper has two lines drawn across it, one 6 cm from the top and one 4 cm from the bottom:

The paper is folded so that the bottom edge is level with the line at the top and the paper creased at the fold. The paper is unfolded and then folded again, this time with the top edge level with the line at the bottom, and another crease made.

When the paper is opened out, how far apart are the crease marks?

A 6 cm   **B** 5 cm   **C** 4 cm   **D** 3 cm

9 This is part of a pattern. Each piece is made from five hexagons fitted together:

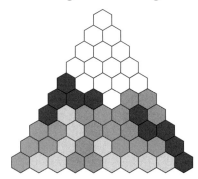

Three of the following pieces can fit together to fill the blank (white) space. Which piece will **not** be used?

  A   **B**   **C**   **D**

10 Jack has a cube with six different faces, including a white face. Here are two views of Jack's cube:

Which could be another view of Jack's cube?

  A   **B**   **C**   **D**

☞ **Answers and explanations on pages 221-222**

Key Points

THINKING SKILLS
Problem solving—Measurement and time

10 MIN

- Some problems involving measurements might need to be solved so it is important to be able to work with basic **units of measurement**.

- Read the question carefully, make sure you understand what is required and take some time to **think**.

- Remember that **time** works differently to other measurements. There are 60 seconds in a minute and 60 minutes in an hour. You need to be able to count forwards or backwards with hours and minutes.

- You should also be familiar with **calendars**. Different months have different numbers of days. Being able to count forwards, or backwards, by 7 will be useful. For example, if you know the date of a particular Monday, counting forward by 7 will give the date of the next Monday.

Example 1

A recipe to make fudge uses 3 cups of sugar, $\frac{1}{2}$ cup of cocoa, 50 g of butter, 1 cup of milk, 1 teaspoon of vanilla and a pinch of salt. Kim is going to use this recipe to make a large amount of fudge for a fete. How many grams of butter should Kim use with 3 cups of cocoa?

A 250 g   **B** 300 g   **C** 350 g   **D** 400 g

Steps to answer the question

1 Read the question carefully and make sure you understand what is required. Here you are given a list of ingredients and need to find the amount of butter needed for a larger amount of fudge.

2 Think carefully. The amounts of the ingredients must always match. For example, if you have twice as much of one ingredient you must have twice as much of all the ingredients. In this case you only need to consider cocoa and butter.

3 Work in steps. First find the amount of butter needed with 1 cup of cocoa.

B is correct. From the question we know that Kim would use 50 g of butter with $\frac{1}{2}$ cup of cocoa, so she would use 100 g of butter with 1 cup of cocoa and 300 g of butter with 3 cups of cocoa.

Example 2

Penny and Molly both read a short story. Penny started reading at 3:30 pm and finished at 4:15 pm. Molly's reading of the story was three times as fast as that of Penny. If Molly began reading at 3:45 pm, when did she finish?

A 4:00 pm   **B** 4:05 pm   **C** 4:15 pm   **D** 6:00 pm

Steps to answer the question

1 Read the question carefully and take the time to be sure that you understand what is required. Here we need to find the time Molly finished reading the story given that she read it three times faster than Penny.

2 Find out how long Penny took to read the story.

3 Understand that if Molly read the story three times as fast then she only took one-third of the time that Penny took to read the story. Find out how long Molly would have taken.

4 Answer the question. You need to find the time Molly finished reading, not just how long she took.

A is correct. Penny started reading at 3:30 and finished at 4:15, so Penny took three-quarters of an hour to finish the story. Now Molly was three times faster than Penny, so she finished the story in one-third of Penny's time. Molly finished in one-quarter of an hour. As Molly began reading at a quarter to 4, she finished at 4:00 pm.

Example 3

Nola goes for a run every day. She runs 3 km on weekdays and 5 km each Saturday and Sunday. How far in total does Nola run in July, if 1 July is a Monday?

A   84 km   B   105 km   C   109 km   D   125 km

Steps to answer the question

1   Read the question carefully. You need to find the total distance that Nola ran in July, remembering that the distance she runs on weekdays is different to the distance she runs on weekends.
2   First work out what day of the week the last day of July is.
3   Find the distance Nola runs each week and the number of full weeks that she runs that distance.
4   Finally work out the distance for the part of the week at the end of the month and the final distance.

C is correct. There are 31 days in July. If 1 July is a Monday, then so is 8, 15, 22 and 29 July. 31 July will be a Wednesday. Now, every week Nola runs a total of 5 × 3 km or 15 km on weekdays and 2 × 5 km or 10 km on weekends. So Nola runs a total of 25 km every week. Nola will run for 4 full weeks which will be 100 km plus 3 km on each of the last Monday, Tuesday and Wednesday. So she will run 109 km altogether.

Checklist

Can you:

1   *read questions carefully and work out what is required?*
2   *understand and work with measurements and speed?*
3   *count forwards or backwards with time and dates?*

Real Test 2

1 A straight fence has 21 posts. The distance between each pair of posts is 5 m.

How far is it between the first and last post?

A 100 m   B 105 m   C 110 m   D 115 m

2 A recipe uses 2 cups of flour, $\frac{1}{2}$ cup of sugar, 125 g of butter and an egg to make 50 biscuits. Jeremy has 7 cups of flour, 2 cups of sugar, $\frac{1}{2}$ kg of butter and 3 eggs and wants to make 175 biscuits.

Which ingredient does he **not** have enough of to make 175 biscuits?

A flour   B sugar
C butter   D eggs

3 A train left Penton at 12 noon to travel to Greenville. A bus left Penton at 8 am and arrived at Greenville at 2 pm. The bus took twice as long as the train to travel between Penton and Greenville.

Which statement is true?

A The train arrived at Greenville an hour before the bus.

B The train arrived at Greenville half an hour before the bus.

C The train arrived at Greenville an hour after the bus.

D The train arrived at Greenville half an hour after the bus.

4 Jennifer is appearing in a play. This month the play will be performed every night from Friday 7th to Sunday 23rd except for Monday and Thursday nights. There will be an afternoon performance as well as one at night every Saturday. How many performances will there be altogether?

A 15   B 16   C 17   D 18

5 Trees will be planted every 10 m on both sides of a straight driveway. The first trees will be beside the gate at the top of the driveway and the last trees will be 120 m away at the bottom of the driveway.

How many trees will there be?

A 20   B 22   C 24   D 26

6 On Saturday, Christopher began mowing his lawn at 3 pm and he finished at 4:30 pm. On Sunday, Christopher mowed the lawn for his grandmother. He finished mowing at 11 am. If Christopher spent twice as long mowing his own lawn than mowing his grandmother's lawn, at what time did he begin mowing on Sunday?

A 10 am   B 10:15 am
C 10:25 am   D 10:35 am

7 The orchestra will be performing on Wednesday, Friday and Saturday each week beginning on Friday 9 January and finishing on 31 January. There will also be a performance on 26 January. How many performances will there be altogether?

A 10   B 12   C 13   D 14

8 Cleo left home at 9:20 am and arrived at her office at 9:45 am. Cleo left her office at 5:10 pm to return home. The return journey was three times slower than the forward journey.

What time did Cleo arrive home?

A 6:00 pm   B 6:15 pm
C 6:25 pm   D 6:35 pm

9 The circus is appearing in town this month from Thursday 4th until Sunday 21st. There will be a performance every night plus extra performances on Wednesday, Saturday and Sunday afternoons. Joel plays the part of a clown every week day (Monday to Friday) and Guy is the clown on Saturdays and Sundays.

How many more times will Joel play the clown than Guy?

A 2   B 3   C 4   D 6

10 A train left Milford at 8:30 am and arrived at Sykes at 11 am. That same day, a helicopter flew from Milford to Sykes, arriving at 2 pm. If the helicopter was five times as fast as the train, what time did it leave Preston?

A 12:30 pm   B 1:00 pm
C 1:15 pm   D 1:30 pm

☞ **Answers and explanations on pages 223-224**

- Often problems that need to be solved can be quite tricky. That doesn't necessarily mean that they are extra hard but they might be **different or unusual**.
- The questions need to be **read carefully**, several times if necessary.
- Take time to **think**. Sometimes it is difficult to see where to begin. In that case, begin with what you do know and what you can then work out.
- Problems might have two (or more) pieces of information that **contradict** each other. One statement is the opposite of the other and only one can be true.
- Always make sure you **answer the question that is asked**.

Example 1

Five girls—Alice, Daisy, Eleanor, Grace and Matilda—are sitting in a row. One of the girls has yellow ribbons in her hair. Daisy is on the far right. There is one girl between Eleanor and Matilda. Grace is sitting next to the girl with yellow ribbons.

Which of these girls **cannot** be the girl with the yellow ribbons?

A Alice **B** Daisy **C** Eleanor **D** Matilda

Steps to answer the question

1 Read the question carefully and think about what is required. In this case we are looking for the girl who cannot be the one with the yellow ribbons. So we know that more than one of the girls might be the one with the yellow ribbons.
2 Begin by placing those girls in position, when we can.
3 Work carefully through the given information. Make assumptions if necessary and see what they would mean. For example, who could be the girl between Eleanor and Matilda?

A is correct. There is one girl between Eleanor and Matilda. She cannot be Daisy because Daisy is on the end. She must be either Alice or Grace. Now, Grace is sitting next to the girl with yellow ribbons. If Grace is the girl between Eleanor and Matilda, then either Eleanor or Matilda must be the girl with yellow ribbons. If Alice is sitting between Eleanor and Matilda, she cannot be sitting next to Grace so cannot be the girl with yellow ribbons. In either case, Alice cannot be the girl with yellow ribbons.

Tip: Take time to think for a moment before rushing into answering a question. It might save you time in the long run!

Example 2

When asked what day last week the big storm had hit, five people all gave different answers. One person's answer was wrong, but the other four answers were correct.

The answers were:

- not Thursday
- Tuesday
- not Wednesday
- not Tuesday
- Friday.

On what day did the big storm occur?

A Tuesday **B** Wednesday **C** Thursday **D** Friday

Steps to answer the question

1 Read the question carefully and determine what is required. In this case we are looking for the day of the week that the storm happened.

2 There were five different answers given but only one was incorrect. Look for contradictions to find which answers might not be correct.

3 When the possible incorrect answers are found, all other answers must then be correct.

4 Answer the question, remembering that you are looking for the day of the storm, not for the day that was the wrong answer.

D is correct. The two answers 'Tuesday' and 'not Tuesday' cannot both be correct. One must be the wrong answer. So the other answers must all be correct. The answer Friday is correct so the storm must have happened on Friday.

The wrong answer must have been Tuesday and the other answers were all correct. So the storm did not happen on Tuesday, Wednesday or Thursday.

Checklist

Can you:

1 *read the questions carefully and understand what is required?*

2 *take time to think and plan how to answer?*

3 *understand what is meant by a contradiction and identify contradictions in given information?*

4 *determine which statements must be true and which false?*

5 *make assumptions and consider different possibilities?*

6 *understand that it is important to answer the question that has been asked?*

Real Test 3

THINKING SKILLS
Problem solving—Tricky problems

10 min

1 Nine people are standing on a field in the positions shown by the diagram.

Bec ●   ● Zac   ● Jill

Bill ●   ● Mo   ● Amy

Jon ●   ● Seb   ● Geri

If Jon is north of Jill, which of these **cannot** be true?

A Zak is south of Bill.
B Mo is west of Bec.
C Seb is north-east of Zak.
D Amy is south-east of Geri.

2 A television program is being shown on Monday, Wednesday and Friday nights every week, beginning on Friday 5th. Each episode will run for three-quarters of an hour and the last episode will be shown on Friday 26th.

For how many hours will the program be shown altogether?

A $6\frac{3}{4}$ **B** 7   **C** $7\frac{1}{4}$ **D** $7\frac{1}{2}$

3 Jethro made a graph of the number of votes given to different colours (red, blue, yellow, green and purple) when his students voted for their favourite colour to paint a statue. Unfortunately Jethro forgot to label the graph.

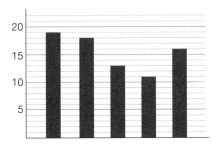

Jethro does remember that more students voted for red than yellow. Fewer voted for green than either purple or blue. More people voted for blue than red and fewer voted for purple than red.

Which must be true?
A 11 students voted for green.
B 16 students voted for purple.
C 13 students voted for yellow.
D 18 students voted for red.

4 Four teams—the Bears, Bulls, Lions and Tigers—played each other twice in a sporting competition, once at home and once away (at the home of their opponent). Each team receives two points for a win, one point for a draw and no points for a loss.

The table shows the winners of the games:

	Home			
	Bears	**Bulls**	**Lions**	**Tigers**
Bears		Bulls	Bears	Tigers
Bulls	Bulls		Lions	Draw
Lions	Draw	Bulls		Lions
Tigers	Bears	Bulls	Lions	

Which team got exactly 7 points?
A Bears   **B** Bulls
C Lions   **D** Tigers

5 Five timber houses are in a row along one side of a street. The houses are painted in three different colours: green, grey and white. No two houses painted the same colour are next to each other. There are exactly two grey houses and they are at each end of the row.

Which must be correct?
A A grey house is next to a white house.
B A green house is next to a grey house.
C The second house from each end is a different colour.
D A white house is to the left of a green house.

☞ **Answers and explanations on pages 224-225**

Real Test 3

THINKING SKILLS
Problem solving—Tricky problems

6 Amy, Noor, Grace and Tammy are sitting on a bus. Two are on one seat and the other two on the seat behind them. Tammy and one other girl are next to the aisle and the other two are next to a window. Grace is not sitting directly in front of, behind or next to Amy.

Which must be true?

A Amy is sitting directly in front of Noor.
B Noor has a window seat.
C Tammy is sitting next to Amy.
D Grace is sitting next to Noor.

7 Hannah has a display case with 16 cubbyholes where she displays her collection of vases. Every row, every column and both diagonals have four vases in four different colours: blue, green, red and white. The top row has blue, green and red in that order in the first three cubbyholes. The vase in B3 is red:

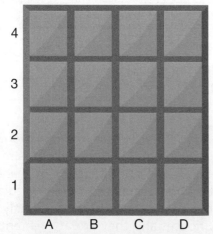

What colour is the vase in D2?

A blue **B** green **C** red **D** white

8 In an old photo, four women—Gwen, Jean, Vera and Daphne—are sitting in a row in some order. Four men—John, Henry, Bert and Frank—are standing behind them. Vera is furthest left and Bert is furthest right. Gwen, who is not sitting next to Daphne, is in front of John. Henry is somewhere to the left of Frank.

Who can be seen to the immediate left of the man standing behind Jean?

A John **B** Henry **C** Frank **D** Bert

9 There are six jars in a row, numbered from 1 to 6. Jars 1, 3 and 5 are full of water and jars 2, 4 and 6 are empty:

It is possible to have three full jars in a row by moving just one jar.

Which of these jars could be moved so that there are three full jars in a row?

A 1 **B** 2 **C** 4 **D** 6

10 The Porter family have five children and a pet named Priscilla. When asked what type of pet Priscilla is, the five children all gave different answers—but only one answer was **not** correct. The answers were:

- rabbit
- not a cat
- dog
- not a guinea pig
- not a dog.

What type of pet is Priscilla?

A rabbit **B** cat
C dog **D** guinea pig

☞ **Answers and explanations on pages 224-225**

MATHEMATICAL REASONING
Symmetry, folding, position and scale

- A **line of symmetry** passes through the centre of a shape and divides it into equal halves.

  Example: How many lines of symmetry does a rectangle have?

1	2	3	4	0
A	B	C	D	E

  The correct answer is **B** (see diagram).

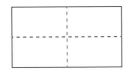

- *Tip:* Practise by cutting out shapes and folding the paper.

- **Grid references** can be used to locate objects on a grid.

  Example: A vertical line is drawn on a grid. What three squares need to be shaded so that the line is a line of symmetry?

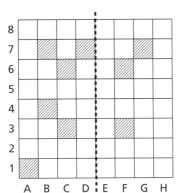

A	E1, G4, F7	B	E1, G3, F7
C	H1, H3, E6	D	E7, E1, G4
E	H1, E7, G4		

  The correct answer is **E**.

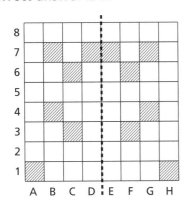

- A shape is **folded** to form a smaller shape.

  Example: Suellen starts with a piece of paper in the shape of a regular pentagon:

  She makes one fold in the paper, without moving it in any other way. Which of the following could **not** be the result?

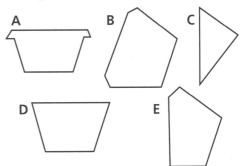

  The correct answer is **C**.

- Locations on a grid can also be described using the **intersection** of the vertical and horizontal lines.

  Example: If B1 and E5 are two vertices of a rectangle, which of these could be another vertex?

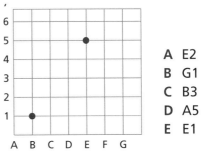

A	E2
B	G1
C	B3
D	A5
E	E1

  The correct answer is **E**. The two possible locations are E1 and B5.

MATHEMATICAL REASONING
Symmetry, folding, position and scale

- A diagram or a map can be drawn using a **scale**.

Example: In the diagram the distance from D3 to G3 is 15 m. What is the distance from C1 to C5?

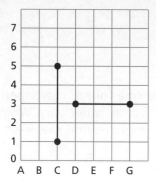

3 m	4 m	20 m	25 m	30 m
A	**B**	**C**	**D**	**E**

The correct answer is **C**. On the grid there are 3 units from D3 to G3. If 3 units represent 15 m, then 1 unit must represent 5 m. As C1 to C5 is 4 units, and 4 × 5 is 20, the distance is 20 m.

- The scale used in the drawing of a **map** allows real distances to be found.

Example: Estimate the distance from Broke to Bulga.

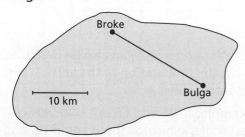

20 km	8 km	60 km	50 km	100 km
A	**B**	**C**	**D**	**E**

The correct answer is **A**. Use the scale to estimate.

- 💡 *Tip:* Use your pen or pencil to measure along the scale and then 'step' along the road.

- **Compass directions** are expressed as North (N), South (S), East (E) and West (W). Halfway between these directions are NE, SE, SW and NW.

Example: A disc is placed on B2. The disc is then moved 4 units north, 5 units east and 2 units south. The disc is then moved in a westerly direction, stopping when it is north-east of its starting point. Where is the disc now?

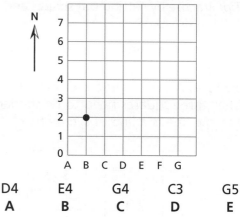

D4	E4	G4	C3	G5
A	**B**	**C**	**D**	**E**

The correct answer is **A**. As D4 is 2 units to the north and 2 units to the east of B2, it is north-east of the starting point:

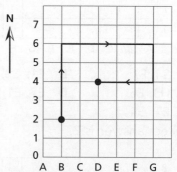

Checklist

Can you:

1 *find the lines of symmetry of plane shapes?*
2 *use grid references to locate objects on a grid?*
3 *use a scale to find the distance between points on a grid or map?*
4 *compare the position of places on a grid or map using compass directions?*

Real Test 1

MATHEMATICAL REASONING
Symmetry, folding, position and scale

10 MIN

1 The shape is made up of four identical triangles. How many axes of symmetry are there?

6	2	1	0	3
A	B	C	D	E

2 The map shows the location of nine towns:

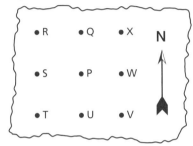

From P, Darren travelled south to a second town. He then travelled north-west to arrive at a third town. This town was

U	W	T	V	S
A	B	C	D	E

3 A map has a scale of 1 cm = 20 km. If the distance from Whereami to Noidea is 80 km, how far apart are the towns on the map?

$4\frac{1}{2}$ cm	4 cm	7 cm	5 cm	16 cm
A	B	C	D	E

4 Kath is shading squares on the grid so that the vertical line is a line of symmetry. She needs to shade three more squares. What are the grid references of the three squares?

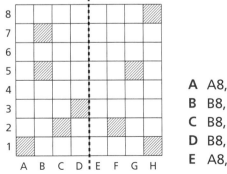

A A8, G7, E3
B B8, G7, E3
C B8, F7, E3
D B8, G7, F3
E A8, G7, F3

5 The grid shows the location of 10 students standing in the playground. Sienna is standing at S4. Her friend Ava is standing more than 20 m from her. If Sienna is south-east of Ava, what is the grid reference for Ava?

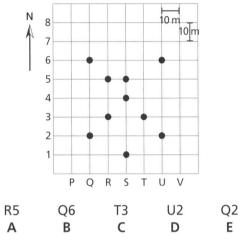

R5	Q6	T3	U2	Q2
A	B	C	D	E

6 Matilda has a piece of paper in the shape of a triangle:

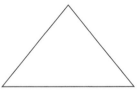

She made one fold in the paper without moving it in any other way. Which of the following shapes could **not** be the result?

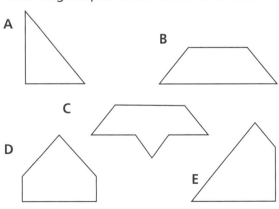

☞ **Answers and explanations on pages 225–226**

Real Test 1

MATHEMATICAL REASONING
Symmetry, folding, position and scale

7 A 4 by 4 grid in the shape of a square is completely covered by three shapes made from small squares:

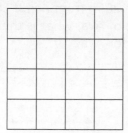

Here are two of the shapes:

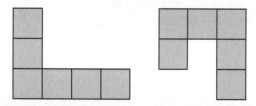

Which of these is the third shape?

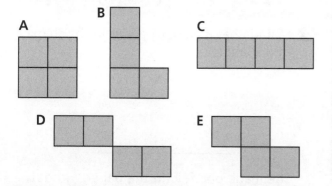

8 Barnaby is standing on *X*. He walks 30 m north, 40 m east, 50 m south and 40 m west. How far is Barnaby away from his starting point?

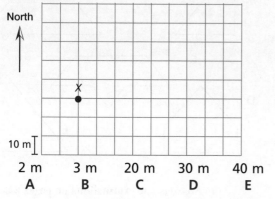

North				
2 m	3 m	20 m	30 m	40 m
A	**B**	**C**	**D**	**E**

9 Sebastian wants to remove one square from this shape:

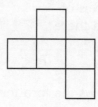

How many of these shapes could he get?

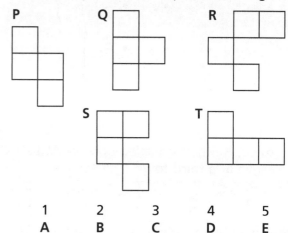

1	2	3	4	5
A	**B**	**C**	**D**	**E**

10 Bryson left V6 and walked in a south-east direction to T4. He then walked the same distance in a south-west direction. He then walked 20 m west, then 30 m north and then 50 m east. What is Bryson's grid reference now?

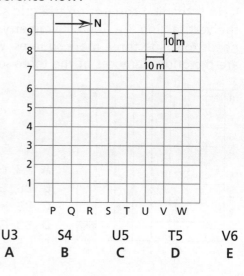

U3	S4	U5	T5	V6
A	**B**	**C**	**D**	**E**

☞ **Answers and explanations on pages 225-226**

Real Test 2

MATHEMATICAL REASONING
Symmetry, folding, position and scale

10 MIN

1 A square has *X* axes of symmetry. The value of *X* is

2	3	4	6	8
A	B	C	D	E

2 How many axes of symmetry has a hexagon with all sides and angles equal?

2	3	4	6	12
A	B	C	D	E

3 The distance from *A* to *C* is 50 km. Estimate the distance from *A* to *B*:

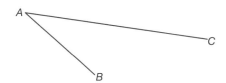

5 km	10 km	25 km	40 km	75 cm
A	B	C	D	E

4 Maryam is standing on *X*. She walks north-west to *Y*. She then walks the same distance in a north-east direction to *Z*. She then walks 30 m south. How far is Maryam away from her starting point?

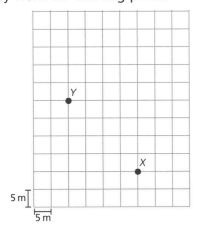

1 m	2 m	10 m	15 m	20 m
A	B	C	D	E

5 Jenny is shading squares on the grid so that the vertical and horizontal lines are lines of symmetry. She needs to shade three more squares. What are the grid references of the three squares?

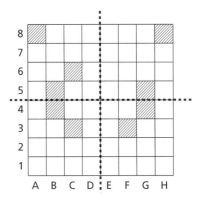

A A1, G1, E5
B D1, H1, F6
C A1, G1, F6
D A1, H1, E5
E A1, H1, F6

6 Harry left D3 and walked 20 m east, 30 m south and 40 m west. He then walked in a northerly direction until he was north-west of his starting point. Which of these is the grid reference of Harry's location?

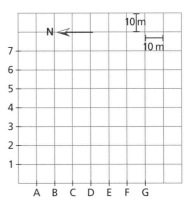

A6	B5	C4	B1	C2
A	B	C	D	E

☞ **Answers and explanations on pages 226-227**

Real Test 2

MATHEMATICAL REASONING
Symmetry, folding, position and scale

7 Charlie has a piece of paper in this shape:

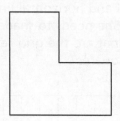

He made one fold in the paper without moving it in any other way. Which of the following shapes could **not** be the result?

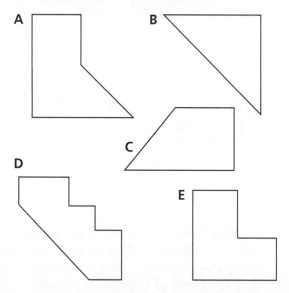

8 The roads near Mason's home run either north–south or east–west. On Wednesday morning Mason left home and rode his bike 3 km east, then 5 km south, 7 km west and 4 km north. Which of these is the path home?

A 4 km east and then 1 km south
B 5 km east and then 2 km north
C 2 km north and then 5 km east
D 3 km east and then 2 km north
E 4 km east and then 1 km north

9 Which three of these five jigsaw pieces can be used to form a square?

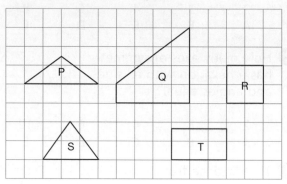

A P, R, S
B P, Q, S
C P, S, T
D R, S, T
E Q, R, S

10 Here are two identical squares:

Which of the following figures **cannot** be formed by gluing the squares together?

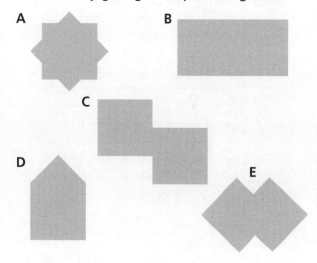

☞ **Answers and explanations on pages 226-227**

MATHEMATICAL REASONING
Statistics and probability

10 MIN

- A **table** summarises data.

  Example: The table shows the number of boys and girls who voted for four students in an election. Which student received the most votes?

Candidate	Boys	Girls
Peter	13	24
Samone	24	15
Cherie	18	21
Gerosha	22	18
Chloe	11	28

  A Peter   **B** Samone   **C** Cherie
  D Gerosha   **E** Chloe

  The correct answer is **D**. Gerosha received 40 votes.

- A table may be a **table of contents** in a book.

  Example: This is the table of contents of a 45-page book:

Contents	
Chapter 1	3
Chapter 2	10
Chapter 3	19
Chapter 4	27
Chapter 5	32
Chapter 6	39

  The largest chapter in the book is
  A Chapter 1
  B Chapter 2
  C Chapter 3
  D Chapter 4
  E Chapter 5

  The correct answer is **B**. Chapter 2 is 9 pages long, while the other chapters are 7 pages (Chapters 1 and 5), 8 pages (Chapter 3) and 5 pages (Chapter 4) long.

- Differences can be highlighted using a **graph**.

  Example: A school conducted a spell-a-thon to raise money for a new interactive whiteboard.

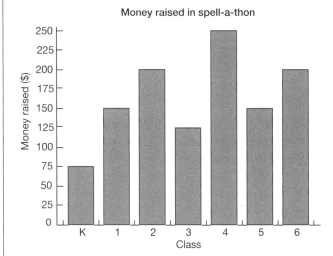

Money raised in spell-a-thon

  The total raised was
  A $1150   **B** $480   **C** $1600
  D $2100   **E** $1350

  The correct answer is **A**, as
  75 + 150 + 200 + 125 + 250 + 150 + 200 = 1150.

- A **pictograph** is a graph that uses symbols. A key shows the number represented by each symbol.

  Example: The pictograph shows the Winter Appeal fundraising amounts for four classes.

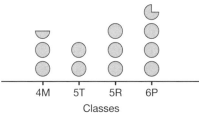

Class fundraising
Key: ◯ = $40

  Here are three statements.
  1 Class 4M raised $20 more than Class 5T.
  2 The classes raised a total of $460.
  3 Classes 4M and 5R together raised less money than Classes 5T and 6P together.

Which of these statements is/are correct?

A statement 1 only

B statement 2 only

C statement 3 only

D statements 1 and 2 only

E statements 1 and 3 only

The correct answer is **E**. Class 4M raised $100, 5T raised $80, 5R raised $120 and 6P raised $150. As 100 – 80 = 20, statement 1 is correct. As 100 + 80 + 120 + 150 = 450, statement 2 is not correct.

As 100 + 120 = 220 and 80 + 150 = 230, statement 3 is correct. This means statements 1 and 3 are correct.

- The **chance** of an event occurring can be found. The study of chance is called **probability**.

Example: The faces of a cube are numbered one to six. If the cube is rolled, what is the chance that an even number appears on the top of the cube?

$\frac{1}{6}$	$\frac{2}{6}$	$\frac{3}{6}$	$\frac{4}{6}$	$\frac{5}{6}$
A	B	C	D	E

The correct answer is **C**. There are three possible even numbers (2, 4, 6) out of six (1, 2, 3, 4, 5, 6).

The answer is 3 out of 6, which is written as the fraction $\frac{3}{6}$ (which could be rewritten as $\frac{1}{2}$).

Checklist

Can you:

1 *read and interpret the data in a table?*

2 *read and interpret the data in a graph?*

3 *determine the chance of simple events taking place?*

Real Test 3

MATHEMATICAL REASONING
Statistics and probability

10 MIN

Circle the correct answer for each question.

The table lists the number of people living in the houses in our street:

People	0	1	2	3	4	5
Houses	1	3	4	5	2	1

Use the table to answer questions **1** to **3**.

1 The number of houses in our street is

5	15	16	20	6
A	B	C	D	E

2 How many people live in our street?

15	16	32	39	40
A	B	C	D	E

3 If a house is chosen at random, what is the most likely number of people living in that house?

4	2	5	1	3
A	B	C	D	E

Thirty-six Year 4 students were surveyed. The graph represents their favourite sports. Use the graph to answer questions **4** to **6**.

4 What was the most popular sport?

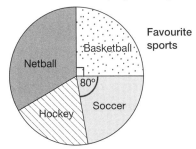

Favourite sports

A basketball   B soccer   C hockey
D netball   E not enough information

5 How many students chose basketball?

9	10	12	15	90
A	B	C	D	E

6 If half the students who chose soccer were girls, how many girls chose soccer?

2	3	4	6	5
A	B	C	D	E

The following graph is to be used to answer questions **7** and **8**. It represents the temperature at Settlers Point throughout one day.

7

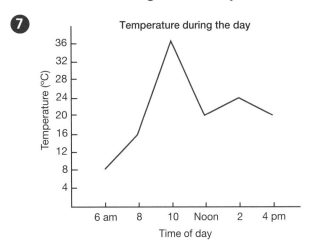

Temperature during the day

Throughout the time period identified, how many times was the temperature 24 °C?

1	2	3	4	6
A	B	C	D	E

8 Over the 10-hour period, what was the range of temperatures?

36 °C	16 °C	24 °C	32 °C	28 °C
A	B	C	D	E

Questions **9** and **10** involve two normal dice numbered 1 to 6. The dice are rolled and the numbers shown on the uppermost face are added together.

9 Which of the following is a possible sum?

1	8	13	36	22
A	B	C	D	E

10 Which of the following is the most likely sum?

2	3	8	12	7
A	B	C	D	E

☞ **Answers and explanations on page 227**

10 MIN

Circle the correct answer for each question.

The graph shows the number of books sold at a second-hand bookstore last week:

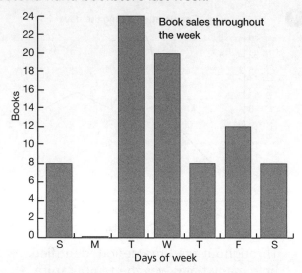

Book sales throughout the week

Use the graph to answer questions **1** and **2**.

1 How many books were sold throughout the week?

12	80	48	14	6
A	B	C	D	E

2 The shop was closed on Monday. On the days the store was open, what was the difference between the most book sales and the least?

8	6	24	4	16
A	B	C	D	E

The graph shows the body temperature of a patient in hospital:

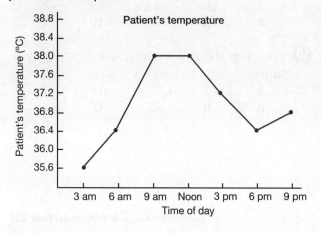

Patient's temperature

Use the graph to answer questions **3** and **4**.

3 How many times was the temperature 36.8 °C?

1	2	3	4	7
A	B	C	D	E

4 How many times was the patient's temperature taken?

A 7
B 6
C 12
D 21
E 18

5 The table shows some of the results of a survey of students' favourite colours.

Favourite colours	
Colour	**Tally**
blue	IIII
yellow	
green	IIII IIII
red	

Three times as many students chose green than yellow and four times as many chose red than blue. Lara wrote these statements.

1 Two more students chose blue than yellow.

2 The second favourite colour was green.

3 A total of 32 students were surveyed.

Which of these statements is/are correct?

A statement 1 only
B statement 2 only
C statement 3 only
D statements 2 and 3 only
E statements 1, 2 and 3

☞ **Answers and explanations on pages 227–228**

Real Test 4

MATHEMATICAL REASONING
Statistics and probability

The graph below represents the results of a survey of workers at a city office to find out the form of transport they took to get to work that morning.

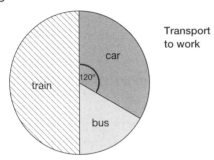

Transport to work

Use the graph to answer questions **6** and **7**.

6 If there were 24 people involved in the survey, how many had travelled by train?

18	8	6	12	48
A	B	C	D	E

7 What fraction of the workers had travelled by car?

$\frac{1}{3}$	$\frac{1}{6}$	$\frac{1}{2}$	$\frac{1}{4}$	$\frac{1}{5}$
A	B	C	D	E

In a television game show, a board contains nine squares. A light flashes randomly on each of the squares. When the flashing stops, a square is lit and the contestant wins the prize amount.

$50	$10	$40
$20	$0	$80
$10	$20	$10

Use the diagram to answer questions **8** and **9**.

8 What is the most likely amount of money to be won on a single turn?

$50	$20	$10	$100	$0
A	B	C	D	E

9 A contestant had two turns at the prize board and won money on both occasions.

Which of the following totals is impossible?

$130	$50	$80	$110	$30
A	B	C	D	E

10 A game is played where two spinners are spun and the results recorded. A score is calculated by multiplying the two results together:

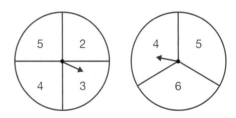

Here are four statements.

1 The most likely scores are 12 and 20.

2 The third smallest score is 12.

3 It is five times more likely that the score is even than odd.

Which of these statements is/are correct?

A statement 1 only

B statement 2 only

C statement 3 only

D statements 2 and 3 only

E statements 1, 2 and 3

☞ **Answers and explanations on pages 227-228**

WRITING
'Agree or disagree' opinion

- You have done some work on writing opinions already (Week 2), so you know many important things about writing your opinion in a test, and have done some practice writing.

- Remember: When you are asked to write your opinion on a topic or question, you always need to **give reasons** for your opinion and be **well organised and clear**.

- As with all test questions, you must **write on the topic or question** you are given. So read the question very carefully.

- You will definitely be asked to write your opinion on a topic in the scholarship test, so it is a good idea to practise writing your opinion **within a time limit**.

- You practised writing opinions in response to *What would you do if … ?* These kinds of questions usually give you a chance to show how imaginative and creative you can be, as they are often about unreal, fun topics.

- In this session, we will practise writing opinions on more **serious topics** in response to questions such as:
  ○ *Do you agree or disagree with … ?*
  ○ *Give your opinion on …*
  ○ *Is … a good or bad idea?*
  ○ *Who or what do you think is … ?*

- Remember that an opinion question will always be on a **very general topic**. It will be something that every student will be able to write about using their own everyday experiences. So you won't be asked to write about something you don't know anything about, and you don't need to study any specific topics before the exam.

- As with all opinion questions, you are expected to give your reasons for your opinions. You are really saying, **'I think that … and here are my reasons …'**

- On the next page is an example of an 'agree or disagree' opinion written in response to a test question, though not under test conditions. In your test, you **might not have time** to produce a polished piece of writing like this. However, if you are **well prepared**, you will be able to aim for this standard.

Question

The government is thinking of increasing how much time schoolchildren spend doing sport. Your teacher is collecting opinions from the class on this question.

Do you agree or disagree that there should be more sport in schools? Give at least **two** good reasons.

Response

Structure

Language

Title—give your writing a title if you are not given one

Introduction to the topic and your opinion

Body—reasons for your opinion (facts, experiences and arguments)

Topic sentences that state main reasons

Paragraphing to separate reasons

Conclusion—sums up opinion and rounds off writing

[No More Sport]

I do not agree that there should be more sport in schools. I think there is enough sport already and not everyone likes it or is good at it anyway.

First of all, in most schools there are plenty of opportunities to play sport and get exercise. In our school we play sport one afternoon or morning a week. We also have a Sports and Healthy Lifestyles Camp once a year where we play different sports each day for a whole week. I haven't even mentioned all the games we play at lunch and recess. I don't think we would have time to do much else if we had even more sport. We wouldn't even have time to learn to read and write!

Also, many children hate sport or are not very good at it. Some of my friends are not interested in playing sport at all. It's like torture for them. They prefer to be inside playing computer games or watching television or even doing schoolwork! I don't think they will do much sport later on in their lives if they are forced to do lots and lots of sport when they are children. It will just turn them off.

I really think the government should think about letting children choose how much sport they do at school. Then everyone would be happy. Teachers wouldn't have to push their pupils to play sport and children would have more time to do the things they really want to do.

'Signpost' words that help the reader follow your ideas

Interesting, imaginative ideas

Precise, vivid language to express ideas

Words to show the **strength of your opinion**

Correct **spelling, grammar** and **punctuation**

Practice Tasks

WRITING
'Agree or disagree' opinion

[50 MIN]

- These tasks will give you some ideas about how to get writing quickly and express your opinion in the short time you have in the test.

- You will have to look back at *No More Sport* to answer some questions and then do some opinion writing yourself. Your writing will be based on the same question, as there are many ways to answer the question and many reasons on both sides. You might agree with the writer of *No More Sport* and want to write on that side. If you do, you should use your own ideas and examples.

- Here is the question again. Look at it now before you start the tasks.

> **Practice question**
>
> The government is thinking of increasing how much time schoolchildren spend doing sport. Your teacher is collecting opinions from the class on this question.
>
> Do you agree or disagree that there should be more sport in schools? Give at least **two** good reasons.

- It is important to take a few minutes to plan your writing but the good news is that this type of writing is easy to structure. You are basically saying to the reader: **I think … and I think this way for these reasons—X, Y and Z.**

- So your first step is to ask yourself: **What do you think about this question**? If you had plenty of time, you could carefully consider the arguments for and against the statement about sport in schools. However, you don't have much time at all. You have to quickly choose a point of view one way or the other. For this question, you could easily argue for more sport or no more sport—there are arguments for both sides. However, for some questions, it might be easier to argue one way than to argue another. So you should think about this before you start.

> **Important:** There is no **one** right answer!

- Your next step is to decide on **two or three good reasons to support your opinion**. You won't have time for more than two or three. Then quickly write down your reasons in a rough plan. Don't waste time on your conclusion when planning—just think about it when you get to it.

Here is the plan for *No More Sport.*

> Introduction (opinion) disagree
> Reasons 1 enough sport already
> 2 some kids hate it—if you make them do it, they will hate it more

Task 1

Make a brief plan for your response to the Practice question in the space below. There is space for three arguments but two is enough if they are good arguments. Give yourself about two minutes.

💡 *Tip:* Don't think up lots of 'little' reasons and then just string them together. It is better to think of two or three strong reasons and then develop them with examples and other details.

Introduction (opinion)

Reasons

1

2

3

Note: It isn't possible to cover in detail all types of questions you could get in the test but the advice here is useful for most questions of **direct** opinion. Look at this question, for example.

What are the **three** best parts of your day and why?

You can still use the advice here but instead of writing one paragraph for one reason, you would write one paragraph for each part of the day you chose.

Practice Tasks

WRITING
'Agree or disagree' opinion—Writing the introduction

- The important thing is to make your opinion perfectly clear at the very start. So in the introduction clearly state your answer to the question, as the writer of *No More Sport* did.

- You might want to begin your opinion sentence with phrases such as:

I think …	I believe …	I agree …	I don't agree …
I disagree	In my opinion …	It is my opinion that …	It is true/not true that

- It can be a good idea to write a sentence to summarise the arguments you are going to make. This gives the reader a kind of 'map' to follow as they read. For example, the writer of *No More Sport* wrote: *I think there is enough sport already and not everybody likes it or is good at it anyway.* This sentence gave a good summary map of the text. However, a map is not absolutely necessary— especially if you are writing a short piece.

Task 2

Write your introduction for the Practice question now. Give yourself about five minutes.

_____

_____

_____

_____

_____

_____

_____

_____

_____

_____

_____

_____

_____

_____

_____

_____

_____

Tip: Use your own experiences to develop your points if you think they make your opinion stronger.

- The main part of your writing will be the **reasons for your opinion**: the arguments for your point of view. Your reasons might be facts or examples, or just sensible arguments for thinking the way you do. Either way, if you don't give any reasons for your overall opinion, your writing won't be very convincing.

- You will probably need to break up your reasons into **paragraphs: one main reason per paragraph**. This helps the reader follow your ideas. In a very short piece of writing, however, you would not need to do this.

- A common way to write your reason paragraphs is to write one sentence that states the reason in a general way. This is called a **topic sentence**. For example, in *No More Sport* the student wrote in paragraph 2: *First of all, in most schools there are plenty of opportunities to play sport and get exercise.*

- After the topic sentence, write **one or two sentences to support or develop the argument**. This makes the argument more convincing.

💡 *Tip:* These kinds of words are useful when writing an opinion and giving reasons.

> issue   question   matter   reasons   point   compare   believe   imagine   difference

Task 3

1 Look back at *No More Sport.* Underline the topic sentences in paragraphs 2 and 3.

2 Write a few words to show what every sentence in paragraph 3 is about.

_____

3 Write a few words to show what every sentence in paragraph 4 is about.

_____

- Always aim to use **precise, expressive language** to express your ideas. Try to avoid common words that you might often use in conversation—words such as *cool*, *stupid*, *mad*, *sick,* etc. These words give only a very general picture of what you are trying to say. They are fine to use to express your opinion in conversation with your friends but they are not precise enough in opinion writing.

- Help your reader follow your ideas by using **'signpost'** words and phrases that show them how your ideas are connected. Here are some examples:

> | firstly | first of all | secondly | thirdly | next |
> |---------|--------------|----------|---------|------|
> | one reason | another reason | for example | in fact | |

- Your opinion will be more powerful and interesting if you use **words that show how strongly you feel or how certain you are about your opinions**. There are many words to help you do this. Some examples are:

very	really	extremely	so much	so many	every	all	most
almost	must	absolutely	completely	certainly	surely	could	totally
might	perhaps	probably	especially	definitely	simply		

☞ **Answers on page 228**

Task 4

Write two or three reason paragraphs now. Give yourself about ten minutes.

_____

_____

_____

_____

_____

_____

_____

_____

_____

_____

_____

_____

_____

_____

_____

_____

_____

_____

_____

_____

_____

_____

_____

_____

_____

_____

_____

Remember: Keep an eye on your grammar, spelling and punctuation, quickly correcting any mistakes you see as you write.

Practice Tasks

● A good conclusion helps to make your opinion more convincing and rounds off the whole text. You may not have time to write very much but if you can, try to state your overall opinion again (varying your words if possible) and to write something interesting or powerful to 'wrap up' all your ideas.

● Some ways to start your conclusion are:

> So …   In conclusion …   To sum up …   In summary …

Task 5

Write your conclusion now. Give yourself about three minutes.

_____

_____

_____

_____

_____

_____

_____

_____

Note: If you like, you can work on your writing some more, improving what you have written so far and writing it out again on your own paper. Use the checklist below to review your writing.

> ## Checklist for writing an 'agree or disagree?' opinion text
> *Have you:*
> 1 *introduced the topic or question and given your overall opinion?*
> 2 *given two or three good reasons for your opinion?*
> 3 *developed your arguments with facts, examples or logical arguments?*
> 4 *used signpost words to help your reader follow your ideas?*
> 6 *written a short conclusion?*
> 7 *checked your grammar, punctuation and spelling?*

Remember: In the test, you won't have time to revise thoroughly and make big changes. You may have time to change a few words but you will really be aiming to do a good piece of writing in one draft.

Choose **one** of the writing tests below to do now. Use your own paper.

If you like, you can do both tests. However, it would be better to do them on different days. For extra practice, you could use the tests again, writing in different ways each time.

Set yourself a time limit of 20 minutes. Use the checklist on page 159 to give it a quick review.

Test 1

Is there too much violence in films and television programs? Yes or no? Give at least **two** reasons for your opinion.

OR

Test 2

What is the best book you have ever read? Give your reasons (at least **two**).

How will we go?

Sample Test Papers

Instructions

1 The Opportunity Class Test has three parts:
   - Reading (25 questions in 30 minutes)
   - Mathematical Reasoning (35 questions in 40 minutes)
   - Thinking Skills (30 questions in 30 minutes).

   There is no Writing test.

2 For the multiple-choice questions, there are four possible answers labelled A, B, C and D. For each question, choose the answer you think is correct. To show your answer, circle one letter (A, B, C or D). In the real test, you will mark your answer on a separate answer sheet.

3 For the questions which are not multiple-choice, follow the examples of the practice tasks.

4 If you decide to change your answer, rub it out completely and mark your new answer clearly. Remember that the answer sheet in the real test is computer marked, so rub it out completely before marking your new answer.

5 You may write on these pages (or on the question booklet in the real test).

6 Do not spend too much time on any one question. Marks are awarded for each correct answer. Incorrect or blank answers score zero.

7 Ask your parent, teacher or an adult if you need any special help.

8 Do not expect to get every answer correct—some questions may be difficult for you.

Read the text below then answer the questions.

From the old and pleasantly situated village of Mayenfeld, a footpath winds through green and shady meadows to the foot of the mountains, which on this side look down from their stern and lofty heights upon the valley below. The land grows gradually wilder as the path ascends, for the way is steep and leads directly up to the summits above.

On a clear sunny morning in June two figures might be seen climbing the narrow mountain path; one, a tall strong-looking girl, the other a child whom she was leading by the hand, and whose little checks were so aglow that the crimson colour could be seen even through the dark, sunburnt skin. And this was hardly to be wondered at, for in spite of the hot June sun the child was clothed as if to keep off the bitterest frost. She did not look more than five years old, if as much, but what her natural figure was like, it would have been hard to say, for she had apparently two, if not three dresses, one above the other, and over these a thick red woollen shawl wound round about her, so that the little body presented a shapeless appearance, as, with its small feet shod in thick, nailed mountain-shoes, it slowly and laboriously plodded its way up in the heat. The two must have left the valley a good hour's walk behind them, when they came to the hamlet known as Dorfli, which is situated half-way up the mountain. Here the wayfarers met with greetings from all sides for the elder girl was now in her old home. She did not, however, pause in her walk to respond to her friends' welcoming cries and questions, but passed on without stopping until she reached the last of the scattered houses of the hamlet.

Here a voice called to her from the door: 'Wait a moment, Dete; if you are going up higher, I will come with you.' The girl thus addressed stood still, and the child immediately let go her hand and seated herself on the ground.

'You must walk bravely on a little longer. In another hour we shall be there,' said Dete in an encouraging voice.

They were now joined by a stout, good-natured-looking woman, who walked on ahead with her old acquaintance, the two breaking forth at once into lively conversation, while the child wandered behind them.

'And where are you off to with the child?' asked the woman. 'I suppose it is the child your sister left?'

'Yes,' answered Dete. 'I am taking her up to Uncle, where she must stay.'

'The child stay up there! You must be out of your senses, Dete! The old man will soon send you and your proposal packing off home again!'

'He cannot very well do that, seeing that he is her grandfather. I have had the charge of the child till now, and I can tell you, Barbel, I am not going to give up the chance which has just fallen to me of getting a good place, for her sake. It is for the grandfather now to do his duty by her.'

'That would be all very well if he were like other people,' said Barbel, 'but you know what he is. The child cannot possibly live with him. He will have nothing to do with anybody. When he does come down once in a while, everybody clears out of the way of him and his big stick. The mere sight of him, with his bushy grey eyebrows and his immense beard, is alarming enough. Few would care to meet him alone.'

Adapted from *Heidi* by Johanna Spyri, 1881

For questions **1–6**, choose the answer (**A**, **B**, **C** or **D**) which you think best answers the question.

1 Which statement is true?
   A The girls were walking in cold and frost.
   B The little girl looked at least five years of age.
   C It was a difficult walk for the little girl.
   D Dorfli was at the top of the mountain.

2 Why were the child's cheeks crimson?
   A because she was happy
   B because she was hot
   C because she had been crying
   D because she was sunburnt

3 Why can't the girl's 'natural figure' be seen?
   A because she is wearing so many clothes
   B because she is wearing a shapeless dress
   C because she is hiding behind the figure of the older girl
   D because she is too far away

4 The information in the extract suggests that Dete
   A is happy about passing over care of the little girl to the grandfather.
   B feels guilty about passing over care of the little girl to the grandfather.
   C is angry about having to pass over care of the little girl to the grandfather.
   D wants to keep the little girl with her.

5 To what does the word 'proposal' refer?
   A an offer of marriage
   B the little girl
   C Dete's plan for the little girl
   D both B and C

6 There is no evidence in the text for which of the following statements?
   A The grandfather will welcome his granddaughter.
   B The little girl will be very lonely living with her grandfather.
   C The grandfather might not want to take care of his granddaughter.
   D The grandfather might frighten his granddaughter.

☞ **Answers and explanations on pages 228-230**

Read the poem below by Judith Wright then answer the questions.

Magpies

Along the road the magpies walk
with hands in pockets, left and right.
They tilt their heads, and stroll and talk.
In their well-fitted black and white

5 they look like certain gentlemen
who seem most nonchalant and wise
until their meal is served—and then
what clashing beaks, what greedy eyes!

But not one man that I have heard
10 throws back his head in such a song
of grace and praise—no man or bird.
Their greed is brief; their joy is long.
For each is born with such a throat
as thanks his God with every note.

For questions **7–11**, choose the answer (**A, B, C** or **D**) which you think best answers the question. There is one extra sentence which you do not need to use.

7 What is the first half of the poem mostly about?
A the greed of magpies at mealtime
B the way magpies walk and move
C the sound of magpies
D the colour of magpies

8 Who do you think are the 'certain gentlemen' the poet refers to in line 5?
A other birds
B farmers
C men in dinner suits
D soldiers

9 What do you think the word 'nonchalant' means in line 6?
A cool and unconcerned
B busy and hurried
C rude and selfish
D dull and boring

10 In lines 7 and 8, what is the poet describing?
A the magpies' behaviour towards humans
B the magpies' singing
C the magpies' feathers
D the magpies' behaviour when they find food

11 What is the last stanza (lines 9–14) mainly about?
A the magpies' greed
B the beauty of the magpies' song
C the magpies' annoying sound
D the difference between man and magpie

☞ **Answers and explanations on pages 228-230**

Read the text below then answer the questions. Six sentences have been removed from the text. Choose from the sentences (**A–G**) the one that best fits each gap (**12–17**).

Nobody really knows exactly how the first kite came to be but when you see pieces of paper or cloth wheeling through the air on windy days, it is not difficult to imagine how someone thought to control this energy by attaching sticks and strings.

The notion of kite flying is generally considered to have first developed in China more than 2000 years ago. Kites at that time were made from silk for the sail and the line, and bamboo for the frame. **12** _____ . It dates from the Mesolithic era (9000 BCE). The cave drawing shows it was made of forest tuber leaves for the sail, bamboo for the frame and twisted pineapple fibre for the rope. Interestingly, people from the island still use kites of the very same kind today.

Around 1500 years ago, kites made of paper rather than silk were being flown in China. We know this from Chinese records which state that a paper kite was used for communication in a battle of that period. The Chinese found many uses for those early kites. **13** _____ . Kites proved to be very useful in many ways: for measuring distances, for signalling and even for frightening the enemy. Other kites were used for religious purposes and some were developed purely as playthings. The kites of China's past were generally flat rather than bowed and often rectangular. **14** _____ . Many were painted with beautiful and brightly coloured designs reflecting the traditions and spiritual beliefs of the people.

The popularity of kite flying soon spread across Asia. The Japanese, Malaysians and Indonesians all developed variations in design and use. The practice even reached Polynesia and New Zealand, where they were used to send prayers to the gods. By the Middle Ages, European explorers and traders had introduced the kite to Europe.

By the 18th and 19th centuries, kites in Europe and America were being used not only for pleasure but also for scientific study, such as experiments proving that lightning is electricity and in measurement of atmospheric conditions for weather forecasting. **15** _____ .

Kite flying is perhaps still more popular in Asian countries than others. In Afghanistan, India, Pakistan, Indonesia, Nepal and Vietnam, for example, it is an important and popular ritual and pastime. In religious festivals all over Asia, kites are still a common sight because of the link they make between heaven and earth. **16** _____ .The participants try to snag each other's kites or cut them down. The kites used for this are usually small, diamond-shaped, and made of paper and bamboo.

While they may be more popular in Asia, kites are used in sport and play throughout the world. They are constructed with a range of materials—nylon, plastic film and carbon fibre for the sail—and synthetic ropes for the cord and kite line. They can be single line, like those your mum or dad might have made for you when you were small, or double, triple or quad line. They come in a range of shapes from a basic diamond shape to a delta or triangular shape to various box and cellular designs.

So now it's your turn to continue in this ancient tradition by learning the basics and to have a fun time with this exciting hobby. **17** _____ .

A In some places the sport is more 'kite fighting' than kite flying.

B Some were fitted with simple whistles and strings so they would make musical sounds as they flew.

C In addition to sending messages in battle, they found other military purposes for them.

D And of course they were instrumental in the early development of aviation.

E However, a cave painting showing a kite has been found on an island off Sulawesi in Indonesia.

F There are many world records for kite flying.

G The possibilities are endless.

☞ **Answers and explanations on pages 228–230**

Read the four extracts below on the theme of children in families.

For questions **18–25**, choose the option (**A, B, C** or **D**) which you think best answers the question.

Which extract …

mentions that sibling rivalry lessens as children get older? **18** _____

suggests that birth order can be an issue for blended families? **19** _____

gives advice to parents about dealing with fights in the household? **20** _____

relates a personal experience related to birth order? **21** _____

explains why the youngest child in the family might be more independent? **22** _____

suggests that sibling fighting helps children solve conflicts as adults? **23** _____

lists the characteristics of oldest, youngest and in-between children? **24** _____

points out that you can't expect small children to be brilliant at solving conflict? **25** _____

Extract A

All parents have experienced those moments when all the kids in the house are getting along just fine and then suddenly war breaks out. There are tears, name-calling and yelling matches. If you are lucky, it will all be over before the day ends but sometimes the feuding goes on for days or even weeks and months. So what can you do? Firstly you should avoid using labels such as 'the athletic one' or 'the smartie' or 'the wild child'. These labels encourage children to compare themselves with their siblings and this creates tension. Secondly, instead of just using time-outs, give your children some strategies to solve the problem themselves. Thirdly try to stay out of fights, unless physical fights break out or furniture is being broken, and don't take sides. Lastly be patient. Solving conflicts is difficult for adults so don't expect miracles from your two or four year old.

☞ **Answers and explanations on pages 228-230**

Extract B

Many experts believe your position in the family can affect your personality and attitude to life. Of course there are many other factors, such as temperament and parenting styles. However, many experts agree on some basic characteristics of first born, last born and those in the middle. Eldest children tend to be high achievers and become leaders after years of bossing their younger siblings around. The middle child tends to be quieter and more of a peacemaker. They may seek attention more than firstborns and look for friendships outside the family. The youngest child is more likely to be outgoing and independent. They are often the charmers in the family. They have often had more freedom than their older siblings and this translates to a willingness to try new things and set out in new directions. So where are you in your family? Does the theory work out for you?

Extract C

When I was eight my mum remarried and I gained two new older siblings to add to the two younger ones I had already. I was not looking forward to losing my position of power and influence and becoming 'the middle child'. Suddenly, overnight, I gained a position of no importance at all. My new big sister was clearly the boss in her family and was not interested in giving up this role. My new big brother looked down on me with total disdain. My baby sister was everyone's darling of course and my little brother was immediately taken under the wing of my new big brother. It was just me—in the middle—who felt alone. It definitely hurt at the time but now I know it didn't really matter. We're all best friends and agree it is definitely our baby sister who is now the big boss.

Extract D

Fighting and arguing between children in the same family is normal. It's how children learn to sort out difficulties and learn strategies which they can use in conflict situations later in life. Sibling rivalry is also how children work out their place in the family and develop their character and personality. Some children struggle more than others in dealing with their anger and frustration. These children are likely to have more feuds with their siblings. Fighting between young children usually decreases as they get older and develop their language and social skills. Some children get on with their siblings all their lives even if they have had the usual arguments and fights. Others might get on well as children but end up having poor relationships as teens and adults. And sad as it is, some just never get on with each other in childhood or adulthood.

1 ⬜ represents a number.

23 + 39 = 81 – ⬜

What number is ⬜ ?

9	11	29	21	19
A	**B**	**C**	**D**	**E**

2 What number is four hundred less than 63 209?

A 57 209
B 58 209
C 62 809
D 62 909
E 63 169

3 Otis works as a security guard. He leaves home at twenty to ten at night and returns the next morning at 7:25 am.

How long is he away from home?

A 8 h 45 min
B 9 h 15 min
C 9 h 45 min
D 10 h 15 min
E 10 h 45 min

4 Scarlett shades one-third of the squares in this shape:

Harriet then shades half of the **remaining** squares.

How many squares now remain unshaded?

2	4	6	8	9
A	**B**	**C**	**D**	**E**

5 These numbers are to be rounded to the nearest hundred.

Which number changes the most?

A 63
B 241
C 478
D 1632
E 2776

6 Elijah is standing at *P* on the grid below:

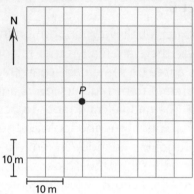

From *P*, Elijah follows these instructions.

• Walk 10 m west.
• Walk 20 m north.
• Walk 35 m east.
• Walk 30 m south.
• Walk 25 m west.

How far is Elijah now from *P*?

0 m	5 m	10 m	15 m	20 m
A	**B**	**C**	**D**	**E**

7 In the squares below, Creed is going to write the numbers 1 to 9:

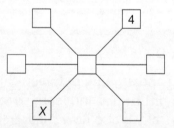

The three numbers in each line must add to 15.

What number must Creed write in the square marked with an *X*?

6	7	8	9	10
A	**B**	**C**	**D**	**E**

8 Lexi is making bunches of 12 balloons for Valentine's Day.

For every red balloon she uses two white balloons and three pink balloons.

☞ **Answers and explanations on pages 230–232**

She needs to make six bunches of balloons. How many pink balloons does she need to inflate?

18	24	30	32	36
A	B	C	D	E

9 Heath has two containers of water.

Container X is half full of water.

When Container X is full it holds 1 L.

Container Y has a capacity of 350 mL of water:

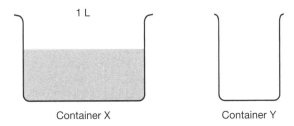

Container X   Container Y

Heath uses Container Y to fill Container X. He needs to fill Container Y twice to do so.

How much water remains in Container Y after Container X is filled?

100 mL	150 mL	200 mL	250 mL	300 mL
A	B	C	D	E

10 A piece of wire is bent to form a rectangle.

The length of the rectangle is three times the width.

If the width is 15 cm, what is the length of wire used?

30 cm	45 cm	60 cm	90 cm	1.2 m
A	B	C	D	E

11 Here are five letters made of vertical and horizontal lines.

Julian is counting the right angles in each letter:

E   F   H   L   T

If he chooses three letters at random, what is the largest possible number of right angles he can count?

8	10	11	12	13
A	B	C	D	E

12 A bakery sells bread rolls.

One bread roll costs 70 cents, a bag of six bread rolls costs $3.50 and a bag of eight bread rolls costs $4.

Rita needs to buy a dozen bread rolls.

What is the lowest amount she can pay?

$6.80	$7.00	$6.20	$8.00	$8.40
A	B	C	D	E

13 This diagram shows 24 = 6 × 4:

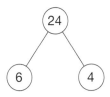

Here is a new diagram that works the same way:

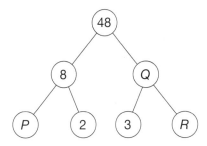

What is the value of P × Q × R?

24	36	48	64	72
A	B	C	D	E

14 Maya used 12 identical cubes to make this solid:

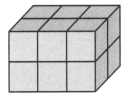

She picks up the solid and looks at it from all directions. How many cube faces cannot be seen?

20	24	28	32	40
A	B	C	D	E

☞ **Answers and explanations on pages 230-232**

15 Maggie writes a sequence of numbers by subtracting 8 and then doubling the result.

One of the numbers in the sequence is 128.

The number before 128 has two digits and Maggie multiplies these digits.

What is her answer?

0	14	6	12	8
A	B	C	D	E

16 Al sells used cars.

The car yard is open Monday to Friday.

The graphs show the sales across two weeks but the data on one of the days is missing:

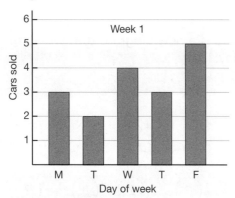

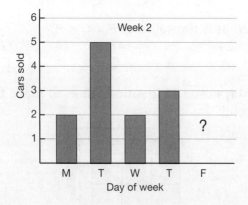

If Al sold two fewer cars in the second week than the first week, how many cars were sold on the Friday in Week 2?

0	1	2	3	4
A	B	C	D	E

17 Lucas has four numbered cards:

Lucas uses the cards to make three-digit numbers.

What is the difference between the largest even and the smallest odd number?

19	397	399	401	409
A	B	C	D	E

18 Here are three squares:

| P | Q | R |

Which of the squares has/have $\frac{2}{3}$ shaded?

A square P only

B square Q only

C square R only

D squares P and Q only

E squares Q and R only

19 Here are some numbers in a sequence:

… 8, 16, 32, 64 …

If 8 is the fourth number in the sequence, what is the sum of the sixth and ninth numbers?

13	72	144	288	576
A	B	C	D	E

20 Charlotte has a bag of small Easter eggs to give away.

She gives $\frac{1}{5}$ of the eggs to her grandmother, and $\frac{1}{10}$ to her neighbour. She gives $\frac{1}{10}$ of the eggs to each of her friends. She has no eggs left over.

How many of Charlotte's friends receive eggs?

7	8	6	4	5
A	B	C	D	E

☞ **Answers and explanations on pages 230–232**

21 Amelia is to shade three more squares on the grid.

She wants the dotted line to be a line of symmetry:

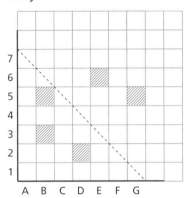

What are the grid references of the squares she needs to shade?

A C6, C1, F4

B C6, B1, F1

C C6, C1, F1

D D6, C1, F4

E D6, B1, F4

22 The grid represents squares drawn on a basketball court.

Jake stands on the court at S4.

Ten other students also stand on the court:

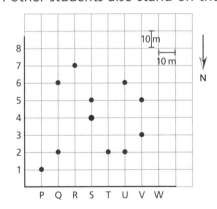

Jake's best friend Archie is standing south-east of him and more than 20 m away.

What is Archie's grid reference?

Q2	U2	V3	U6	Q6
A	B	C	D	E

23 The mass of six identical blocks is 24 kg.

The mass of 12 identical cylinders is 24 kg.

What is the total mass of 12 blocks and six cylinders?

36 kg	48 kg	60 kg	66 kg	72 kg
A	B	C	D	E

24 Florence folds a square piece of centimetre-squared paper as shown:

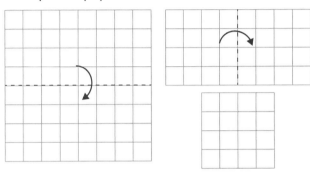

She cuts off the parts of the folded paper that are shown in purple and throws them away:

Florence now opens the folded paper completely.

What is the area of the paper remaining?

28 cm²	32 cm²	36 cm²	38 cm²	40 cm²
A	B	C	D	E

25 An eraser costs 80 cents and a glue stick costs $2.40.

Freya buys an eraser and a glue stick and pays with a $10 note.

She receives change of 20-cent coins and 10-cent coins only.

If she was given six 10-cent coins, how many 20-cent coins did she receive?

16	21	26	31	36
A	B	C	D	E

☞ **Answers and explanations on pages 230–232**

26 25 June 2021 was a Friday. Which day of the week was 25 August 2021?
A Tuesday
B Wednesday
C Thursday
D Friday
E Saturday

27 A gym runs fitness classes throughout the week.

The graph shows the results of a survey of gym members and the number of fitness classes attended:

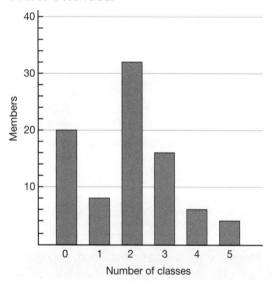

Grace reads the graph and makes these claims:

1. 26 members attend at least three classes.
2. Twice as many members attend two classes as three classes.
3. One-quarter of the members do not attend any classes.

Using the information on the graph, which of Grace's claims is/are correct?
A claim 1 only
B claim 2 only
C claim 3 only
D claims 1 and 2 only
E claims 1, 2 and 3

28 Avery makes this solid using 12 identical small cubes:

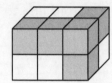

She picks up the solid, looking at it from all directions and counts the cube faces she can see.

She then breaks the solid into two smaller solids:

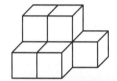 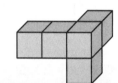

Avery now picks up both solids, looking at them from all directions, and counts the total cube faces she can see.

How many more faces can Avery now see?

8	16	18	24	28
A	B	C	D	E

29 There are red, blue, green and yellow balls in a box.

There are twice as many red balls as blue balls.

There are three more blue balls than green balls.

A quarter of the balls in the box are yellow.

There are three green balls in the box.

How many balls are in the box?

28	30	32	36	40
A	B	C	D	E

30 Gideon starts with a piece of paper in the shape of a parallelogram:

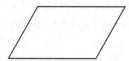

☞ **Answers and explanations on pages 230-232**

He makes **just one fold** in the paper, without moving it in any other way.

Which of these shapes could **not** be the result?

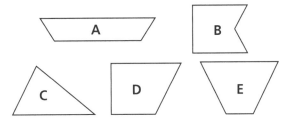

31 Here is a pattern of shapes drawn on centimetre-squared paper:

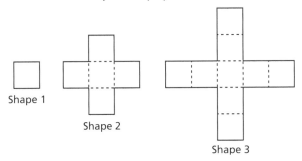

Shape 1

Shape 2

Shape 3

If Ange continues the pattern, what will be the perimeter of Shape 5?

24 cm	28 cm	32 cm	36 cm	40 cm
A	**B**	**C**	**D**	**E**

32 Aurora had cards numbered 1 to 15 and placed them in a bag. Without looking, she took a card from the bag.

Which of the following statements is/are correct?

1. Aurora is more likely to pull out an odd number than an even number.
2. Aurora is equally likely to select a number less than 5 than a number greater than 10.
3. Aurora is less likely to take the number 11 than the number 12.

A statement 1 only

B statements 1 and 2 only

C statements 2 and 3 only

D statements 1 and 3 only

E statements 1, 2 and 3

33 Bruce's boss gave him a Christmas bonus of $1000.

He gave each of his four children $105.

He also gave his sister some money.

He still had $380 remaining.

How much money did Bruce give his sister?

$105	$200	$220	$415	$515
A	**B**	**C**	**D**	**E**

34 Chris has drawn this shape:

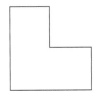

He draws one straight line to split the shape into smaller shapes.

Which of these can he make with the cut?

X. two quadrilaterals

Y. three triangles

Z. a quadrilateral and a hexagon

A X only

B Y only

C Z only

D X and Y only

E X, Y and Z

35 Hazel made these two spinners:

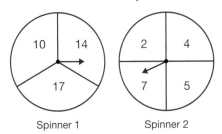

Spinner 1   Spinner 2

She spins the arrows on both spinners. A score is the difference between the two results. Which of these scores is **not** possible?

8	9	10	11	12
A	**B**	**C**	**D**	**E**

☞ **Answers and explanations on pages 230–232**

1 Abigail, Bella, Fiona, Cooper, Daniel and Edward are sitting at a round table. Abigail is directly opposite Bella. Cooper is next to Daniel:

Which must be true?
A Daniel is next to Bella.
B Cooper is next to Abigail.
C Abigail is next to Edward.
D Edward is next to Fiona.

2 Students were given the option to hand in their project in hard copy or digitally. The deadline for completing the work is Friday at 5 pm.

On Friday morning the teacher, Mr Flint, announced: 'I found ten hard copy projects in my hand-in box this morning. That means fifteen of you have decided to send me your projects digitally. I'm looking forward to reading them all.'

Which of the following shows the mistake Mr Flint has made?
A He did not announce which students had handed in their projects.
B Some of the students might hand in hard copy projects later that day.
C He did not include projects that had already been completed.
D Some of the students might have decided to do a different project.

3 Rachael, Meg, Jaxson and Brock take turns visiting at each other's homes to play board games. Their turns are in alphabetical order.

Brock is away on holiday for a fortnight and won't be attending and Rachael has just told the others she won't be able to have her turn at her home this week as she's having some renovations done.

Whose home will they meet at this week?
A Rachael   B Meg   C Jaxson   D Brock

4 Some students did two tests. Here are their results but Mia's mark in the second test is missing:

Name	Test 1	Test 2
Alex	72	69
Polly	67	75
George	76	71
Mia	64	
Henry	70	73

A prize was awarded to the student with the highest total for the two tests. Mia won the prize.

What is the lowest mark that Mia could have scored in Test 2?
A 78   B 80   C 82   D 84

5 Many Chinese restaurants in Australia serve fortune cookies. People think they are a Chinese tradition but fortune cookies were actually invented in Japan. They were introduced to the United States by the Japanese and from there they spread globally. In China, fortune cookies are considered by many to be an American invention.

Which of the following sentences best expresses the main idea in the text?
A Fortune cookies were invented in Japan, not in China or America.
B Many Chinese restaurants in Australia serve fortune cookies.
C In Australia many people think fortune cookies are a Chinese tradition.
D In China, fortune cookies are considered by many to be an American invention.

☞ **Answers and explanations on pages 233–236**

6 Which two squares have the same six pieces? (They might be turned around or over.)

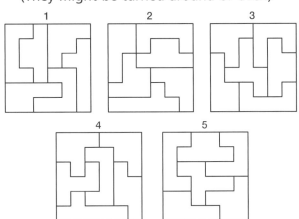

A 1 and 2
C 2 and 4
B 1 and 3
D 3 and 5

7 A flag has five horizontal stripes in three colours: red, yellow and blue. Two of the stripes are red. The top stripe is red and the bottom stripe is yellow.

Which must be correct?

A A red stripe is next to a blue stripe.
B A yellow stripe is next to a red stripe.
C Two of the stripes are blue.
D Two of the stripes are yellow.

8

Diane: 'I've just read *Anne of Green Gables* by LM Montgomery and I really liked it. It was about a feisty, talkative and imaginative girl named Anne. I told Sam I thought he'd probably enjoy reading it because it is very funny and I know he enjoys humorous books.'

Tahlia: 'I've read that book. I'm sure Ilona would enjoy it. Ilona is not much of a reader and it's difficult to get her to stick with a book to the finish but *Anne of*

Green Gables is an entertaining story with a great female protagonist who makes mistakes but learns from them. I know Ilona would read the book to the end.'

Whose reasoning is correct?

A Diane only
B Tahlia only
C Both Diane and Tahlia
D Neither Diane nor Tahlia

9 Yassie enrolled Peaches in puppy school.

To graduate from puppy school, puppies must demonstrate achievement of any two of the three core skills:

• to walk with a loose leash
• to play politely with other dogs
• to stay on command.

Based on the information above, which of the following **cannot** be true?

A Peaches will not graduate because she did not stay on command or walk with a loose leash.
B Peaches will graduate because she performed well in all three skill areas.
C Yassie was keen to learn how to train Peaches and help her graduate from puppy school.
D Peaches will not graduate because she could not walk with a loose leash even though she could stay on command and play politely.

10 Five girls—Hailey, Isla, Jenna, Kahlia and Laura—are sitting in a row at the movies.

• Laura is somewhere between Hailey and Isla.
• Jenna and Kahlia are beside each other.
• Kahlia is left of, but not beside, Hailey.
• There is one girl sitting between Jenna and Hailey.

Who is sitting in the middle?

A Hailey **B** Isla **C** Jenna **D** Laura

☞ **Answers and explanations on pages 233-236**

11 Pashmina said: 'We have an English bull terrier named Fifi. English bull terriers are sweet and placid most of the time but sometimes they get overexcited and run around crazily, crashing into things and spinning in circles without any thought to their own safety. When they do this, they are very entertaining and funny to watch.'

Which statement best supports Pashmina's claim?

A English bull terriers can destroy your furniture if they are bored or neglected.

B English bull terriers are rowdy and clownish.

C English bull terriers are very muscly and strong so need good training.

D English bull terriers have a short, easy-to-maintain coat.

12 The yo-yo must be the greatest toy ever invented. It's been around since at least 400 BCE and is still a popular toy today. In ancient times yo-yos were made of wood, metal or terracotta (clay) but since the 1960s yo-yos have often been made of plastic. They are cheap, lightweight, easy to carry around and fun to use so it's no wonder their popularity has endured.

Which statement **weakens** the above argument?

A The first World Yo-Yo Contest was held in 1932 and now yo-yo contests are held annually in different parts of the world.

B The world's biggest yo-yo weighs 115 kg and has to be dropped by a crane.

C You can do tricks with a yo-yo such as 'walk the dog', 'rock the baby' and 'around the world'.

D Over the years the yo-yo has gone in and out of fashion and popularity.

13 The positions of some towns are shown on this map but the names have been left off:

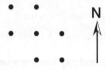

Malven is east of Bankston and west of Araluen. Portland is north of Bankston and west of Rosewood. Rosewood is north of Fenton, which is south of Malven. Hapville is south of Araluen and east of Fenton.

What direction is Portland from Hapville?

A north-east   B north-west

C south-east   D south-west

14 **Pearl:** 'I need to go shopping after school. There's a dance concert coming up and I have to wear a plain white t-shirt and leggings.'

Marc: 'You're going to buy a plain white t-shirt and leggings, then.'

Which assumption has Marc made?

A Pearl will go shopping with her mother after school.

B The dance concert is after school.

C Pearl does not own a plain white t-shirt and leggings.

D Pearl is annoyed about shopping after school.

15 Joe is building a fence. He places posts at each end of the straight fence line. A third post is then placed in the middle of those two posts. Two more posts are placed in the centre of the two gaps. Finally, posts are placed in the middle of all the other gaps.

If the posts are 4 m apart, how long is the fence line?

A 28 m   B 32 m

C 36 m   D 40 m

☞ **Answers and explanations on pages 233-236**

16 This is the net of a cube:

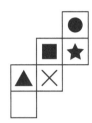

When the net is folded, what will be on the face opposite the blank face?

A star   **B** square

C cross   **D** circle

17 When caught outside in a blizzard there are lifesaving actions you can take to protect yourself. First find shelter. If there is no shelter nearby then build a simple snow cave. It will protect you from the wind. Don't eat snow. It will lower your body temperature. Instead, melt snow and drink it. Every so often briskly move your fingers, toes, arms and legs.

Which of the following best expresses the main idea of the text?

A Do not eat unmelted snow.

B In a blizzard, try to keep out of the wind.

C There are lifesaving actions you can take if caught in a blizzard.

D Moving your fingers, toes, arms and legs will keep the blood circulating.

18 A scientist says: 'The hunting of elephants for their ivory tusks is a major problem. Now there is evidence that this human activity is causing a population of African bush elephants to evolve without tusks. This lack of tusks can stop an elephant being killed for its ivory. But this comes at a cost. The evolution of elephants without tusks has lasting negative impacts on the ecosystem.'

Which one of these statements most strengthens the scientist's argument?

A Tuskless elephants are evolving faster than anyone thought possible.

B Elephants use their tusks in ways that help the long-term health of the ecosystem.

C Some people think the tuskless elephants are stressed, rather than evolving.

D There have always been a few naturally tuskless elephants.

19 Natalie goes to netball training every Monday, Wednesday and Friday afternoon except on the Fridays that there is a game.

How many training sessions will there be in March, if the Friday games are 5 March and 26 March?

A 10   **B** 11   **C** 12   **D** 13

20 When Alice said she wanted to win a Scout of the Year award, the unit leader told her: 'To have even a chance of winning a Scout of the Year award, you must be a youth member of Scouts NSW and have made a major contribution to scouting as well as a difference in the wider community.'

If the unit leader is correct, which one of these statements will be true?

A All members of Scouts NSW will win a Scout of the Year award.

B Some of the scouts who have not made a difference in the wider community might win a Scout of the Year award.

C None of the scouts who have not made a major contribution to scouting will win a Scout of the Year award.

D All the scouts who have made a difference in the wider community will win a Scout of the Year award.

☞ **Answers and explanations on pages 233-236**

21 Are you curious about things in space? You need our astounding new Night Sky app! It's the best thing to expand your night-time astronomical explorations. Simply stand under the dark night sky with your phone and the app open. Then watch the screen and be astounded by all the things in space you can track.

Which statement most **weakens** the advertisement's argument?

A Indigenous Australians were the world's first astronomers.

B The number of visible shooting stars is greater during a meteor shower.

C Stars make up only 4% of the Milky Way.

D Looking at the bright screen of your phone will ruin your night vision.

22 A contestant in a game show can choose one of five boxes, numbered from 1 to 5, to win a voucher. The values of the vouchers are $5, $10, $20, $50 and $100:

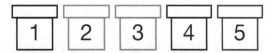

The contestant has won these three clues as he played the game.

• The $50 voucher is in an odd-numbered box.

• There are two boxes between the one holding the $5 voucher and the one holding the $20 voucher.

• The $10 voucher is somewhere between the $50 and the $100 vouchers, and is in a lower numbered box than the $100.

Which box should the contestant choose to win $100?

A box 2　　B box 3　　C box 4　　D box 5

23 Finn left home at 1:50 pm. He walked to a friend's house, arriving at 2:50 pm. Later, Finn's friend drove him home. The return journey was four times faster than the outward journey.

If Finn arrived home at 4:50 pm, how long did he spend at his friend's house?

A $\frac{3}{4}$ h　　B $1\frac{1}{4}$ h　　C $1\frac{3}{4}$ h　　D 2 h

24 When Eric's parents told him to go to bed, he said he wanted to stay up and watch his favourite television series.

He argued there was nothing wrong with staying up late to binge the whole series because all his friends at school do this.

Which assumption has Eric made in order to draw his conclusion?

A If everyone else does something, it's okay for you to do it too.

B It is not yet his bedtime.

C His parents do not like to watch that television series.

D Tomorrow is not a school day.

25 Dominoes from a set have been used to create this square, with one domino missing. No number is repeated in any row, column or diagonal. Each domino is only used once in the square, although not all dominoes in the set are used:

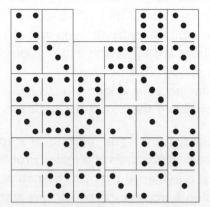

Which of the following could be the missing domino?

A　　B　　C　　D

☞ **Answers and explanations on pages 233-236**

㉖ | Only those students who have completed and handed in last night's homework will be allowed to go to the book fair in the library at lunchtime.

Hugo: 'I've completed and handed in last night's homework so I'll definitely be allowed to go to the book fair.'

Mila: 'I left my homework at home so I won't be allowed to go to the book fair.'

If the information in the box is true, whose reasoning is correct?

A Hugo only   **B** Mila only

C Hugo and Mila

D Neither Hugo nor Mila

㉗ Zena is making a pattern. She is using one colour from each group:

Group 1	Group 2	Group 3	Group 4
red	pink	red	green
blue	white	white	black
green	blue	orange	orange
yellow	black	grey	purple

She is using blue, green and purple.

What colour can Zena **not** use?

A orange   **B** black   **C** white   **D** red

㉘ Six cupboards in a kitchen are all in a row. One holds bowls, one has cups, one has plates, one has saucepans, one has cookbooks and one has staples (flour, sugar, salt, sauces etc.):

The cupboard that has plates is two cupboards away from the staples and three cupboards from the one holding cookbooks. The staples are not next to the cookbooks.

The cupboard holding the saucepans is next to both the bowls and cookbooks.

The cupboard holding cups is further left than that holding the bowls.

What is found in the third cupboard from the right?

A bowls   **B** cups

C plates   **D** saucepans

㉙ When completed, every row, every column and the two diagonals will all have the same set of five different symbols: a circle, star, triangle, square and diamond:

Which of these will be the bottom row?

A ◆ ■ ● ◆ ▲   **B** ■ ▲ ● ◆ ◆

C ■ ● ◆ ◆ ▲   **D** ◆ ● ■ ◆ ▲

㉚ There is a difference between a need and a want. Things like housing, food and medicine are all needs. We need them to survive. Things like toys, eating out and new clothes are wants. We wish we could have them. We'd even be disappointed if we can't have them. But we don't need them to survive.

Which of the following best expresses the main idea of the text?

A We cannot have everything we want.

B No matter what we have, we always want more.

C It is disappointing when you want something but can't have it.

D Needs and wants are different.

☞ **Answers and explanations on pages 233-236**

Instructions

1 The Reading and Viewing test contains 25 questions to be answered in 30 minutes.
2 Read each passage and then answer the questions.
3 For each question, there are four possible answers labelled **A**, **B**, **C** and **D**. For each question, choose the ONE answer you think is correct. To show your answer, circle one letter (**A**, **B**, **C** or **D**). In the real test, you will mark your answer on a separate answer sheet.
4 If you decide to change your answer, rub it out completely and mark your new answer clearly. Remember that the answer sheet in the real test is computer marked, so rub it out completely before marking your new answer.
5 You may write on these pages (or on the question booklet in the real test).
6 Do not spend too much time on any one question. Marks are awarded for each correct answer. Incorrect or blank answers score zero.
7 Ask your parent, teacher or an adult if you need any special help.
8 Do not expect to get every answer correct—some questions may be difficult for you.

Read the story extract and answer questions 1–5.

More than anything else, Andrew wanted to be like other kids. But that silly, old, lifeless right leg—which wasn't really lifeless, but might as well have been—made sure that he was not. When he looked at his reflection in the mirror after showering and dressing, he looked almost normal. It was only the crutches that betrayed the bone-crushing car accident when he was fourteen months old.

He couldn't remember that, but he could remember the many times he'd been in hospital since. There had been numerous operations, the last one just three months ago, but the bones were still not right. The doctors could promise nothing. 'It is all a matter of time,' they said. Time! It would never end, thought Andrew. Here he was, in the last year of primary school, and still hobbling about.

As well, there were the fittings for new crutches as he had grown. And of course the physiotherapy.

Some years it seemed he had spent more time in hospitals and clinics than in school, but it was school that remained most in his mind. There, his difference from the other children would always be made apparent in all sorts of little ways. He was overwhelmed by what lay before him on this first day back at school, and this is what made him feel so sick. The painful memories of sitting on sidelines watching others play cricket or football came back. And could he take being the wallflower during dance practice again? Or the 'special place' he was given at school assemblies and speech days?

He felt an impulse to crawl back into bed and hide under the covers. But Andrew had spent far too long struggling to make his body do what he wanted it to do. Now, when faced with an unpleasant task, he couldn't give up. So, with a little sigh, he turned his gaze away and resolved himself to school.

From *Perfect Timing* by Jeremy Fisher, Harcourt Brace Jovanovich, Sydney, 1992

1 Why doesn't Andrew want to go back to school?
  A because the children make fun of him
  B because at school it is so clear he is different from other kids
  C because he is tired and wants to go back to bed
  D because the teachers make a fuss of him

2 When will Andrew's leg be completely right
  A never
  B It is not certain.
  C next year
  D by the end of primary school

3 How long had Andrew been dealing with his injury?
  A about fourteen months
  B about fourteen years
  C about ten years
  D about two years

4 Which statement is **not** true?
  A Andrew's injury is only noticed by others because of his crutches.
  B Andrew has no feeling in his right leg.
  C Andrew is given special treatment at school.
  D Andrew does not give in to his anxiety about school.

5 How does Andrew have the strength to carry on?
  A He thinks of how long he has fought to get this far.
  B He thinks of how much his parents have worked to get this far.
  C He thinks of getting back to his friends at school.
  D He thinks it might be better tomorrow.

☞ **Answers and explanations on pages 237-238**

Read the poem below and answer the questions 6–10.

Tractor

Dragging an iron rake
the tractor wallows
across the ocean of the paddock
with a fine excitement of gulls
5   in its wake.

It has two large paddle wheels,
a funnel, with smoke;
and the captain is on the bridge.
Having cast off a couple of moments ago,
10 he sets a course for the opposite hedge.

William Hart-Smith

6 What does the poet imagine the tractor to be throughout the whole poem?
A   a garden rake
B   a steam-train
C   a paddle-steamer
D   a speedboat

7 Line 2 says the tractor 'wallows'. What does this tell you about how the tractor moves across the paddock?
A   smoothly and fast
B   backwards
C   unevenly and with difficulty
D   evenly and in a regular way

8 What word is used instead of 'flock' in stanza 1?
A   wake   B   excitement   C   ocean   D   gulls

9 Who is the 'captain' the poet refers to in line 8?
A   the owner of the farm
B   a sea captain who lives nearby
C   the person driving the tractor
D   none of the above

10 What does 'cast off' refer to in line 9?
A   starting the motor
B   getting rid of the gulls
C   dumping a load of fertiliser
D   losing a wheel

☞ **Answers and explanations on pages 237-238**

Read the text below and answer the questions 11–16.

Thales of Miletus

Thales of Miletus (circa 635 – 543 BCE) was an engineer, astronomer and mathematician. He predicted an eclipse and knew that the moon was a sphere. He is considered the father of science because, before Thales, the world was only understood in myths.

5   Thales thought that water was really the origin of everything. This was very significant because he was the first person recorded in history who tried to explain the physical world by rational thinking. Up till then it was only ever explained by reference to mythical gods—the gods and goddesses of fire, oceans, the sun, the moon and so on. Of course, his explanation about water was incorrect, but he had a huge influence on the way humans thought, and many scientists followed his example of seeking for explanations in nature.

10   Some stories about Thales show that he was also a practical person. He was able to use his intelligence to become wealthy. He bought all the olive presses in the city after predicting a good harvest. This way he controlled the production of olive oil.

Another story about Thales told how he solved a problem with a cunning mule. Salt was loaded on a mule and as they were travelling, the mule fell in a stream and the heavy load of
15   salt was partly dissolved by the water. This mule must have been smart because it soon realised that this was a way to make the load lighter. At every opportunity the mule would roll over when it came to water. Thales found a way to stop this habit. He loaded the mule with sponges instead of salt. Then when the mule rolled over, the sponges absorbed water and the load became much heavier. In due time it is said that this cured the mule of its bad habit.

20   On the other hand, there is a story of how Thales was not all that smart. One night Thales was looking at the sky and as he walked along, he fell into a ditch. A servant helped him up and said to him 'How do you expect to understand what is going on up in the sky if you do not even see what is at your feet?'

11 What was Thales's main contribution to the world's knowledge?
  A his contribution to mathematics
  B his contribution to astronomy
  C his contribution to science
  D his contribution to engineering

12 What was important about Thales's explanation that water was the origin of everything?
  A It explained the world through myths.   B It was wrong.
  C It referred to supernatural ideas.   D It was based on rational thinking.

13 How do we know that Thales was a practical person?
  A because he was the father of science
  B because he used his knowledge to make money
  C because he travelled on a mule
  D because he fell into a ditch while looking at the stars

☞ **Answers and explanations on pages 237-238**

14 What does 'circa 635 – 543 BCE' (line 1) mean?

- **A** Thales was born in 543 BCE and died in 635 BCE.
- **B** Thales was born in 635 BCE and died in 543 BCE.
- **C** Thales was born around 543 BCE and died around 635 BCE.
- **D** Thales was born around 635 BCE and died around 543 BCE.

15 What does 'rational thinking' mean (lines 5–6) as it is used in the text?

- **A** clear thought and reason
- **B** clever guessing
- **C** belief in the gods
- **D** imagination

16 How did Thales solve the problem with the mule?

- **A** He gradually put more and more salt in the mule's load.
- **B** He replaced the sponges with salt.
- **C** He gradually put more and more sponges in the mule's load.
- **D** He replaced the salt with sponges.

Read the text below and answer questions 17–21.

It seems very natural to you that if you have two dollars and you add two dollars to them, you have four dollars. But did you know that it may have taken human beings millions of years to be able to think this way? In fact, one of the most difficult things to teach children is the concept of numbers.

In very ancient times, when a man wanted to tell how many animals he owned, he had no system of numbers to use. Instead, he put a stone or a pebble into a bag for each animal. The more animals he had, the more stones he had.

Later on, man used tally marks to count. He would just scratch a line for each object he wanted to count, but he had no word to tell the number.

The next step in the development of the number system was probably the use of fingers. The word 'digit' comes from the Latin word *digitus*, which means 'finger'. And since we have ten fingers, this led to the general use of '10' in systems of numbers.

But in ancient times there was no single number system used all over the world. Some systems were based on 12, others were based on 60, others on 20 and still others on 2, 5 and 8. The system invented by the Romans about 2000 years ago was widely used by the people of Europe until about the 16th century. In fact, we still use the Roman numeral system on clocks and sometimes to show pages or chapters in books. But it was a very complicated system.

The number system we use today was invented by the Hindus in India thousands of years ago and was brought to Europe around the year 900 by Arabic traders. In this system, all numbers are written with the nine digits 1, 2, 3, 4, 5, 6, 7, 8, and 9 to show how many, and the zero. It is a decimal system, that is, it is built on the base of 10.

Adapted from *The Big Book of Tell Me Why* by Arkady Leokum, Barnes & Noble Books, New York, 1965; reproduced with permission

☞ **Answers and explanations on pages 237-238**

17 What do you think is the title of this text?

A *How Do We Count?*

B *Counting with Pebbles, Stones and Fingers*

C *How Did Our System of Counting Begin?*

D *The Roman Numeral System*

18 What reason is given for why number systems are generally based on the number 10?

A That was the biggest number that people could count to.

B People usually had no more than ten animals to count.

C It is the easiest system.

D We have ten fingers.

19 Who invented the number system we use?

A Romans

B Hindus

C Arabic traders

D Europeans

20 Which statement is true?

A There were many different number systems in ancient times.

B The Roman system is only used in Rome nowadays.

C Our system is called a digital system.

D Children very easily learn the concept of numbers.

21 How old is our number system?

A thousands of years old

B 1200 years old

C 2000 years old

D 400 years old

☞ **Answers and explanations on pages 237-238**

Read the text below and answer questions 22–25.

There are three main fingerprint patterns: loops, whorls and arches. In a loop pattern, the ridges enter from either side, re-curve and pass out either on the side they entered or the other side. In a whorl pattern, the ridges are usually circular. In an arch pattern the ridges enter from one side, make a rise in the centre and exit generally on the opposite side. Loop patterns have two focal points: the core or the centre of the loop, and the delta. The delta is the area of the pattern where the ridges come to a triangular point. The loop has a core and a delta, the whorl has two or more deltas, and the arch has neither a core nor a delta.

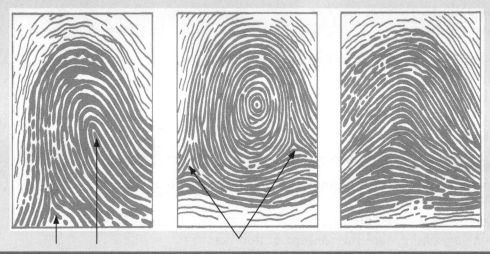

22 Which label would you put above the third diagram?

A arch   B whorl   C loop   D none of these

23 In the first diagram, you can see two arrows pointing to parts of that diagram. Looking at the arrow on the left, how would you label the part pointed to?

A arch   B whorl   C loop   D none of these

24 Keep looking at the first diagram and the two arrows. Looking at the arrow on the right, how would you label the part pointed to?

A arch   B delta   C core   D loop

25 In the second diagram, you can see an arrow pointing to two parts of the diagram. How would you label the parts pointed to?

A delta   B whorl   C core   D none of these

☞ **Answers and explanations on pages 237-238**

1 Pitar plays this maths game.

Think of a number. Double it. Add 3. Subtract 1. Take away the original number you thought of. Add 2. Take away the original number you thought of. Subtract 2. Add 4.

The answer Pitar gets is

3	4	5	6	8
A	B	C	D	E

2 Xan is in square F5 marked with an X.

Samuel is in C3, Alexis is in H1 and Frankie is in H8:

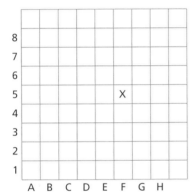

Which one of these statements is true?

A Alexis is closer to Xan than Samuel is.
B Alexis is closer to Xan than Frankie is.
C Frankie is closer to Xan than Samuel is.
D Samuel and Frankie are the same distance from Xan.
E Alexis and Samuel are the same distance from Xan.

3 Here are five cards with numbers:

Mia selected cards and added the numbers.
Which of these totals is impossible?

95	115	120	135	145
A	B	C	D	E

4 Rose is driving from Caddick to Beauty Point.

At 2:40 pm Rose is 85 km from Beauty Point.

At 3:10 pm she is 40 km from Beauty Point.

At what average speed has Rose been driving?

A 90 km/h **B** 80 km/h **C** 75 km/h
D 45 km/h **E** 30 km/h

5 The temperature in our classroom at 9 am was 23 °C.

The temperature rose half a degree every 15 min until 2 pm.

When did the temperature reach 30 °C?

A 12:00 pm **B** 12:30 pm **C** 1:30 pm
D 2:30 pm **E** 3:00 pm

6 Here is a number puzzle where *A*, *B* and *C* represent numbers:

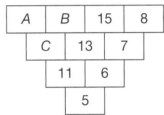

What is the value of *A* + *B* + *C*?

52	60	84	96	104
A	B	C	D	E

7 If six people take 8 h to paint a fence, how long would it take 16 people?

A 2 h **B** 2 h 20 min
C 3 h **D** 3 h 20 min
E 3 h 40 min

8 What fraction of this shape is shaded?

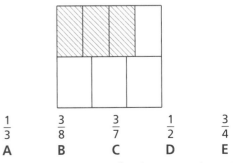

$\frac{1}{3}$	$\frac{3}{8}$	$\frac{3}{7}$	$\frac{1}{2}$	$\frac{3}{4}$
A	B	C	D	E

☞ **Answers and explanations on pages 238–239**

9 Noah, Daphne and George share a box of chocolates.

Noah has twice as many chocolates as Daphne. George has three times as many chocolates as Daphne.

If George has 12 chocolates, how many chocolates were in the box?

16	18	24	36	48
A	B	C	D	E

10 A pencil costs 80 cents. A pen costs $1.30 and a pencil case costs $4.20.

Harriet has $10 to spend. She buys two pens and a pencil case.

What is the maximum number of pencils Harriet can buy?

1	2	3	4	5
A	B	C	D	E

11 Eva has a 10:45 doctor's appointment. She arrives 8 min before the appointment time. Eva sits in the waiting room for 25 min. If she sees the doctor for 12 min, what time does she leave?

11:04	11:09	11:10	11:11	11:14
A	B	C	D	E

12 Mario, Rafael and Bruno are comparing the number of goals they had scored in a season.

Mario scored three more than twice as many as Rafael.

If Bruno had scored two more goals he would have scored half as many as Mario and Rafael together.

What was the total number of goals scored by the three players if Rafael had scored 11 goals?

52	33	45	48	50
A	B	C	D	E

13 Lucy has a container of $2 coins.

If she arranges the coins in piles of 3 she has 2 left over.

If she arranges the coins in piles of 4 she has 3 left over and if she arranges the coins in piles of 5 she has 2 left over.

If she has fewer than 50 coins in the container, what is the exact value of her coins?

$47	$54	$64	$76	$94
A	B	C	D	E

14 A sequence of numbers is changing by the same amount each time.

The fifth, sixth and eighth numbers are 12, 15 and 21.

What is the sum of the first and the one hundredth numbers in the sequence?

300	297	296	270	267
A	B	C	D	E

15 A pair of normal dice are rolled and the numbers on the uppermost sides are added.

Which of these totals is most likely?

4	5	6	7	8
A	B	C	D	E

16 Bronson was counting the number of toy cars in his collection.

The cars are red, green, blue and yellow.

One-third of the cars are red.

He started to draw a column graph to record the colours, but the column for red cars is missing:

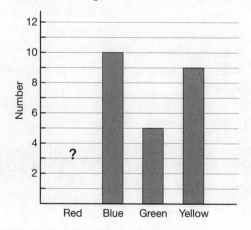

How many cars are in Bronson's collection?

23	28	32	33	36
A	B	C	D	E

☞ **Answers and explanations on pages 238-239**

Instructions

1 In the Writing test, you are asked to write two short pieces of writing. You will have 20 minutes for each piece. One piece will be a true or imaginary story, and the other will ask you to give your opinion about something.
2 Write your answer on the following pages.
3 Remember that the amount you write is not as important as the quality of your writing. Make your writing clear, lively and interesting to read. Be careful to write on the topic you are given.
4 Ask your parent, teacher or an adult if you need any special help.
5 If you finish writing before the time is up, use the rest of the time to go over your work and make changes you think might improve it.

Story

Imagine you are a scientist and that you have made a great discovery or invention. Perhaps it is something you have daydreamed about—a medical cure or a clever invention to save people time and energy.

Describe your discovery and its importance. Write about some experiences you had and your feelings about your discovery.

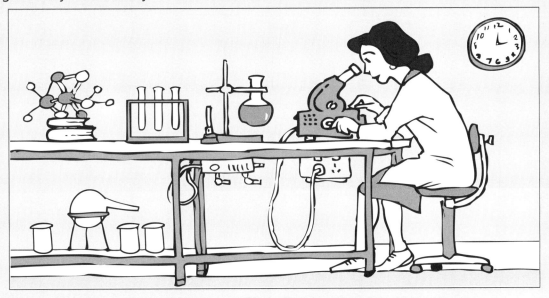

Opinion

City life is much better than country life. Do you think this statement is true or not? Give at least two reasons.

Your writing will be judged on:

- what you have to say
- how well you organise the way you say it
- how clearly and effectively you express yourself.

Parents and teachers might like to use the checklists in the Answer section on page 240 to give you some feedback. Remember: This is just practice, so don't worry too much if they suggest you need to improve in some way. You can use this page for planning and rough work.

START YOUR RESPONSE ON THE NEXT PAGE

WEEK 1

READING
Literary texts   Pages 4–11

Practice Task 1

1 A **2** B **3** D **4** C **5** A **6** C

EXPLANATIONS

1 You have to work this out from the conversation between the two children. 'Watch it, you stupid thing' suggests the correct answer. The boy does not speak very kindly (so does not seem happy to be with his sister), but he does not want her to get hurt (so he cares about her).

2 Although clouds are mentioned, there is no evidence that a storm is coming, so not A. 'The wind had dropped and the powdery dust on the road lay undisturbed' tells you it is not D. There is evidence that it is very hot and still, and much more than just warm, so not C: the clouds did not give them 'any relief', meaning the clouds did not bring rain to make it cooler; there is a heat haze ('hazy monotony'); and the trumpeter says 'bloomin' hot'.

3 There is good evidence for this answer if you look for it: 'Occasionally, a ute or truck from one of the nearby farms' (so a country area); 'hazy monotony'; the 'undisturbed' dust on the road; and the children's eagerness to see what is approaching (nothing much happens).

4 Carol repeats that the truck is 'not from around here' and says 'you can tell', but does not say how. This suggests that it is simply because she knows all the trucks from around there. 'Anyway, there's a few of them' makes her feel more certain (they rarely see a convoy of trucks on their roads), but it is not the main reason.

5 There is plenty of evidence for this one, but you need to look for it: 'moved slowly'; 'the trucks laboured' (worked hard); 'the trucks ground up the road' ('grind' can mean to work hard); the trumpeter 'lurched' with the truck and the children were surprised she didn't fall off; the truck pulled up 'with a groan'.

6 It helps if you know the meaning of the word from other contexts. Speechless means not having any words to react to what you see or hear because your feelings are so strong. The children could feel all these things and had strong reactions to them, so A, C and D are possible, but C is the most likely answer. The text strongly suggests the children are bored and in the middle of nowhere, and would probably be unable to express their surprise when they see a woman lying on top of a truck playing a trumpet!

Practice Task 2

1 B **2** A **3** C **4** C **5** C **6** A

EXPLANATIONS

1 Lines 5 to 8 should tell you this clearly. The writer mentions 'tiny, itchy blisters', 'red and lumpy skin', 'scratching' and 'sores'. Then there is the doctor's comment about a 'very nasty allergy' (lines 10–11).

2 Lines 10–11 tell you this. The doctor says, 'Whatever chemical it is, is in the smog, and gives Stuart a very nasty allergy, indeed'.

3 Line 12 tells you this. You might be confused by the words 'wasting his money' and choose B, but the father does not say that he thinks the doctor charges 'too much money'. He calls the doctor a 'witchdoctor' because she did not really know what the problem was, and she tried all sorts of treatments, which did not work, and so wasted his money.

④ The first paragraph tells you this clearly. The narrator mentions 'previous visits' so we know it is not the first time. He also says he has read 'all the comics' so it seems he has been there many times, not just once. We also know that the doctor has tried many treatments, so this also suggests the narrator has been there many times before.

⑤ In this type of question, you have to check each answer choice—look for evidence that it is true or not. It is a good idea to tick those there is evidence for (e.g. A, B and D) and cross any you don't find evidence for or find evidence against. Lines 23–24 tells you quite clearly that the narrator's mum is not very happy about the new home.

⑥ You should get the answer easily from lines 18 to 21, but you need to read the text carefully to make sure all parts of your chosen answer match the text. The narrator says that the house is 'flaky' (old paint), the gutters are 'leaky' and 'over-flowing with peppercorn leaves', the tanks are 'filled with smelly green algae'. There are mice and possums in the house and the fruit trees have not been pruned. If this evidence is not enough, the narrator says, 'The house was a picture of tangled neglect'.

Practice Task 3

1 C 2 B 3 D 4 A 5 C 6 A

EXPLANATIONS

❶ You should find this answer easily in line 3. However, you have to read carefully to avoid being tricked into answer A (magician). He is a famous magician of legend, but you are asked what people said about him when he was a young boy.

❷ You will find the answer in the second paragraph (lines 20–21). If you expected the answer to be in the first paragraph and did not read carefully beyond this, you

might have got it wrong. Remember that questions are not always asked in the order in which the answers appear in the text.

❸ The answer is at the end of the first paragraph (lines 17–19). You need to be careful here. He did not laugh *at* the people, he laughed *to himself*.

❹ The last two lines give the best clue to the answer: 'he had known that this would happen to him'. Also, you know that Merlin has never worried about people staring at him and gossiping about him, and that he waited for the horsemen at the city gates (so expected them to come).

❺ If you have never heard of 'set spurs' or 'steed' before, you have to work harder to get this right. It seems likely from the sentence that a 'steed' is a horse, so that means A or C. The sentence says the horseman 'galloped off', so it seems likely that the setting of the spurs is connected to the horse's movement.

❻ All these things are mentioned in the text but A, C and D are what people said about Merlin (gossip and rumour). Only A is presented as fact.

Real Test

1 D 2 C 3 B 4 A 5 D 6 B

EXPLANATIONS

❶ The answer is given in paragraph 3, though you have to read that paragraph carefully to get it. Be careful not to choose B instead—because the Royal George (inn) is also mentioned. There is more than one clue that it is an inn so not A or C.

❷ Any of these answers seem reasonable at first glance. However, there are many clues that he is a sailor, so C. You might be tricked into choosing D as the writer mentions he 'seemed like a mate or a skipper' but this is only his opinion. We don't know for sure he is a captain (or 'skipper').

3 Evidence for all the other statements can be found. There is no evidence that he seeks the company of others; in fact there is evidence for the opposite. For example, he asks the narrator if there is much company at the inn and is pleased that the answer is no: 'This is the berth for me.' What they learn from the barrow man supports this view. Also the narrator says that at first they thought he was looking around to seek out men like himself from the sea but later realised he was wanting to avoid them ('desirous to avoid them').

4 The answer to question 5 gives some clues but the words around 'connoisseur' are the main clue. The narrator and his father are probably used to sailors drinking quickly and heavily and displaying no manners or particular interest in how good the rum is—as long as it is rum. This sailor drinks slowly and seems to appreciate the taste. He is not desperate to swig the rum down quickly.

5 You have to draw your own conclusion here; it is not clearly stated. We read that the man threw down his money in a careless way as he said these words: 'he threw down three or four gold pieces on the threshold'. This suggests he does not care if he spends it all or not. His actual words—'You can tell me when I've worked through that"—suggest he doesn't mind being asked for more because he has more to spend.

6 The answer lies in this sentence: 'And indeed bad as his clothes were and coarsely as he spoke, he seemed like a mate or skipper accustomed to be obeyed or to strike.' You need to avoid the tricky A to get this right. It is close but not quite accurate.

THINKING SKILLS
Critical thinking—Identifying the main idea Pages 13–15

Real Test 1

1 A **2** A **3** C **4** D **5** B **6** A **7** C **8** B **9** D **10** C

EXPLANATIONS

1 The creator of the text wants you to accept that knights were expected to live by a code of chivalry and A is the statement in the list that best expresses this. The rest of the text gives you reason to believe the main idea; it gives supporting information about what chivalry means.

2 The creator of the text wants you to accept that guinea pigs need a rich, stimulating environment and A is the statement in the list that best expresses this. The rest of the text gives you reasons to believe the main idea by providing supporting information about why it is important and about some of the natural behaviours guinea pigs should be able to express in their environment. The final sentence is a call to action to provide this environment for your pet guinea pigs.

3 The creator of the text wants you to accept that different countries and cultures celebrate birthdays in different ways and C is the statement in the list that best expresses this. The rest of the text gives you reasons to believe the main idea by providing supporting information about some of the different traditions around the world.

4 The creator of the text wants you to accept that, even though brush turkeys have a reputation for destroying gardens, they can actually be good for gardens. D is the statement in the list that best expresses this. The rest of the text supports the main idea by detailing the ways brush turkeys are good for gardens.

The final sentence is a call to action to consider letting a brush turkey move into your garden.

5 The creator of the text wants you to accept there are many fascinating facts about elephants and B is the statement in the list that best expresses this. The rest of the text gives you reasons to believe the main idea by listing some of those fascinating facts.

6 The main idea the creator of the text wants you to accept is that Venus is inhospitable to human life. All the information in the text supports that idea.

7 The main idea the writer of the text wants you to accept is that *The Secret Garden* is a wonderful story about friendship, family and love. Other information in the text supports this idea.

8 The main idea the creator of the text wants you to accept is that they do not want to change schools. The writer gives reasons to support this main idea.

9 The main idea the creator of the text wants you to accept is that swamps and other types of wetlands are vitally important for the environment. The rest of the text supports this main idea.

10 The main idea the writer of the text wants you to accept is that the dam poses unacceptable risks to the environment. The rest of the text supports this main idea.

THINKING SKILLS
Critical thinking—Assessing the impact of further evidence to strengthen an argument   Pages 17–19

Real Test 2

1 C 2 A 3 C 4 B 5 D 6 C 7 D 8 C 9 A 10 B

EXPLANATIONS

1 The argument the government wildlife spokesperson is making is when venomous snakes need to be removed from a property only a suitably qualified, licensed person should do this. The statement that a licensed reptile handler must have completed a reptile-handling course and have two years experience handling venomous snakes strengthens the spokesperson's claim.

2 The health expert claims that physical exercise is good for the brain as well as the body because it increases blood flow, which brings more oxygen to the brain for it to work well. The statement that strengthens the importance of exercise for the brain is that the brain uses about 20% of the body's oxygen. The other statements do not specifically apply to the beneficial effects of exercise on the brain.

3 Davy needs to support his claims in the advertisement in order to sell his tent quickly. The statement that the tent has barely been used strengthens his claims. A and B weaken the advertisement and D is a call to action that strengthens the advertisement but not the claims made in them about the tent.

4 The podiatrist claims everyone should take proper care of their feet to avoid foot problems. The statement that most strengthens this claim tells what could happen if you don't take care of your feet: your muscles, bones and joints can weaken.

5 The argument is that Harry Houdini is one of the most famous magicians of all time because of his amazing stunts. The statement that strengthens this argument is that audiences around the world sat on the edges of their seats as they watched him perform. D best supports the argument because to become one of the most famous magicians in the world requires a large, impressed audience worldwide.

6 The politician's argument is that balloons should be banned because they pose a threat to wildlife. The statement that wildlife can become entangled in the strings on balloons is another example of a threat to wildlife and so most strengthens this argument.

7 Ali's argument is that pets can make us physically and mentally healthier. The statement that research shows pet owners make fewer visits to the doctor most strengthens this argument.

8 Jade's argument is that a robot that moves like a cockroach could be a good design for a robot that rescues people in rubble after an earthquake. The statement that cockroaches can squeeze into tiny places by redistributing their exoskeleton sections most strengthens her argument.

9 The student council's argument is that the school should honour the vision of the Olympic Games and include the arts in the annual sports carnival. The statement that the founder of the modern Olympics had included plans for athletics and the arts most strengthens this argument. The statement about ancient trumpet competitions is an example of the arts being central to the ancient Olympics but is not the statement that **most** strengthens the argument.

10 The spokesperson's argument is that people should urgently donate money to train koala detection dogs because the organisation needs exact information about where koalas live. The statement that, by successfully training dogs, the organisation can work faster and more accurately to protect koalas most strengthens this argument.

THINKING SKILLS
Critical thinking—Assessing the impact of further evidence to weaken an argument Pages 21–23

Real Test 3

1 B **2** C **3** D **4** A **5** D **6** A **7** B **8** C **9** B **10** D
EXPLANATIONS

1 The argument is that bananas are a complete health-food package. The statement that most weakens Hilda's argument is that bananas are deficient in protein so would not provide adequate nutrition for long-term survival.

2 The argument is that eating cauliflower is good for your health. The statement that weakens the argument is that cauliflower can cause abdominal discomfort in a small number of people. For these people, cauliflower would not be good for their health.

3 Cody's argument is that he'd be hopeless at table tennis because his reflexes are slow. The statement that weakens his argument is that you can develop quick reflexes to improve at table tennis.

4 Jeffrey's argument is that Willem is a great role model and sets a good example of being a good sport. The fact that Willem argued with the referee undermines Jeffrey's argument and therefore weakens it.

5 Ashleigh's argument is that she uses antihistamines which make her drowsy because it's better for her to be sleepy than constantly sneezing. The statement that Ashleigh works as a forklift operator weakens her argument because forklift operators need to be mentally alert at work and should not take any medication that might make them drowsy. The fact that a potential side effect of Ashleigh's particular antihistamine is drowsiness would put Ashleigh and others at risk in the workplace.

6 Ruby's argument is that cats make the best pets because they don't need a lot of space and the way they chase things is cute. The statement that studies estimate each roaming pet cat kills 115 native animals per year weakens this argument. The fact that pet cats roam undermines the argument that they don't need a lot of space and killing native animals undermines the argument that chasing things is cute.

7 Tom's argument is that shark nets keep swimmers safe from sharks. The statement that most weakens this argument is that around 40% of sharks are caught on the 'wrong side' (beach side) of nets. If the sharks are on the beach side of the net, it means the net did not prevent them from reaching the beach and potentially biting a human. The statement about other marine species also getting caught and killed in the nets weakens the argument in favour of the nets but it does not weaken the argument that the nets keep humans safe from sharks.

8 Nina's argument is that email is better than post because email is faster. The statement that it is exciting to anticipate and receive a letter in the post weakens this argument about speed.

9 Cooper's argument is that all snakes are awful because they bite. The statement that most weakens this argument is that snakes will normally only bite when provoked or hurt.

10 The argument is that floods are bad for the environment. The statement that floods replenish groundwater weakens the argument, since replenishing groundwater is of benefit to the environment.

MATHEMATICAL REASONING
Whole numbers and money   Pages 27–28

Real Test 1

1 C **2** C **3** D **4** A **5** C **6** B **7** C **8** B **9** D **10** E

EXPLANATIONS

1 115 rounds to 100 (changes by 15), 183 rounds to 200 (17), 238 rounds to 200 (38), 277 rounds to 300 (23) and 326 rounds to 300 (26). This means the number with the largest change is 238 which drops by 38.

2
$$\begin{array}{r} 265\ 893 \\ +\quad 600 \\ \hline 266\ 493 \end{array}$$

3 The largest number 852 is formed using the digits in descending order. The smallest number 258 is formed using the digits in ascending order. To find the difference use subtraction.

$$\begin{array}{r} 852 \\ -\ 258 \\ \hline 594 \end{array}$$

4 $2.38 rounds to $2.40. Adding 10 cents gives $2.50, then 50 cents gives $3 and then another $2 makes $5. This means Harry will receive a $2 coin, a 50c coin and a 10c coin. He receives 3 coins as change.

5
$$\begin{array}{r} 246 \\ -\ 120 \\ \hline 126 \end{array}$$
Edick has 126 more stickers than Clint. Half of 126 is 126 ÷ 2 which is 63. Edrick gives Clint 63 stickers.

6

130	520	1200
× 4	+ 430	− 950
520	950	250

The cost of a hotel is $250.

7

152	152
− 79	+ 79
73	231

The two numbers are 73 and 231.

8 As 2 × 3 + 2 is 8, Kate bought 2 lots of 3 punnets and then 2 punnets. Now, 2 × $6 is $12, plus 2 × $2.50 is $5, so the total is $17.

9 As 4 + 1 is 5, from 4 °C a drop of 4 degrees is 0 °C and then another 1 degree is −1 °C. If the temperature drops another 2 degrees it must be −3 °C at 6 am.

10 The cost will be 360 ÷ 5. Doubling gives 720 ÷ 10 which is 72. Each of the friends pay $72.

Real Test 2

1 B **2** C **3** D **4** A **5** D **6** E **7** D **8** E **9** C **10** C

EXPLANATIONS

1 As 6 × 4 is 24 and 24 + 18 is 24 + 10 + 8 = 34 + 8 = 42, Idris picked 42 oranges on the weekend.

2 As 80 × 4 is 320, the bananas cost $3.20. This means William received $1.80 as change. As 2 × 9 is 18, then 20 × 9 = 180. William received 9 coins.

3 36 + 18 is 36 + 10 + 8 = 46 + 8 = 54. This means that Wilma has 54 teapots. 36 + 54 is 36 + 50 + 4 = 86 + 4 = 90. The sisters have a total of 90 teapots altogether.

4 As 35 × 2 is 70 and 120 + 70 is 190, Jordie has spent $190. As 200 − 190 is 10, Jordie has $10 remaining.

5 25 is a multiple of 5 and when 25 is divided by 6 there is a remainder of 1.

6 First, 6 + 12 is 18 and 12 × 6 is 72. As 72 − 18 is 72 − 12 − 6 = 60 − 6 = 54, Amelia's answer is 54.

7 The number is eighteen thousand three hundred and sixty-four. This means the value of the 8 is 8000 and the value of the 6 is 60.

8000
− 60
7940

The difference is 7940.

8 As 12 × 2 is 24, then 120 × 2 is 240. This means the necklace cost $240. As 120 + 240 is 360, the total amount was $360.

9 Leo bought one more salad roll than Oscar and paid $3 more. This means the cost of a salad roll is $3 and so a bottle of water costs $2. As 3 + 2 × 2 is 7, Harry will pay $7.

10 If Charlotte had 40 points then Scarlett had 40 + 30 = 70 points. This means Billie had 70 ÷ 2 = 35 points. Also, Doneta had 50 + 35 = 85 points. The finishing order was Doneta, Scarlett, Charlotte and Billie. Also 40 + 35 is 75 which is less than 85. Statement 3 is the correct statement.

MATHEMATICAL REASONING
Fractions and decimals   Pages 31–33

Real Test 3

1 C **2** A **3** B **4** A **5** C **6** D **7** E **8** C **9** D **10** E

EXPLANATIONS

1 There are 20 squares in the diagram. As $\frac{4}{5} = \frac{4 \times 4}{4 \times 5} = \frac{16}{20}$, Shannon has to shade 16 out of the 20 squares. She has already shaded 11 squares. This means she has to shade another 5.

2 There are 8 sectors. Four are unshaded. $\frac{4}{8} = \frac{4 \times 1}{4 \times 2} = \frac{1}{2}$

3 Half of a half of 24 = half of 12 = 6

4 0.2, 0.6, 1.2, 1.4 is increasing in size.

5 As $\frac{3}{4}$ is $\frac{9}{12}$, and 9 – 4 is 5, Anonna needs to shade another 5 rectangles.

6 As one-fifth is $\frac{1}{5} = \frac{2}{10}$, Angelo has read two-tenths of the book. As $1 = \frac{10}{10}$, and 10 – 2 = 8, Angelo will take 8 nights to read the rest of the book.

7 If $\frac{2}{3}$ of a number is 24, then, by division, $\frac{1}{3}$ of the number is 12. By multiplication, $\frac{3}{3}$, or the whole number, is 36. Twice the number is 36 × 2 = 72.

8 $\frac{1}{3}$ is $\frac{4}{12}$ and 1 is $\frac{12}{12}$. The number line has been marked in twelfths. As $\frac{3}{4}$ is $\frac{9}{12}$, the fraction is located at C.

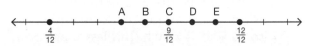

9 There are 6 multiples of 4: 4, 8, 12, 16, 20 and 24. As 24 – 6 is 18, the fraction of numbers that are not multiples is $\frac{18}{24}$, which is $\frac{3}{4}$.

10 First, $\frac{3}{10} = 0.3$ and $\frac{1}{2} = 0.5$. This means 0.08, 0.20, $\frac{3}{10} = 0.30$, 0.31, $\frac{1}{2} = 0.50$. As 8, 20, 30, 31, 50 are from smallest to largest then the order is 0.08, 0.2, $\frac{3}{10}$, 0.31, $\frac{1}{2}$.

Real Test 4

1 D 2 B 3 D 4 A 5 B 6 E 7 C 8 B 9 E 10 E

EXPLANATIONS

1 Two-thirds shaded would mean the first two rows. This leaves 4 squares in the unshaded row.

2 Difference = 2.0 – 1.6 = 0.4.

3 Three-quarters of 8 = 3 × a quarter of 8 = 3 × 2 = 6. This means Uncle Peter eats 6 slices and 2 remain.

4 If Jack's mother is 36, Jack is 12 (by dividing 36 by 3), and so Jack's father is 48 (by multiplying 12 by 4).

5 As $\frac{1}{4}$ of 12 is 12 ÷ 4 = 3, Alyssa shades 3 squares. This leaves 9 unshaded squares. As $\frac{1}{3}$ of 9 is 3, so $\frac{2}{3}$ of 9 is 6. Hanna shades 6 squares, leaving 3 out of 12 squares unshaded. This can be written as $\frac{3}{12}$, or $\frac{1}{4}$ of the rectangle.

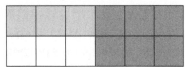

6 Use $1 = \frac{8}{8}$, and $\frac{1}{4} = \frac{2}{8}$. As $\frac{8}{8} - \frac{2}{8} - \frac{1}{8} = \frac{5}{8}$, Adam gave $\frac{1}{8}$ of the cupcakes to his friends. If each friend received $\frac{1}{8}$ of the cupcakes, Adam gave 5 friends some cupcakes.

7 The top rectangle is $\frac{1}{2}$ of the original square and $\frac{1}{2}$ of this rectangle is shaded. As $\frac{1}{2}$ of $\frac{1}{2}$ is $\frac{1}{4}$, the large shaded triangle is $\frac{1}{4}$ of the square. The small square is $\frac{1}{4}$ of the large square and $\frac{1}{2}$ is shaded. As $\frac{1}{2}$ of $\frac{1}{4}$ is $\frac{1}{8}$ the small shaded triangle is $\frac{1}{8}$ of the original square. As $\frac{1}{4} + \frac{1}{8}$ is $\frac{2}{8} + \frac{1}{8} = \frac{3}{8}$, then $\frac{3}{8}$ of the original square is shaded.

8 As $\frac{7}{10}$ is $\frac{14}{20}$, there must be 14 red balls in the bag. As 20 – 14 is 6, there are 6 balls that are not red. There could be 1 green, 1 yellow and 4 blue balls but this is not an option. There could be 2 green, 2 yellow and 2 blue balls. This is one of the options.

9 As $1 - \frac{7}{10}$ is $\frac{3}{10}$, then $\frac{3}{10}$ of her original number of lemons is 12. As $12 \div 3$ is 4, then $\frac{1}{10}$ of her original lemons is 4. This means she sold $7 \times 4 = 28$ lemons. As 7×3 is 21, Emma made $21.

10 In the fifth shape, 5 out of 9 squares are shaded which is more than half. The other shapes have half or less than half of the squares shaded.

WRITING
'Imagine if …' story   Pages 38–39

Practice Task 3

Who? A child about to turn 10 years old

When? The year 2522

Where? A home on planet Earth

What? A surprise birthday celebration about to take place

Task 6

1 a phantasmagorical

b KX99—android from Jupiter

c wham, whiz, pow, whoosh

2 mindblaster, timezapper, timezapped

WEEK 2

READING
Poetry   Pages 46–50

Practice Task 1

1 C 2 A 3 A 4 B 5 C

EXPLANATIONS

The questions for 'Corroboree' are all a little different, but to get any of them right you need to understand the general meaning of the whole poem—what is being described and what is important to the poet.

1 In this type of question, you have to look for clues about each of the possible answers. In this poem, lines 1 and 2 tell you it is early evening: 'Hot day dies', 'cook time comes', and 'between the sunset and the sleep-time'. If you need more clues, the dancers dancing by 'firelight' (line 4) and 'the great surrounding dark' (line 11) should help you.

2 In this type of question, you have to look at more than one line, and think about the meanings of words you might not know (e.g. 'compels' in line 7 means 'forces'). Lines 7 and 8 tell you the answer, but you have to read both lines: the didgeridoo 'compels … eager feet to stamp'.

3 You have to look at the following line to get the answer correct. If you do not, you might think it is the dancers (C) as the line before (line 10) mentions the dancing corroboree. Or you might think it is B as 'ghosts' are similar to 'spirits'. Or you may be tricked into D—'those watching'—because of the word 'watching'.

4 You have to work out that the word 'weave' is not being used normally (weaving wool or cotton). If you are not sure whether it is A or B, 'stories of the tribe' tells you the dancers are expressing stories from the past, not new stories. Using your own experience and knowledge will also help.

5 From line 10 to line 15 the image created is a ghostly, other-worldly scene – 'spirit things', 'surrounding dark', 'ghost-gums', 'eerie the scene', eerie the sounds', 'wild setting' – so C. The energy (A) and the rhythm (D) are mentioned but in the first half of the poem. A viewer might find the scene magical (B) but the poet does not say or suggest this. Her emphasis is on the eerie, unearthly atmosphere.

Practice Task 2

This poem is a good example of how poets use imagery—comparing one thing to another—to create a picture for us. It is also a good example of how they link smaller images to make one big picture. You may find this poem quite difficult, and you may need to read it a few times to understand the imagery.

1 A **2** C **3** A **4** A **5** D

EXPLANATIONS

1 Lines 1 and 2 tell you the answer to this question: 'The beach is … A soft ripe melon'. Remember, you sometimes need to read a few lines to get an answer—one idea is not always expressed within one line.

2 Again you have to read a few lines to get the answer (from line 6 to line 8): 'the sea … / With its sharp, / Sharp white teeth'. You then need to connect the idea of 'teeth' (for the waves) to the idea of a mouth (for the whole sea). The tricky part here is that the word 'mouth' is not mentioned by the poet.

3 If you got Question 2 right, you should get this right. The colour of the 'teeth' (white) should help you work out that the poet is talking about the waves.

4 Answers A, B and C are all green so you might find this a little difficult. It would help you to think about a melon and its rind, and to realise that the rind is behind the pale yellow of the fruit (the sand).

5 If you have worked out the images of the melon for the beach, the mouth for the sea and the teeth for the waves, you will realise the waves are eating the beach.

Practice Task 3

1 A **2** B **3** A **4** D **5** A

EXPLANATIONS

1 The poet likens the ant to a person at many points—'explorer', 'made up his mind', 'he had his ma's consent'—and tells the tale of his adventures in his small world as though he is a human exploring a vast and difficult landscape. If you understand this, you will get the right answer. By seeing the ant's life from down there on the ground with him and imagining what it must be like—perhaps for the first time—he is aiming to help us understand an ant's challenging life. You might have chosen D but the poem does not 'contrast' the life of a human and an ant.

2 It helps to be familiar with the word 'consent'. However, you can also work it out. The answer is not A, as this does not quite make sense here with the line following. It is not C, as there is no evidence that she encouraged the ant. It is not D, as 'permission' perfectly matches 'consent' here.

3 If you understand the poem as described in the answer to question 1, you will get this right. He goes down a small dip in the ground but because he is so small, it seems like a dark and gloomy gully (or valley). It is not B or D as the poet is not describing a landscape that we might walk in. The word 'down' tells you it is not C, as a shadow would not send the ant down anything.

4 Again, if you understand the overall meaning of the poem you will answer this correctly. The desert was 'feet and feet across' (using the old system of measurement in feet and inches, which you probably know), so we know it is not really a desert (so not C); instead it is just a stretch of ground (maybe 3 feet, or about a metre). Describing it this way helps us appreciate how vast the distance seems to the ant. We know the ant is wandering a long way from home (A) and we know the ant is getting tired (B) but these lines do not give us this information.

5 All these answers seem reasonable but C and D are too general and do not really explain the poem's effectiveness. B is

probably true—most of us find ants interesting—but again this does not really explain why the poem works well. The only one that does is A. Most of us have spent time watching little ants climbing over rough dirt, sometimes climbing leaves and sometimes carrying bits of twig or leaf on their backs, and wondered what it must be like to be so small and down so low, and carrying on so busily in what must look like a huge dangerous world.

Real Test

1 B **2** D **3** D **4** B **5** C

EXPLANATIONS

1 The last two lines give the answer. He would prefer the people upstairs to live downstairs so he wouldn't hear their noise. He does not mention moving himself (so not A) and there is no evidence he might want to meet the people upstairs or go to their parties (so not C or D).

2 The poet does not really think the people are doing ballet or any other activities described (so not A, B, or C); it just sounds like this is what they are doing. They are just ordinary people doing everyday things but they make a lot of noise doing them, or perhaps the building just carries the noise easily. So D is the answer.

3 You have to use your own experience here. Line 10 mentions people are going to the bathroom so we can guess he is talking about the end of the night (perhaps after a party but perhaps after an ordinary evening of moving around the flat) and we can guess that the noise might get less or even stop for a while late in the evening (so D) rather than increase (so not A). B and C do not make sense in this context.

4 All of the answers are mentioned in the poem but only one—pogo sticks—are mentioned as being supplied by the residents to their guests (line 8). You have

probably heard of pogo sticks but if you haven't, they are sticks on springs. You stand on them and jump around, a bit like a kangaroo.

5 We know the poet is irritated by the noises because he says he wishes his neighbours would move downstairs. If we think about the whole poem, and about the way the poet uses his imagination to come up with funny things the neighbours might be doing, you should conclude that he enjoys doing this. It is a lighthearted, fun poem about something many people experience when living in flats or apartments. So the answer is both A and B (so C).

THINKING SKILLS
Critical thinking—Drawing a conclusion
Pages 52–54

Real Test 1

1 D **2** C **3** C **4** A **5** B **6** A **7** B **8** D **9** C **10** D

EXPLANATIONS

1 The only stamps collected by Mia that are not collected by either Yoshi or Mahesh are stamps from Greece and Singapore.

2 John likes stories that could be true so he should also like stories that Rasha likes (real-life stories about creepy humans) and stories that are Evie's favourites (survivalist or adventure stories that are plausible enough to be true).

3 If Cinnamon does not go out for a ride, all three of the other horses will ride so the conclusion is that Sugar and Phantom will ride with Oakie.

4 The main conclusion that can be drawn from the text is that house dust comes from everywhere and can cause problems for people's health. C and D are also conclusions that can be drawn from the text but neither of these is the main conclusion.

5 If it's correct that you need to exercise at least every second day to regain muscle strength within six weeks then none of the elderly people recovering from pneumonia who do less exercise than every second day will regain their muscle strength within six weeks.

6 The information tells us that if the remote car is not cleaned, it has no chance of selling for the best price. So this conclusion that it sold for the best price is not possible.

7 The plants grown by Chloe that are not grown by either Levi or Na are beans and lettuce.

8 According to the climbing instructor, if a climber has not had at least 10 hours practice then they do not have a chance of progressing to the next level. Therefore none of the climbers who have had less than 10 hours practice will progress to the next level.

9 If Max does not have a clown, then he must have a pinata. And since he has a pinata, he must also go to the skate park.

10 Since everyone had to vote for two out of the three genres, knowing that no drama club member voted for both musical and historical drama tells you all students must have voted for comedy. Comedy must also have been the only genre that all drama club members voted for because each genre got at least one vote.

THINKING SKILLS
Critical thinking—Identifying an assumption   Pages 56–57

Real Test 2

1 B 2 C 3 D 4 D 5 A 6 B 7 C 8 A 9 D **10** D

EXPLANATIONS

1 Ella's conclusion is that there is nothing wrong with dropping rubbish. She has based this conclusion on the evidence that everyone else does it. So for her conclusion

to hold it must be assumed that it is okay do something if everyone else does it: everyone else drops rubbish + it's okay to do something if everyone else does it = there's nothing wrong with dropping rubbish.

2 Josh's conclusion is that Ying is a good goal shooter. He has based this conclusion on the evidence that Ying scored four goals on Saturday. So for his conclusion to hold it must be assumed that anyone who scores four goals is a good goal shooter: Ying scored four goals on Saturday + anyone who scores four goals is a good goal shooter = Ying is a good goal shooter.

3 Lee's conclusion is that students should wear the proper school uniform. He has based this conclusion on the evidence that not wearing the proper school uniform would hurt the reputation of the school. So for his conclusion to hold it must be assumed that students should not do something that would hurt the reputation of the school: not wearing the proper school uniform would hurt the reputation of the school + students should not do something that would hurt the reputation of the school = students should wear the proper school uniform.

4 Lily's conclusion is that Jun loves working on the project. She has based this conclusion on the evidence that Jun is staying home to work on it. So for this conclusion to hold it must be assumed that anyone who stays home to work on a project must love working on the project.

5 Ben's conclusion is that Dad must not scratch the car. He has based this conclusion on the evidence that Mum will get really upset if he scratches the car one more time. So for this conclusion to hold it must be assumed that Dad should not do something that would upset Mum.

6 Isaah's conclusion is that Annabel's diet enables her to perform so well. The evidence for this conclusion is that Annabel is one of the top triathletes in Australia and she uses a nutritionist to help with her diet. For Isaah's conclusion to hold true his assumption must be that the nutritionist is an expert in diet and athletic performance.

7 Fern's conclusion is that Halyna will look terrific in a Mad Hatter hat. The evidence is that Liam is going to help his mum make a hat for Halyna to dress as her favourite book character for a school party and Halyna loves the Mad Hatter. For Fern's conclusion to hold true it must be assumed that Liam is going to make a Mad Hatter hat for Halyna to wear.

8 Patrick has drawn the conclusion that there will be tasty dog treats provided for the dogs. The evidence is that it's a birthday party for dogs. For Patrick's conclusion to hold, his assumption must be that parties always have appropriate party food for guests and, because this is a party for dogs, there will be dog treats provided. C and D could also be assumed from Tilda's information but these are not the assumptions that have led to Patrick's conclusion.

9 Chad has concluded that the storm on Tuesday must have damaged the tree limb. The evidence is that the limb fell off on Saturday and there had been a storm on Tuesday. For Chad's conclusion to hold true, his assumption must be that it can take days for a damaged tree limb to fall down after a storm.

10 Octavia's conclusion is that Gabbi must think she's improved enough to make it onto the team this year because she was really upset last year when she tried out and failed. The evidence that has led to this conclusion is that Gabbi was devastated about failing last year and so

has been practising before trying out again this year. For Octavia's conclusion to hold true, the assumption must be that Gabbi would only try out if she felt she would make it onto the team (and not fail again).

> **THINKING SKILLS**
> *Critical thinking—Checking reasoning*
> *to detect errors*   Pages 59–61

Real Test 3

1 D **2** A **3** B **4** B **5** C **6** B **7** D **8** C **9** B **10** A

EXPLANATIONS

1 Neither Ria nor Faisal's reasoning is correct. Uma reasons that the tracks are large and in sets of three. However, the tour guide does not say that the Pluto beast is the **only** three-footed creature outside the compound. So Ria cannot say the tracks **must** come from a Pluto beast. Faisal's reasoning is flawed because the tour guide says each foot can be **up to** 60 cm long so it could be possible that a 30-cm footprint is from a Pluto beast.

2 Only Ilja's reasoning is correct. We know that Ms Street always gives an early mark when she is in a good mood. And she's always in a good mood if it has been windy when she is on lunchtime playground duty. Therefore Ilja's reasoning is correct. However, Livvy's reasoning that Friday must have been windy is incorrect. There might have been another reason why Ms Street was in a good mood and gave the early mark.

3 We know that any student who does not return their permission slip by Monday will not be allowed to go on the excursion to the zoo. However, Jim has made a mistake by saying he **definitely** will be allowed to go since, even though he has returned his slip, there may be other reasons why a student is not allowed to go to the zoo.

4 Only Hank's reasoning is correct. Hank practises for at least the minimum time required but correctly reasons he **might** pass, since doing the minimum required to have *a* **chance** of passing does not guarantee he will **definitely** pass. Ava also practises for at least the minimum time required but incorrectly reasons she will **definitely** pass the exam.

5 The sales assistant has found a dress that matches the description from Loren's mother and assumes it **must** be the one Loren wants. However, it might not be the correct dress because there might be other dresses that are blue with crocodiles.

6 Serena is correct when she reasons that because Lance has not collected ten tokens he definitely won't be able to enter the competition. Eddie's reasoning is incorrect because, although Nathan has collected ten tokens and is therefore allowed to and likely to register for entry to the competition, it does not mean he **will** register to enter the competition.

7 If the mixture spreads well, it would be a mistake to add more lime juice as that would make it runny. Keisha's reasoning is incorrect.

8 Both Eric and Will use correct reasoning based on the information Leesa has given them.

9 Hanna correctly reasons that crocodiles can be active at any time of day or night and, if it's a known crocodile habitat, there could be crocodiles there even if you can't see them.

10 Charlie is correct in reasoning that because all tortoises are turtles and because tortoises live on the land then tortoises must be turtles that live on land. Sam's reasoning is incorrect in concluding that because it lays eggs it must be a tortoise because the information says all turtles lay eggs.

MATHEMATICAL REASONING
Patterns and algebra Pages 64–66

Real Test 1

1 C **2** C **3** A **4** E **5** B **6** B **7** E **8** D **9** A **10** B

EXPLANATIONS

1 The left column is increasing by one, and the right column is increasing by 4. This means X equals 18.

2 The sequence is 4, 8, 12, , 20, The missing number is 16.

3 The numbers are going up by 2, then 3, then 4, then 5, then 6, then 7, and so on. This means the missing numbers are 15 and 21.

4 Start with the small numbers on the vertices on the triangles. Here is the completed puzzle:

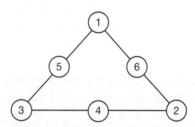

As 1 + 6 + 2 is 9, the sum is 9.

5 As $6 + X = 10$, the value of X is 4. This means $Y = 3$. Also, $2 + Z = 6$, so the value of Z is 4. $Y \times Z = 3 \times 4 = 12$.

6 For every 3 grey blocks used there are 2 purple blocks. As $24 \div 3 \times 2$ is 16, Oscar has used 16 purple blocks.

7 Use the inverse operations to find the previous numbers. From 20, add 4 to get 24 and then halve 24 to get 12. This means the fourth number is 12. Now from 12, add 4 to get 16, and then halve 16 to get 8. The third number in the pattern is 8.

8 The numbers are doubling. The next three terms are 64, 128 and 256.
Now $256 - 32 = 256 - 30 - 2$ which is 224.

9 Look at the multiples of 6. As **4** × 6 is 2**4**, and **8** × 6 is 4**8**, then Q is either 4 or 8. If Q = 4, then 6 × P + 2 is 44. This means that P is 7. (Trying Q = 8 means 6 × P + 4 and this cannot give 88. You could have instead worked out Q = 4 and then divided 444 by 6 to get 74, which means P = 7.)

10 First, 75 − 9 is 66. The number sentence can be rewritten as 38 + 7 × ☐ = 66.

As 66 − 30 − 8 = 28, then 7 × ☐ = 28.

As 28 ÷ 7 is 4, the missing number is 4.

Real Test 2

1 D **2** C **3** B **4** D **5** D **6** C **7** E **8** E **9** B **10** E

EXPLANATIONS

1 Count the matches used: 4, 7, 10, 13 …. The numbers are increasing by 3. This means the fifth number will be 16.

2 The sequence is 1, 2, 4, 8, 16, 32, 64, 128. This means there are 128 grains on the eighth square.

3 Each number on the bottom row is the number on the top row doubled and with 1 added. This means double 13 plus 1. The answer is 27.

4 The numbers are going up by 2, then 3, then 4. This means the next number goes up by 5: 10 + 5 = 15.

5 For the numbers 1 to 7, the middle number is 4. This number is written in the middle circle. Now pair the smallest and largest numbers (1 and 7) and write them in opposite circles. Continue this pattern by pairing the next smallest and largest numbers:

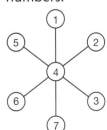

As 1 + 4 + 7 is 12, the sum is 12.

6 For the numbers 6 to 14, the middle number is 10. This number is written in the middle circle. (Now pair the smallest and largest numbers (6 and 14) and write them in opposite circles. Continue this pattern by pairing the next smallest and largest numbers.)

Here is the completed puzzle:

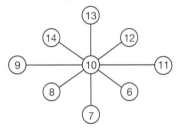

The middle number is 10.

7 As 4 × 3 = X, the value of X is 12. Also, 12 × Y = 72, which means Y = 6. Finally, 2 × Z = 6, which means Z = 3. $X + Y + Z$ = 12 + 6 + 3 = 21.

8 As 36 ÷ 4 is 9, Cassie has repeated the pattern 9 times. As 9 × 3 is 27, there are 27 squares in the finished pattern.

9 Use the inverse operations to find the previous numbers. From 32, add 8 to get 40 and then halve 40 to get 20. This means the second number is 20. Now from 20, adding 8 gives 28, and then halving 28 gives 14. The first number in the pattern is 14. Adding 14 and 20 results in 34.

10 The sequence is … 63, 70, X, 84 … The rule is adding 7. As 14 − 8 = 6, the difference between the fourteenth and eighth terms is 6 × 7 which is 42.

MATHEMATICAL REASONING
Length and area   Pages 69–72

Real Test 3

1 D **2** A **3** B **4** C **5** D **6** D **7** E **8** C **9** D **10** E

EXPLANATIONS

1 A normal school ruler is about 30 cm in length and about 3 cm wide. As 30 + 3 + 30 + 3 = 66, the perimeter is about 66 cm.

2 The perimeter in units is a sequence: 4, 6, 8, ... This means the perimeter will be 10 units.

3 The two 'lengths' add to 8 cm. This means the two 'widths' add to 4 cm. Each width must be 2 cm.

4 If the perimeter is 28 cm, then the sum of the length and width is 14 cm. The dimensions must be 8 cm and 6 cm. As 8 × 6 is 48, the area is 48 cm².

5 Each square has an area of 1 cm². There are 5 squares and 2 half squares.
As $5 + \frac{1}{2} + \frac{1}{2} = 6$, the area is 6 cm².

6 There are 9 squares and 4 half-squares remaining. As 2 half-squares = 1 square, then a total of 11 squares remain. As there were 4 layers and 4 × 11 is 44, the sheet of paper will have an area of 44 cm².

7 The sum of the length and width is 16 cm. The length is 12 cm and width is 4 cm. As 12 × 4 = 48, the area is 48 cm².

8 The square will have a side length of 3 cm. As 4 × 3 is 12, the perimeter is 12 cm.

9 The longer piece is three-quarters of the original piece, and the shorter piece is one-quarter. As 60 ÷ 4 is 15, the shorter piece is 15 cm long. As 15 × 3 is 45, the longer piece is 45 cm.

10 As each square has an area of 4 cm², the side length is 2 cm. Half a side length is 1 cm. Adding the side lengths gives 40 cm:

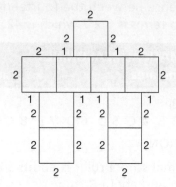

Real Test 4

1 E **2** C **3** A **4** B **5** A **6** E **7** B **8** D **9** A **10** D
EXPLANATIONS

1 Adding the lengths of each side: 3 + 1 + 1 + 3 + 1 + 1 + 1 + 3 = 14. The perimeter is 14 units.

2 As the area is 36 cm², the dimensions are 12 cm by 3 cm.
The perimeter is 12 + 12 + 3 + 3 = 30. This means the perimeter is 30 cm.

3 As 4 × 4 = 16, the length of each side is 4 cm. As 4 × 4 = 16, the perimeter is 16 cm.

4 As 8 × 3 is 24, the perimeter of the triangle is 24 cm. As 24 ÷ 4 is 6, each side of the square is 6 cm.

5 Each square has an area of 1 cm². The shape covers 14 squares and 4 half squares. As 2 half-squares form a square, the area is 16 cm².

6 There are 4 shapes removed. These have areas of 2 cm², 4 cm², 1 cm² and 4 cm². As 2 + 4 + 1 + 4 is 11, then 11 cm² has been removed. As 8 × 4 = 32, originally the shape had an area of 32 cm². As 32 − 11 = 21, the area of the remaining paper is 21 cm². There were 2 layers and as 21 × 2 = 42, then the area of the unfolded sheet is 42 cm².

7 As 7 + 3 + 7 + 3 = 20, the perimeter of the rectangle is 20 cm. As 20 ÷ 4 = 5, the square will have a side length of 5 cm. Comparing the areas, 5 × 5 − 7 × 3 = 4 which means that the square has an area 4 cm² bigger than the rectangle.

8 As 4 + 6 + 6 + 3 = 19, James rode 19 km.

9 The large squares have a side length of 6 cm and the small square has a side length of 2 cm. As 6 + 6 + 4 + 4 + 6 + 6 + 4 + 4 is 40, the perimeter is 40 cm.

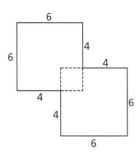

10 The triangle is half a square which is made from 9 small squares. As 9 × 4 is 36, and half of 36 is 18, the area of the triangle is 18 cm². As 18 + 4 + 4 is 26, the shaded area is 26 cm².

WRITING
'What would you do if ...?' opinion   Page 78

Practice Task 3

1 First I would like to experience what it is like to travel through space.

2 space travel

WEEK 3

READING
Factual texts   Pages 84–88

Practice Task 1

1 E **2** B **3** A **4** C

EXPLANATIONS

1 The sentence follows the theme about Aboriginal communities hunting dugongs and sharing their meat. This sentence is about how many communities the food provides for. You have to make the link, however. There is no linking word like 'and'.

2 This sentence fits well between the sentence before it and the one that follows: both are about where the dugongs are seen (or not seen).

3 This sentence links with the one before it which is about what dugongs look like. Again, there is no clear linking word to help you.

4 You have to read the sentences that follow this one to get it right. The whole of the last paragraph is about the vulnerability of dugongs. The linking word 'however' helps you too. This contrasts the information in this sentence with the paragraph before about how well they hear and communicate.

The unused sentence is D. This sentence might appear in a text about dugongs but it would have to go in the second paragraph and there is no space for it there in this text.

Practice Task 2

1 D **2** E **3** A **4** C **5** B **6** F

EXPLANATIONS

1 'These peoples' indicates you are looking for mention of a group of people in a previous sentence to the gap. The phrase 'in turn' tells you there is more than one group of people to look for. 'These peoples' refers to the 'merchants in Timor'.

2 'These vessels' tells you to look in the previous sentence for a mention of vessels or ships of some kind—you can find it with 'Malay vessels"

3 The pronoun 'they' directs you to look back at previous sentences for a likely thing or person being referred to (so 'the Macassans'). The information in the sentence links directly to the information about the Macassans returning to the same spots.

4 You need to look for mention of 'two groups' and you can find it in the previous sentence about the Macassans and the Aboriginal people. You also have to look at the following sentence. The missing sentence is about the bad relationship but

the following sentence includes the important linking word 'however' and focuses on when the relationship was good.

5 You have to look at the sentences that follow the missing one to get the answer. If you know the word 'reciprocal' it will help you but if not, you can still understand that you are looking for benefits to the traders. You can find these in the sentences that follow.

6 You might think that F matches gap 3 but, although it makes some sense, the sentences before and after 3 are connected to the topic of their campsites (not the traders themselves) and so the missing one must be also. It matches better to 6 as the paragraph ends with a description of the positive influence of the Macassans in the art and stories of the region.

The unused sentence is G. The only place this sentence could possibly go is in paragraph 1 where the trepang or sea slugs are introduced. However, this would not really make sense in the first gap as the writer has moved the text on to the trepang traders.

Practice Task 3

1 C **2** E **3** A **4** B **5** F **6** G

EXPLANATIONS

1 The pronoun 'this' shows you that the sentence refers back to a previous sentence. The words 'system' and 'becoming an artist' show you it refers to the young Leonardo and the apprentice arrangement he learnt within.

2 Again, a pronoun ('it') shows that the sentence refers back to a previous sentence. 'It' refers to the painting of The Last Supper.

3 This sentence fits the theme of the paragraph: Leonardo's work as a scientist. 'He described and drew' links back to 'His approach' in the previous sentence and to the following sentence about his notebooks.

4 This sentence relates back to the description of his mirror writing in the previous sentences. The linking word 'also' shows you the sentence is building on information already given.

5 Again, 'also' is an important clue here. It shows that the sentence links closely to the one before where the link words 'not only' are used—so 'not only … but also'.

6 This sentence fits the theme of the last paragraph. You have to look at the sentence following which describes what he did when he moved to Venice.

The unused sentence is D. There is no gap in the text where you could place this sentence that would make sense.

Real Test

1 C **2** D **3** B **4** A **5** E **6** G

EXPLANATIONS

1 This sentence makes sense in the basic explanation of bartering in the first paragraph.

2 The word 'modern' links this sentence to the one before it and gives you the clue. The linking word 'however' is also an important clue. It contrasts the idea in this sentence to the one before.

3 The pronoun 'they' at the start of this sentence shows it is linking back and standing in for people or things in the previous sentence. In this case 'they' refers back to 'certain things' and 'these things' in the previous sentence. The sentence also makes sense in the paragraph.

4 You have to look back a bit further than the sentence before it to get this correct. The previous sentence about salt might stop you seeing that this sentence refers back to the sentence 'For example, cows, tobacco, grains, skins, salt and beads were all used as money at some time' to see that this is what 'these kinds of money' refers to.

5 The repetition of 'money' at the start of the sentence and the general theme of the paragraph, which is about modern-day 'money', show that this is the right answer.

6 This sentence links to the one following, which gives an example of how we learn that money has value.

The unused sentence is F. This sentence makes sense and could be used in a text about bartering. However, a sentence like this would normally lead to at least two sentences giving reasons for and against the system in a balanced way. There are no sentences which do this and so the sentence does not fit.

THINKING SKILLS
Problem solving—Word problems Pages 91–92

Real Test 1

1 C **2** B **3** A **4** B **5** C **6** D **7** D **8** C **9** D **10** A

EXPLANATIONS

1 Zara is younger than both Lily and Maddy, so Zara is the youngest. Maddie might be the oldest or Lily might be the oldest or they might be the same age. There is not enough information to determine which is the case. So A, B and D are not options that **must** be true.

2 Angus's bike isn't blue because it is either red or green. Neither Lauren nor Emily has a blue bicycle. Kylie's bike is not blue because it is pink. So the blue bicycle can only belong to Dylan. Dylan's bike is blue.

3 The plates are above the cookbooks. The cups are below the plates, so the plates are also above the cups. This means that the plates must be on the top shelf.

The cookbooks and the cups are below the plates but there is no further information about where they are placed. So the statements in B, C and D might be true but we cannot say that they **must** be true.

4 Annabel and Khalid are the same age and are older than Theresa, Salim and Marlee but younger than Victor. So Victor is the oldest, Annabel and Khalid are the equal second oldest and Salim is younger than Annabel. Marlee might be the youngest but Salim might also be the youngest. The statement that might not be true is that Marlee is the youngest.

5 The sports that Logan can choose in Term 3 are soccer, hockey and baseball. The only one of these that Logan has chosen is soccer, so soccer must be the sport chosen in Term 3.

Logan could have chosen swimming in Term 4, basketball in Term 1 and tennis in Term 2. So A, B and D are not options that must be correct.

6 Bailey is older than Timothy but younger than Nicholas. So Nicholas is older than both Bailey and Timothy. Louis is younger than Nicholas, so Nicholas is also older than Louis. So Nicholas must be the oldest.

Timothy is younger than both Bailey and Nicholas, but he might or might not be younger than Louis. Either A or B will be true but we cannot say that either must be true. Similarly, Bailey is younger than Nicholas and older than Timothy so he might be the second oldest, but he might also be the third oldest. C might be true but is not the option that must be true.

7 Georgia must choose a shape from Box 3, but Box 3 contains no parallelogram, hexagon, rectangle or octagon. So Georgia cannot have chosen those four shapes.

Georgia could have chosen a rectangle from Box 2, square from Box 1, kite from Box 4 and circle from Box 3. She could have chosen a triangle from Box 2, a hexagon from Box 4, an octagon from Box 1 and a circle from Box 3. Georgia could have chosen a kite from Box 3, a triangle from Box 4, a trapezium from Box 2 and a hexagon from Box 1. So Georgia could

have chosen the shapes in the options A, B and C.

8 If the second child is a boy, then the first child, a girl, threw the frisbee to that boy. If the second child is a girl, then that child threw the frisbee to the last child, a boy. In either case a girl must have thrown the frisbee to a boy.

The possible outcomes are girl, boy, boy or girl, girl, boy. So some of the other options might be correct but none of them **must** be correct.

9 The boxes holding clothes and toys are diagonally opposite each other, so one of these is on the top and one on the bottom. The box holding shoes is also on the bottom, so the remaining box, the one holding papers, must be on the top.

There is no information about which of the boxes holding toys and clothes is on the top and which is on the bottom. So Sharon cannot know the things in options A, B and C.

10 As Irene is next to both Tayla and George, those three children are at desks all in a row with Irene in the centre. If either Tayla or George was next to Julian, who is at one end, then at the other end Dana would have to be next to Harry and that is not correct. If either Tayla or George was at the other end of the row that would also mean that Dana would have to be next to Harry. So the other end of the row must belong to either Harry or Dana and either Dana or Harry must be next to Julian. So George, Irene and Tayla are between Harry and Dana. Dana is not next to George (or Irene) so she must be next to Tayla.

Harry might be next to Julian but B is not the option that **must** be true. Julian cannot be next to George so C is not correct. Tayla must be between Dana and Irene so cannot be next to Harry so D is not correct.

THINKING SKILLS
Problem solving—Position, order and direction   Pages 95–96

Real Test 2

1 A **2** C **3** B **4** C **5** D **6** B **7** B **8** A **9** C **10** D
EXPLANATIONS

1 Ryan can be placed in any position. Meg is on his left. The other two positions at the table belong to Elizabeth and Vincent. Elizabeth must be on Vincent's right so Elizabeth will be opposite Ryan and Vincent will be opposite Meg. Elizabeth will be on Meg's left and Ryan will be on Vincent's left.

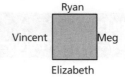

The correct statement is Elizabeth is on Meg's left.

2 Jill chose brown. Brown is only in Bucket 3, so she cannot choose any other colour from Bucket 3. Jill also chose red. Red only appears in Buckets 3 and 4, so she must have chosen the red marble from Bucket 4. Pink only appears in Bucket 4, so Jill cannot have chosen pink.

As well as brown from Bucket 3 and red from Bucket 4, Jill could choose green from Bucket 1 and orange from Bucket 2. So Jill could have chosen orange. She could have chosen green from Bucket 2 and either blue or white from Bucket 1, so Jill could also have chosen blue or white. So A, B and D are not correct.

3 The pins and needles, thread and scissors are in the top row. The material is above the patterns so the patterns are in the bottom row. The patterns are left of the buttons and the material is right of the ribbons. So the material and patterns must be in the centre of their rows. The patterns are in the centre of the bottom row.

The pins and needles are in the top row, but might not be in the centre. The ribbons must be furthest left in the middle row and the buttons must be furthest right in the bottom row. So A, C and D are not correct.

4 Eli, Sophie and Polly all got lower marks than Frances. So Frances must be either first or second. But Frances got a lower mark than Abdul. So Frances came second. Abdul must have come first. Eli must have come either third or fourth. Sophie could have come third, fourth or fifth and Polly came either fourth or fifth. A, B and D might be correct but are not options that must be correct.

5 As Patra and Wyatt have stables furthest apart, they must have the two end stables. Diva's stable is next to Patra's, so is not next to Wyatt's. Flowerpot and Carter have the two middle stables, neither of which is next to Wyatt's. So the only horse whose stable can be next to Wyatt's is Magic.

6 Maria can only try pottery on Day 1. If she does pottery on Day 1, she can only play board games on Day 2. If she does pottery on Day 1 and board games on Day 2, she can only do drama on Day 4. So Maria can also only do the activities that are available on Day 3. Photography is not available on Day 3 so Maria cannot also do photography. The activities in the other options are all available on Day 3, so A, C and D are not correct answers.

7 If Phoebe is sitting diagonally opposite Erin, then John and Mitchell must also be sitting diagonally opposite each other. As John is facing the beach, Mitchell must be facing the other way. Mitchell must be facing the park.

Phoebe might be sitting next to John or she might be sitting next to Mitchell. Erin might be directly opposite Mitchell or she might be directly opposite John. John might be sitting directly opposite Phoebe or Erin. A, C and D are not options that **must** be correct.

8 The grey house is to the left of the green house. The yellow house is to the right of the grey house, so the grey house is left of the yellow house. The white house is to the right of the yellow house so the grey house is also left of the white house. The grey house must be furthest left.

B is not correct. The yellow house is not the furthest left. C and D are not the correct options because there is not enough information to say they **must** be true. Either the white or green house will be furthest right.

9 Rogan is south-west of Joyville.

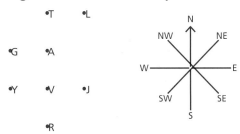

10 Nathan and Mary are sitting as far apart as possible. So they must be sitting at the opposite ends of the rows on opposite sides of the table. Geri is seated directly opposite Mary. So Geri is on the same side of the table as Nathan, at the other end of the row. Daisy is next to Nathan. So Daisy is sitting between Nathan and Geri. The remaining seats are for Jackie and Jess and, as Mary is at one end of the row, Jackie and Jess must be seated next to each other.

Either Jackie or Jess must be sitting next to Mary. Jackie and Jess must be opposite Nathan and Daisy in some order, but Nathan might be opposite Jess and Daisy might be opposite Jackie. A, B and C are not the options that **must** be true.

THINKING SKILLS
Problem solving—Numerical reasoning
Pages 99–100

Real Test 3

1 A **2** D **3** B **4** A **5** B **6** D **7** C **8** C **9** C **10** B

EXPLANATIONS

1 To complete the pattern 4 more times, Trent would need 4 × 5 = 20 green tiles, 4 × 3 = 12 grey tiles and 4 × 4 = 16 white tiles. So he can complete the pattern 4 more times. He would then only have 3 white tiles left which is not enough to complete another pattern. Trent can complete his pattern another 4 times.

2 The red car is not first or last and is not next to the white car or the black car. So the red car must be between the blue and silver cars. As the blue car is last, the red car must be fourth and the silver car must be in the middle. The red car is in fourth place, the white is two places away, so it is second. The black car will be first. The car in second spot is the white car.

3 Find the total marks for everyone:

Name	Round 1	Round 2	Round 3	Total
Emma	18	15	18	51
Max	15	16	17	48
Joe	17	17	19	53
Sara	16	18	20	54
Zane	19	20	16	55
Rose	20	19	15	54

So Emma scored 51 points and Zane scored 55 points. The person who scored 2 more points than Emma and 2 less than Zane must have scored 53 points. That person is Joe.

4 The new numbers of balloons were:

Colour	Number
red	24 + 2 = 26
white	15 + 8 = 23
green	21 + 5 = 26
yellow	18 + 7 = 25

So there were the same number of red and green balloons.

5 The total number of beads that Fiona has already used is 35 + 14 + 21 = 70. So, as each pattern uses 10 beads, Fiona has completed 7 patterns. Now 35 ÷ 7 = 5, 14 ÷ 7 = 2 and 21 ÷ 7 = 3. This means that each pattern uses 5 pink beads, 2 blue beads and 3 white beads. As 5 × 8 = 40 and 5 × 9 = 45, Fiona has enough pink beads for 8 more patterns, but not enough for 9. As 8 × 2 = 16 and 8 × 3 = 24, Fiona has more than enough blue and white beads to complete 8 more patterns. So, although Fiona has more blue and white beads, she only has enough pink beads for 8 more patterns, so Fiona can only complete 8 more patterns.

6 Shea got a higher mark than Samuel. Shea also got a higher mark than Lucy and Lucy's mark was higher than Toby's. So Shea had the highest mark. Shea got 97 marks.
Lucy's mark was higher than Toby's but there is not enough information to determine where Samuel's mark fits in compared to Lucy and Toby. Toby got either 91 or 94 marks, Lucy got either 94 or 96 marks and Samuel got either 91, 94 or 96 marks. Options A, B and C are not the options that must be correct.

7 Gaby is using more yellow than blue blocks and fewer blue blocks than red ones, so blue is the colour of the smallest number of blocks. So Gaby is using just 10 blue blocks.

Gaby is using more yellow and more red blocks than blue blocks but there is no further information. So she might be using 15 red blocks and she must be using either 15 or 12 yellow blocks, but we cannot say that any of the other options, A, B or D, must be correct.

8 Mohammad won the race. Elton, Lachlan and Jayden all finished between Sean and Wes. Sean finished before Wes so Sean came 2nd and Wes came 6th. Elton finished between Lachlan and Jayden so Elton came 4th. Jayden finished ahead of Lachlan, so Jayden came 3rd and Lachlan was the boy who finished in 5th place.

9 As 48 − 39 = 9, Kevin improved his time by 9 min.
As 49 − 41 = 8, Jake improved his time by 8 min.
As 54 − 44 = 10, Roger improved his time by 10 min.
As 56 − 47 = 9, Adam improved his time by 9 min.
So the greatest improvement was 10 min. The person who improved his time the most was Roger.

10 The total scores are:

Molly	10 + 7 = 17
Kate	7 + 8 = 15
Amelia	9 + 5 = 14
Stella	5 + 9 = 14
Tilly	8 + 6 = 14
Ivy	7 + 6 = 13

So Molly did come first, Tilly did come equal third and Ivy did come last. But Kate came second, not Stella.
The statement that is not correct is Stella came second.

MATHEMATICAL REASONING
Volume, capacity, mass and time
Pages 103–105

Real Test 1

1 E **2** B **3** A **4** C **5** C **6** B **7** A **8** B **9** B **10** E

EXPLANATIONS

1 Count the days: 5 in April and 11 in May means 5 + 11 = 16. A fortnight after Tuesday 25 April is 9 May. This means 11 May is a Thursday.

2 There are 21 days in three weeks. As 21 − 15 = 6, and there are 31 days in May, use 31 − 6. This is 25, so the date was 25 May.

3 The 19th is the only Saturday between the 13th and Thursday 24th.

4 2 × 50 + 3 × 80 = 100 + 240 = 340. This means the mass is 340 g.

5 1000 − 420 = 580. This means Fran has 580 g remaining.

6 Ten to nine is 8:50 pm. From 8:50 pm to 6:50 am is 4 + 5 = 10 h. As he got out of bed 5 min before 6:50 he was in bed for 9 h 55 min.

7 *P* has 10 mL and *Q* has 40 mL. Halfway between 10 and 40 is 25. As 40 − 25 is 15, then 15 mL needs to be poured from *Q* to *P*.

8 As 32 − 20 = 12, the water that half fills the tank has a mass of 12 kg. The mass of water that fills the tank is 24 kg. As 32 − 24 = 8, the fish tank has a mass of 8 kg.

9 The mass of a cylinder is less than 11 kg. The mass of 2 cylinders is more than 18 kg so more than 9 kg each. This means each cylinder has a mass of 10 kg, and so $X = 10$.

10 From 7 am to 9 am is 2 h, or 120 min. As 120 ÷ 10 is 12, then 12 trams leave the station. This means 7:10, 7:20, and so on. You also need to count the tram that left at 7 am, so 12 + 1 is 13 trams.

Real Test 2

1 B 2 C 3 D 4 C 5 D 6 E 7 A 8 B 9 A 10 E

EXPLANATIONS

1 There are four Sundays in September on the calendar. As 4 × 6 = 24, Adam jogged 24 km.

2 Three weeks after Tuesday 5 March is Tuesday 26 March. This means that 28 March is a Thursday.

3 As 2 h = 120 min, and from 14 to 36 is 22, the total is 120 + 22 = 142. The running time is 142 min.

4 As the mass of 1 block = mass of 3 discs, the total mass on the first side would be 2 × 3 + 3 = 9. This means there must be 9 discs on the other side.

5 As 40 – 6 = 34 and 34.0 – 0.8 = 33.2, there is 33.2 kg remaining in the bag.

6 From quarter to one to 1:00 is 15 min. Another 11 h is midnight. Then add 5 h to 5 am and 30 min to reach 5:30 am. As 11 + 5 = 16 and 15 + 30 is 45, it is switched on for 16 h 45 min.

7 Container X has 700 mL and Container Y has 420 mL. As 1000 mL is 1 L, and 1000 – 700 is 300, Ariana needs 300 mL from Container Y. As 420 – 300 is 120, there will still be 120 mL remaining in Container Y.

8 As 1000 g is 1 kg, Jacob could buy 8 small bags which would cost $16. He would have more than 4 kg of rice if he bought 2 large bags which would cost $18. If he bought 1 large bag and 3 small bags it would cost him $9 + 3 × $2 which is $15.

9 As 24 ÷ 6 is 4 and 12 ÷ 6 is 2, a floor tile has a mass of 4 kg and a wall tile 2 kg. As 10 × 4 + 8 × 2 is 40 + 16 = 56, the total mass is 56 kg.

10 As 1000 mL is 1 L then 2000 mL is 2 L. As one-quarter is 2000 ÷ 4 = 500, there is 500 mL of juice in the jug. As 200 × 2 is 400 and 500 – 400 = 100, only 100 mL remains. As 2000 – 100 is 1900, Aleesha needs 1900 mL to fill the jug.

MATHEMATICAL REASONING
2D and 3D shapes   Pages 107–110

Real Test 3

1 E 2 A 3 D 4 A 5 E 6 D 7 B 8 A 9 C 10 B

EXPLANATIONS

1 There are the obvious four rectangles, then the large rectangle and then four overlapping rectangles inside. This means nine rectangles in total.

2 A hexagonal prism has a front and back face, and six side faces. This means eight faces in total.

3 A cube has six faces, eight corners, is a solid but has 12 edges, not 10 as stated.

4 The two bases will no longer be seen. There will be eight faces remaining.

5 There are 17 cubes in the solid and 12 of the cubes are visible.
As 17 – 12 = 5, there are 5 cubes hidden.

6

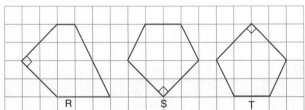

7 There are 6 cube faces on the front and 6 on the back. From the top there are 6 and there are 6 from the bottom. There are 5 from the left and 5 from the right. As 6 + 6 + 6 + 6 + 5 + 5 is 34, Logan can see 34 cube faces.

8 The 3 shapes form a regular pentagon:

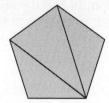

9 There are 24 cubes in the original solid. The new solid only has 9 cubes. As 24 – 9 is 15, there have been 15 cubes removed.

10 *R* is opposite *T* and *P* is opposite *S*. This means *Q* is face down on the table.

Real Test 4

1 C **2** B **3** C **4** E **5** D **6** E **7** A **8** D **9** E **10** D

EXPLANATIONS

1 There are eight obvious squares and then three across the rectangle. This means there are 11 squares.

2 The small shape is a row of the front of the large shape. There are three of these rows and the shape is three thick. As 3 × 3 = 9, there are nine small shapes.

3 Four on its base and four coming down from its apex. This means eight edges.

4 Jayden should choose E and H. The letters both have 4 right angles. This means the most number of right angles is 8.

5 These are the 6 cubes with only 3 red faces:

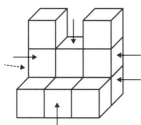

6 Each right angle measures 90°. The other two angles measure more than 90° and look like about 130°. 3 × 90 + 2 × 130 is 270 + 260 which is 530. The closest answer is 540°.

7 There are 7 cube faces on the front and 7 on the back. From the top there are 4 and there are 4 from the bottom. There are 2 from the left and 2 from the right. As 7 + 7 + 4 + 4 + 2 + 2 is 26, Ella can see 26 cube faces. Now 7 × 6 = 42, so the cubes have a total of 42 faces. As 42 – 26 is 16, Ella cannot see 16 cube faces.

8 There are 4 cube faces on the front and 4 on the back. From the top there are 3 and there are 3 from the bottom. There are 4 from the left and 4 from the right. As 4 + 4 + 3 + 3 + 4 + 4 is 22, there are 22 grey cube faces:

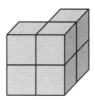

9 Here are three straight-line cuts:

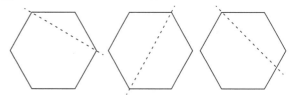

All 3 cases can be made.

10 This shape cannot be made because one of the coloured squares is in the wrong position:

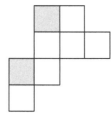

WRITING
Narrative story Pages 115–116

Task 3

… he thinks he is too old to have one (a teddy) and that other kids at school will not still have one.

Task 5: a

Task 6

1 a old, ratty
   b peculiar

2 a tossed
   b eyeing off

WEEK 4

READING
Varied short texts   Pages 122–129

Practice Task 1

1 C **2** D **3** B **4** D **5** C **6** D **7** A **8** B

EXPLANATIONS

1 This extract gives many reasons why people love fantasy fiction. Extract B demonstrates a love of fantasy fiction too but only really gives one reason: 'the other worlds and the fantastical creatures in them'.

2 This extract has two sentences about the attraction of reading fiction: 'Fiction also allows me to live life in another person's shoes … And this helps me understand'.

3 This extract gives the names of four books read as a small child.

4 This extract includes the sentence: 'Fiction helps me forget other problems, big and small'.

5 The sentence 'Villains can flourish in this genre like no other' gives you the answer. The following words reinforce this idea: 'And we love them'.

6 This extract mentions learning about different places and other time periods through fiction.

7 This extract is about how the writer learnt to read from the backs of bathroom products and cereal packets.

8 The last three sentences of this extract compare the fantastical characters in fantasy fiction to ordinary boys and girls in other types of fiction.

Practice Task 2

1 C **2** A **3** B **4** A **5** D **6** C **7** B **8** D

EXPLANATIONS

1 This extract includes the words 'and they always do', which refers to things going wrong in your own holidays.

2 This extract from a holiday activity website is advertising snorkelling and surfing activities.

3 This extract relates a disastrous horseriding holiday.

4 The last line of this extract ends with a question which suggests to the reader that everyone's holiday should have some adventure.

5 This extract is clearly all about the history of holidays.

6 The last line of this extract mentions two films which will appeal to young people who 'might find it hard going' being on family holidays, suggesting this is true for at least some young people.

7 The writer of this extract only wants to read on holidays and in the end she does this in hospital with an injury sustained on the horseriding trip.

8 This extract mentions more than once that travel was, and is, difficult for people who have to give up work and money to go away on holiday.

Practice Task 3

1 C **2** D **3** A **4** B **5** D **6** D **7** A **8** B

EXPLANATIONS

1 This extract focuses almost totally on past technologies for entertainment and ends with a comment comparing this to children's entertainment today.

2 This extract begins by saying the speaker will talk about the benefits of technology and then goes on to talk about how technology can benefit learning.

3 In this extract, as part of the second point, the writer says that screen time should not interfere with making time for playing with your child.

4 This extract mentions the danger of communication technology leading to a lower attention span for children and affecting their ability to learn.

5 This extract mentions that technology can help children to multitask effectively. Multitasking means doing more than one thing at a time.

6 The two sentences at the beginning refer to parents in the audience probably being negative about any benefits and being 'sick and tired' of managing their children's use of technology.

7 The second-last line of the extract, after listing how to manage technology with small children, tells parents to look for good applications and says there is a great choice of these.

8 The last two sentences are about the dangers for social interaction with the constant use of screens. Children who frequently use screens may be less able and more reluctant to interact with others face to face.

Real Test

1 C **2** B **3** D **4** B **5** A **6** D **7** A **8** C

EXPLANATIONS

1 This extract explains the need to communicate in netball as players work in their positions and work out how to score a goal.

2 The last line of this extract mentions the competitiveness of playing video games.

3 The writer of this extract says he gradually realised that the grand final match was only a game and that there were more important things in life than who wins and loses. Extract A also mentions winning and losing but does not focus on this particular aspect.

4 The writer of this extract, who is not a sports lover, points out he is not a 'couch potato' and in fact goes to the gym.

5 This extract acknowledges there are other ways to develop teamwork skills but that physical participation in team sports is the best way.

6 The writer of this extract shows his passion for sport by saying how much he was affected by his team's loss and revealing how he shouts at the television 'like a maniac' and gets dressed up in his team's colours.

7 The last two sentences of this extract mention 'mental spin-offs' (benefits) of sports participation and the benefit of sport on students' concentration in the classroom.

8 This extract mentions one unusual aspect of netball: that players cannot move once they have the ball. The writer explains what players must learn to do because of this.

THINKING SKILLS
Problem solving—Shapes and objects
Pages 132–133

Real Test 1

1 C **2** A **3** C **4** B **5** D **6** C **7** D **8** B **9** A **10** A

EXPLANATIONS

1 When the net is folded, 2 is opposite 7, 3 is opposite 6 and 4 is opposite 5. Now 2 + 7 = 9 and 3 + 6 = 9 and 4 + 5 = 9. So the numbers on each pair of opposite sides add to 9.

2 No two squares use the same five pieces. (The first square has a cross and none of the others has that. The second square has a T shape and neither of the two remaining squares has that. The third square has a U shape and the fourth does not have that.)

3 The cube formed from the net in C has the star opposite the circle, the triangle opposite the square and the heart opposite the cross. So C could be the net of Charlie's cube.
The cube from the net in A has the star opposite the circle, but the triangle is opposite the heart and the square opposite the cross.

The cube from the net in B has the star opposite the cross, the triangle opposite the heart and the square opposite the circle. The cube from the net in D does have the triangle opposite the square, but the circle is opposite the heart and the star opposite the cross. None of these could be Charlie's cube.

4 Pieces 1, 2 and 3 can be placed together to form a square. Piece 4 cannot:

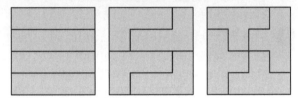

5 All of the nets have the numbers 4, 5, 6, 7, 8 and 9. Now 4 + 9 = 13, 5 + 8 = 13 and 6 + 7 = 13. So 4 must be opposite 9, 5 must be opposite 8 and 6 must be opposite 7. This only occurs on the net in D.

In A, 4 is opposite 9 but 5 is opposite 7 and 6 is opposite 8. In B, 4 is opposite 9 but 5 is opposite 6 and 7 is opposite 8. In C, 6 is opposite 7 but 4 is opposite 5 and 8 is opposite 9.

6 Square number 2 and square number 5 are made up of the same five shapes:

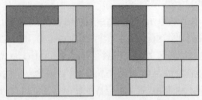

7 The front view gives the height and width of the books. The top view gives the length and the width, but not the height. So the top view must be the one where the books have the same width as the front view. This only happens in option D.

8 The first crease mark is made halfway between the top line and the bottom edge. As 6 cm has been left out when the paper is folded, the fold line will be 3 cm below the middle of the paper. The

second crease mark is made halfway between the top edge and the bottom line. It will be 2 cm above the middle of the paper. So altogether the two lines will be 5 cm apart:

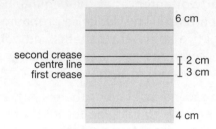

9

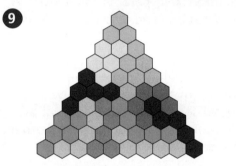

10 In the two views of Jack's cube, the face opposite the purple face cannot be seen. Neither can the white face be seen. So the white face must be opposite the purple face. The white face is on the left side in the second view of Jack's cube. If the cube is turned to the right through a quarter of a turn the white face will be at the front, the black dot at the top and the purple diamond on the right side. So the view in option A will be another view of Jack's cube.

If the white face is on the right side and the purple cross at the front, the face with two black lines will be at the top, but they would need to run from front to back, not from side to side. So B cannot be Jack's cube. If the white face was at the top and the black dot at the front, the purple diamond would be on the left side, not the right side. So C cannot be Jack's cube. If the white face was at the top and the black dot on the right side, the purple diamond would be at the front. So D cannot be a view of Jack's cube.

THINKING SKILLS
Problem solving—Measurement and time
Page 136

Real Test 2

1 A **2** D **3** C **4** B **5** D **6** B **7** B **8** C **9** A **10** D

EXPLANATIONS

1 If there are 21 posts there will be 20 gaps between the posts. Each gap is 5 m. So the total distance will be 20 × 5 m or 100 m.

2 As 3 × 50 = 150, Jeremy only has enough eggs to make 150 biscuits.
To make 175 biscuits, Jeremy would need 7 cups of flour, $1\frac{3}{4}$ cups of sugar and 437.5 g of butter, so he has enough of each of those ingredients.

3 From 8 am until 2 pm is 6 h. So the bus took 6 h to travel from Penton to Greenville. The train took half of that time, so it took 3 h. Now, 3 h after 12 noon is 3 pm. 3 pm is 1 h after 2 pm, so the train arrived at Greenville an hour after the bus.

4 Each week there are performances on 5 nights, plus an extra performance on Saturday afternoons. So there are 6 performances every week. Now, from Friday 7th until Thursday 20th is 2 weeks, so that will mean 12 performances. There are then performances on Friday 21st, two on Saturday 22nd and one on Sunday 23rd. So there are another 4 performances. The number of performances is 12 + 4 or 16.

5 The driveway is 120 m long and the trees are planted every 10 m. Now 120 ÷ 10 = 12. There will be 12 gaps between trees on each side of the driveway. There will be a tree before the first gap and another at the end of the last gap. So there will be 13 trees on each side of the driveway. As 2 × 13 = 26, there will be 26 trees altogether.

6 From 3 pm until 4:30 pm is an hour and a half. That is 60 min plus 30 min or 90 min in total. So Christopher spent 90 min mowing his own lawn. Now Christopher only spent half that amount of time mowing his grandmother's lawn. Half of 90 is 45, so Christopher spent 45 min, or three-quarters of an hour, mowing his grandmother's lawn. He finished at 11 am, so he began three-quarters of an hour earlier, at 10:15 am.

7 There are performances on 3 days each week (Friday, Saturday and Wednesday). Now, if 9 January is a Friday, then so is 16, 23 and 30 January. 31 January is a Saturday, so there is no Wednesday performance in the final week. However, there is a performance on Monday 26 January. So there will be the equivalent of 4 weeks of performances. As 4 × 3 = 12, there will be 12 performances altogether.

8 From 9:20 until 9:45 is 25 min. So the forward journey took 25 min. Now 3 × 25 = 75. So if the return journey took 3 times longer, it took 75 min. Now 75 min is 1 h 15 min. An hour after 5:10 pm is 6:10 pm and 15 min after that is 6:25 pm. So Cleo arrived home at 6:25 pm.

9 Joel will be the clown 6 times every week. As there are 2 full weeks from Thursday 4th until Wednesday 17th, he will be the clown 12 times over that period. He will then also be the clown on Thursday 18th and Friday 19th. So altogether Joel is the clown 14 times. Guy is the clown 4 times every week. The circus is in town for three weekends so Guy is the clown 12 times. This means that Joel is the clown 2 more times than Guy.

10 From 8:30 am until 11 am is $2\frac{1}{2}$ h. So the train took $2\frac{1}{2}$ h to travel from Milford to Sykes. The helicopter was 5 times as fast, so it took one-fifth of the time.

Now $2\frac{1}{2}$ h is $(2 \times 60 + 30)$ min or 150 min. $150 \div 5 = 30$. So the helicopter took 30 min or half an hour to fly from Milford to Sykes. It left half an hour before 2 pm, so at 1:30 pm.

THINKING SKILLS
Problem solving—Tricky problems
Pages 139–140

Real Test 3

1 C **2** D **3** D **4** C **5** D **6** B **7** C **8** A **9** A **10** A

EXPLANATIONS

1 The statement Seb is north-east of Zak cannot be true because Seb will be north-west of Zak:

Bec •   Zak •   • Jill

Bill •   Mo •   • Amy

Jon •   Seb •   • Geri

(compass showing E, SE, S / NE, SW / N, W / NW)

The statements in A, B and D will all be true.

2 Friday 26th is 21 days or 3 weeks after Friday 5th. The program is shown 3 times a week for 3 weeks plus one extra show on the final Friday. So it is shown 10 times altogether for three-quarters of an hour each time. Now 10 times three-quarters is 30 quarters or 15 halves which is seven and one-half. The total time is $7\frac{1}{2}$ h.

3 More students voted for blue than red. More students voted for red than for yellow or purple or green, as more voted for purple than green. So blue must have received the most votes and red the second most. So 18 students must have voted for red.

More students voted for purple than green, but there is no information about the number who voted for yellow compared to those who voted for purple or green. So either 13 or 16 voted for purple, either 13 or 11 voted for green and either 16, 13 or 11 voted for yellow. A, B and C are not options that must be true.

4 The Bears won 2 games and had 1 draw, so got 5 points. The Bulls won 4 games and had 1 draw, so got 9 points. The Lions had 3 wins and 1 draw for 7 points and the Tigers had 1 win and a draw for 3 points. The team that got exactly 7 points was the Lions.

5 The two grey houses are at each end of the row, so the middle three houses are either two white and one green, or two green and one white. Because no two of the same colour are next to each other, the middle house must be the one of which there is just one colour. The possibilities are: grey, white, green, white, grey or grey, green, white, green, grey. In either case a white house is to the left of a green house.

A and B might or might not be correct. So they are not the option that **must** be correct. C is not correct.

6 Because Grace is not sitting directly in front of, behind or next to Amy she must be sitting diagonally away from Amy. This means that Tammy and Noor must also be sitting diagonally from each other. So, as Tammy is sitting next to the aisle, Noor must be sitting next to a window.

Amy might be sitting directly in front of Noor, but she also might be sitting directly behind Noor or next to Noor. Tammy might be sitting next to Amy, but she also might be sitting next to Grace. Grace might be sitting next to Noor, but she also might be sitting next to Tammy. A, C and D are not options that **must** be true.

7 As there is blue in A4, green in B4 and red in C4, the vase in D4 must be white. So D1 cannot be white. Nor can it be blue or red as A4 is blue and B3 is red and D1 lies on the same diagonal. So D1 is green. D3 cannot then be white or green because they are already in column D and D3 cannot be red because B3 is red. So D3 is blue and D2 must be red:

4	B	G	R	W
3	W	R	G	B
2	G	B	W	R
1	R	W	B	G
	A	B	C	D

8 Vera is furthest left and Bert is furthest right. Gwen is in front of John, so is not at the end of the row. She is not sitting next to Daphne so must be sitting between Vera and Jean. Daphne must be furthest right, in front of Bert. Jean is second from the right with Gwen on her left. So the man who is on the immediate left of the man behind Jean is the man behind Gwen. It is John:

Henry	John	Frank	Bert
Vera	Gwen	Jean	Daphne

9 If jar 1 is picked up and the water in it is tipped into jar 4, then there will be three full jars, 3, 4 and 5 in a row.
(Jar 5 could also be tipped into jar 2 to have the same result, but 5 is not one of the options.)

10 Two answers were 'dog' and 'not a dog'. They cannot both be correct, so one of those is the answer that is wrong. All the other answers must be correct. The answer 'rabbit' is correct, so Priscilla is a rabbit.
'Dog' is the answer that must be wrong. Priscilla is not a cat, not a guinea pig and not a dog.

MATHEMATICAL REASONING
Symmetry, folding, position and scale
Pages 143–146

Real Test 1

1 E **2** E **3** B **4** A **5** B **6** D **7** E **8** C **9** D **10** A

EXPLANATIONS

1 The four triangles form a triangle which has three axes of symmetry. The shading in one small triangle does not affect the answer.

2 Darren travelled from P to U and then to S.

3 We divide 80 by 20 to get 4. This means the distance on the map is 4 cm.

4
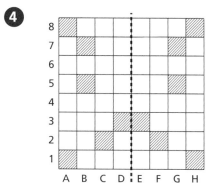

5 As Sienna is south-east of Ava, then Ava is north-west of Sienna. This means she could be at R5 or Q6. As the girls are more than 20 m apart, Ava must be at Q6.

6
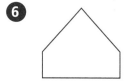

7
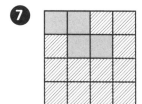

8 The finishing point is 2 units from *X*.
As 2 × 10 = 20, the distance is 20 m:

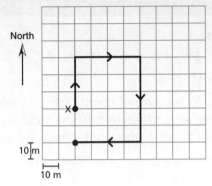

9 All shapes can be made except for shape *S*.

10
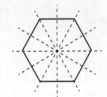

Real Test 2

1 C **2** D **3** C **4** C **5** E **6** D **7** E **8** E **9** B **10** D

EXPLANATIONS

1 A square has four axes of symmetry. This means that *X* is 4.

2 A hexagon with all sides and angles equal has six axes of symmetry:

3 By measurement, *A–B* appears to be half the length of *A–C*. This means *A–B* is about 25 km.

4 The finishing point is 2 units from *X*.
As 2 × 5 = 10, the distance is 10 m:

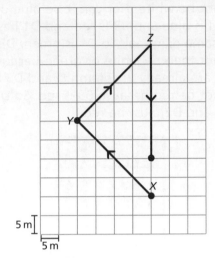

5
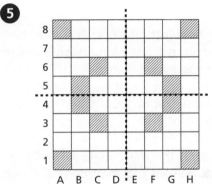

6
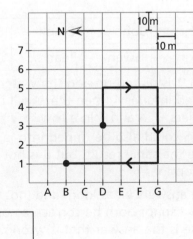

7

8 Mason needs to ride 4 km east then 1 km north (or 1 km north then 4 km east—but this is not one of the options):

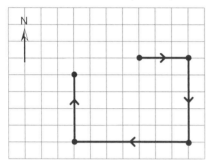

9

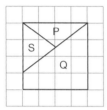

10 The squares used to form shape D are not identical.

MATHEMATICAL REASONING
Statistics and probability　　Pages 149–151

Real Test 3

1 C　**2** D　**3** E　**4** D　**5** A　**6** C　**7** C　**8** E　**9** B　**10** E

EXPLANATIONS

1 Counting the number of houses:
1 + 3 + 4 + 5 + 2 + 1 = 16.

2 Multiply the houses by the people and then add: 1 × 0 + 3 × 1 + 4 × 2 + 5 × 3 + 2 × 4 + 1 × 5 = 39.

3 The most popular number of people living in a house is 3 (which occurs 5 times).

4 Netball is the most popular sport, as it has the largest angle.

5 Basketball is represented by an angle of 90°. This means $\frac{1}{4}$ of the students favour basketball: $\frac{1}{4}$ × 36 = 9.

6 A circle has 360° and soccer is $\frac{80}{360} = \frac{8}{36}$. This means 8 students chose soccer and so 4 girls chose soccer.

7 By counting, three times.

8 The range of temperatures = 36 – 8 = 28 which is 28 °C.

9 The only possible sum is 8 (2 + 6, 3 + 5, 4 + 4, 5 + 3, 6 + 2).

10 Look at each alternative:
2: 1 + 1
3: 1 + 2, 2 + 1
7: 1 + 6, 2 + 5, 3 + 4, 4 + 3, 5 + 2, 6 + 1
8: 2 + 6, 3 + 5, 4 + 4, 6 + 2, 5 + 3
12: 6 + 6

Real Test 4

1 B　**2** E　**3** C　**4** A　**5** D　**6** D　**7** A　**8** C　**9** D　**10** E

EXPLANATIONS

1 The number = 8 + 0 + 24 + 20 + 8 + 12 + 8
= 80

2 The difference = 24 – 8 = 16.

3 The temperature was 36.8 °C three times.

4 The temperature was taken seven times (at 3 am, 6 am, 9 am, noon, 3 pm, 6 pm and 9 pm).

5 As 9 ÷ 3 is 3, then 3 students chose yellow. As 4 × 4 is 16, then 16 students chose red:

Favourite colours	
Colour	**Tally**
blue	IIII
yellow	III
green	~~IIII~~ IIII
red	~~IIII~~ ~~IIII~~ ~~IIII~~ I

As 4 – 3 = 1, statement 1 is not correct. As the second highest number is 9, green is the second favourite and so statement 2 is correct. As 4 + 3 + 9 + 16 = 32, then statement 3 is correct. The correct statements are 2 and 3.

6 Half the graph represents the train travellers. As half of 24 is 12, 12 people travelled by train.

7 The car travellers are represented as an angle of 120°, out of a possible 360°. This can be written as $\frac{120}{360} = \frac{1}{3}$.

8 $10 appears three times and $20 twice, while everything else appears once. The most likely amount is $10.

9 $130 is possible by winning $80 and $50; $50 is possible by winning $10 and $40; $80 is possible by winning $40 and $40; $30 is possible by winning $20 and $10; but it is impossible to win $110.

10 Here is a table which shows all possible scores:

	4	5	6
2	8	10	12
3	12	15	18
4	16	20	24
5	20	25	30

From the table 12 and 20 both appear twice. This means they are the most likely and so statement 1 is correct. In order the scores are 8, 10, 12 … This means the third smallest score is 12 and so statement 2 is correct. There are 10 even scores and only 2 odd scores. As 5 × 2 is 10, it is 5 times more likely that the score will be even, so statement 3 is correct. This means all statements are correct.

WRITING
'Agree or disagree' opinion Page 157

Practice Task 3

1 Paragraph 2: First of all, in most schools there are plenty of opportunities to play sport and get exercise.

Paragraph 3: Also, many children hate sport or are not very good at it.

2 not everyone likes sport

3 children should choose how much sport they do

OPPORTUNITY CLASS TEST
Part 1: Reading Pages 162–167

1 C **2** B **3** A **4** B **5** D **6** A **7** B **8** C **9** A **10** D
11 B **12** E **13** C **14** B **15** D **16** A **17** G **18** D
19 C **20** A **21** C **22** B **23** D **24** B **25** A

1 The main clue to the correct answer is in the third paragraph: 'Slowly and laboriously she plodded along in the heat.' This, as well as the references to the heat, her age and her clothing, suggests she walked with difficulty. It is not B, as the story says she didn't look more than five 'if as much', so she was probably less than five. 'At least five' means she would have been five or more. It is not D as, although Dorfli is in the mountain area, Dete and the little girl pass it on their way to the top. A is obviously wrong: it is clearly summer.

2 Getting question 1 right will help you with this one. Although all the answers make some kind of sense, paragraph 2 tells you clearly how much the little girl was wearing in the heat and so we know she would be red-faced from such clothing.

3 As in the answer above, paragraph 2 tells us how much the little girl was wearing. This is why we can't see her figure.

4 The answer is not clearly stated. You have to draw your own conclusions from what is in the text and eliminate the clearly wrong answers. The main clue that B is correct is that Dete does not want to talk to anyone from her hometown, which suggests she is embarrassed or ashamed that she is giving the little girl to someone who is clearly not an ideal carer for her. Her behaviour does not suggest she is happy about the situation (so not A) or angry (so not C) and we know she wants to take up a job offer (so not D).

5 The word 'proposal' can mean an offer of marriage but that does not make sense here so not A. 'Proposal' also means an idea or plan of action so C could be correct. However, Barbel says the grandfather will soon send Dete and her proposal 'packing off home again!', which suggests she is using the word to refer to the little girl. The little girl *is* the plan or proposal. Barbel is really using the word to mean both so the best answer is D.

6 In these types of questions, you should examine the text for evidence for each one. Then tick off each statement as you go so you won't get confused. In this case, there is evidence for all statements except A. We know the grandfather never sees anyone so this is evidence for B. We know from Barbel's words that he is likely to send her away instantly so this is evidence for C. We know he frightens everyone on the mountain so this is evidence for D. So the only one left is A. There is absolutely no evidence he will welcome his granddaughter.

7 Stanza 1 is all about the way they look when they walk along (e.g. 'hands in pockets', 'They tilt their heads'). Lines 5 and 6 (stanza 2) continue the description. Only the last two lines of stanza 2 are about their greed, so not A. Only lines 4 and 5 are about their colour, so not D, and there is no mention in this first half of their sound, so not C.

8 The poet is comparing the magpies with their black and white colours and their way of walking to gentlemen in black dinner suits and white shirts strolling around at a social event.

9 You have to think of magpies and the way they stroll around, as well as understand the way men at a party might appear before the food appears! Even if you have never seen a magpie, you can probably work this out from the other clues in the

description—it is the opposite of how magpies look when the food arrives.

10 This should be clear. Line 7 says 'until their meal is served—and then', and line 8 focuses on the way they fight in a greedy way.

11 There are many words about the way magpies sing in the last stanza, and it should be clear the poet is praising it, and not criticising it (so not C).

12 The linking word 'However' shows you have to look backwards. You need to go beyond the sentence about what the kites were made of to the sentence saying that kite-flying is 'generally considered' to have been invented in China. Sentence E goes against that claim.

13 Again, you have to look two sentences back to find the link to this sentence, which talks about using the kite in battle and refers to military uses. The phrase 'as said' indicates you must look backwards.

14 This sentence fits the meaning of the sentences before and after, which are about how the kites of old China looked.

15 The linking words 'And of course' are the main clue. They direct you right back to the sentence before about the use of kites for science.

16 Here the sentence links to the one following it. In this following sentence we get details of what kite-fighting means.

17 This is the only sentence that works here. It is a general 'wrapping up' kind of sentence that you often find at the end of factual texts like this. The 'possibilities' relate to the 'fun' you can have with kites. F is the unused sentence. The sentence is about world records and so could only go in a paragraph about modern times; in other words the last two. The only available gap is at 17 and sentence F does not continue the meaning of the previous sentence.

18 The middle part of this extract mentions that fighting usually decreases as siblings get older and develop their language and social skills.

19 This extract demonstrates the effect of losing your position in a family when you join another family.

20 This extract lists some points of advice about how to deal with fighting between siblings. The question 'So what can you do?' and the linking words (firstly, secondly) give you an immediate clue.

21 This extract is about a personal experience related to birth order: 'When I was eight' directs you quickly to this answer.

22 This extract explains that youngest children have often had more freedom than their older siblings and this can lead to a willingness to try new things and set out in new directions (to be independent).

23 The second sentence of this extract makes this claim quite clearly.

24 This extract goes through the general characteristics of 'first born, last born and those in the middle'.

25 The last two sentences of this extract make this warning: 'be patient'; 'don't expect miracles'.

OPPORTUNITY CLASS TEST
Part 2: Mathematical Reasoning Pages 168–173

1 E **2** C **3** C **4** B **5** B **6** C **7** A **8** E **9** C **10** E
11 C **12** A **13** C **14** E **15** B **16** D **17** D **18** B
19 D **20** A **21** A **22** E **23** C **24** D **25** D **26** B
27 D **28** B **29** A **30** C **31** D **32** A **33** B **34** E
35 D

1 As 23 + 40 is 63, then 23 + 39 is 62.
To find 81 − ▢ = 62, as 81 − 20 is 61, then 81 − 62 is 19.

2
```
  63 209
−    400
  62 809
```

3 As twenty to ten is 9:40 pm, there are 20 min to 10 pm. Another 2 h is midnight, and then 7 h 25 min takes the time to 7:25 am. As 2 + 7 = 9 and 20 + 25 = 45, the amount of time is 9 h 45 min.

4 One-third of 12 squares is 4 squares. As 12 − 4 = 8 there are 8 squares remaining. As half of 8 is 4, and 8 − 4 is 4, there will be 4 squares unshaded:

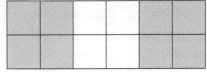

5 Look at each of the options: 100 − 63 = 37, 41, 500 − 478 = 22, 32, 100 − 76 = 24. As the biggest number is 41, then 241 changes the most.

6 Elijah finishes 2 units, or 10 m, from his starting point *P*:

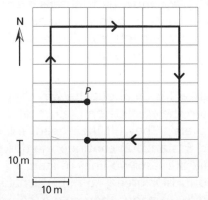

7 The number in the centre is the middle number of 1 to 9 which is 5.
As 15 − 4 − 5 = 6, the value of *X* is 6. Here is the completed puzzle:

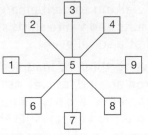

X is the number 6.

8 As 1 + 2 + 3 = 6, then each bunch will have 2 red balloons, 4 white balloons and 6 pink balloons. As 6 × 6 = 36, Lexi will need 36 pink balloons.

9 As 1 L is 1000 mL, then half a litre is 500 mL. Container X needs another 500 mL to fill. As 350 × 2 is 700, and 700 − 500 = 200, there is still 200 mL remaining in Container Y.

10 As 15 × 3 = 45, the length is 45 cm. As 45 + 45 + 15 + 15 = 120, the wire is 120 cm, or 1.2 m long.

11 E has 4 right angles, F has 3, H has 4, L has 1 and T has 2. As 4 + 3 + 4 is 11, the largest number is 11.

12 As 8 + 4 = 12, Rita should buy a bag of 8 and then another 4. As 70 × 4 is 280, then $2.80 + $4 is $6.80. This is the lowest amount.

13 As 8 × 6 is 48, then $Q = 6$. As 4 × 2 is 8, then $P = 4$ and as 3 × 2 is 6, then $R = 2$. Now, $P \times Q \times R = 4 \times 6 \times 2 = 48$.

14 Each cube has 6 faces. As 12 × 6 is 72, there is a total of 72 faces. Looking at the solid, there are 6 cube faces on the front and 6 on the back. There are 4 cube faces on the right, and 4 on the left. There are 6 cube faces on the top, and 6 on the bottom. As 6 + 6 + 4 + 4 + 6 + 6 is 32, and 72 − 32 is 40, there are 40 cube faces that cannot be seen.

15 Half of 128 is 64. As 64 + 8 is 72, the number in the sequence before 128 is 72. As 7 × 2 is 14, Maggie's answer is 14.

16 As 3 + 2 + 4 + 3 + 5 = 17, Al sold 17 cars in Week 1. As 17 − 2 = 15, Al sold 15 cars in Week 2. As 2 + 5 + 2 + 3 = 12, and 15 − 12 = 3, Al sold 3 cars on Friday Week 2.

17 The largest even number is 864 and the smallest odd number is 463. The difference is 864 − 463 = 401.

18 Square P has 4 out of 8 triangles shaded which is $\frac{1}{2}$. Square Q has 6 out of 9 small squares shaded which is $\frac{6}{9} = \frac{2}{3}$. The circle in Square R has $\frac{2}{3}$ shaded, but there is more space outside the circle. This means that Q is the only square.

19 Here are more numbers in the sequence: … 8, 16, **32**, 64, 128, **256**, 512 … The sixth number is 32 and the ninth number is 256. As 56 + 32 is 88, then 256 + 32 is 288.

20 $1 = \frac{10}{10}$ and $\frac{1}{5} = \frac{2}{10}$. As 10 − 2 − 1 = 7 she has $\frac{7}{10}$ of the eggs to give to her friends. This means she has 7 friends.

21 The squares to be shaded are C6, C1 and F4:

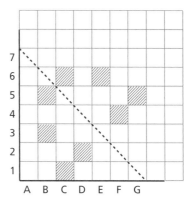

22 Using the compass rose and scale, Archie must be standing at Q6:

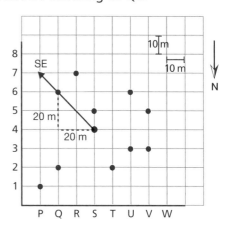

23 As 24 ÷ 6 is 4, each block has a mass of 4 kg. As 24 ÷ 12 is 2, each cylinder has a mass of 2 kg. As 12 × 4 + 6 × 2 is 48 + 12 which is 60, the total mass is 60 kg.

24 The area of the small square was 16 cm² before the sections were cut away. The purple sections are $\frac{1}{2}$ cm², 2 cm² and 4 cm². This is a total of $6\frac{1}{2}$ cm². As $16 - 6\frac{1}{2}$ is $16 - 6 - \frac{1}{2}$ is $9\frac{1}{2}$, the area is $9\frac{1}{2}$ cm². As there are 4 layers of paper and $9\frac{1}{2} + 9\frac{1}{2} + 9\frac{1}{2} + 9\frac{1}{2}$ is 38, the area is 38 cm².

25 $2.40 plus 80 cents is $3.20 and $10 − $3.20 is $6.80. Now six 10-cent coins is 60 cents, and $6.80 − 60 cents is $6.20.
There are five 20-cent coins in a dollar, and as 6 × 5 + 1 is 31, Freya will be given 31 20-cent coins.

26 There are 30 days in June and 31 days in July. By adding 7 days each time, here are the Fridays: 2, 9, 16, 23, 30 July. Also, 6, 13, 20, 27 August are Fridays. This means 25 August is a Wednesday.

27 20 attend 0 classes, 8 attend 1 class, 32 attend 2 classes, 16 attend 3 classes, 6 attend 4 classes and 4 attend 5 classes. As 16 + 6 + 4 = 26, then 26 members attend at least 3 classes. Claim 1 is correct. 32 is twice 16, and so twice as many members attend 2 classes as 3 classes. Claim 2 is correct. 20 + 8 + 32 + 16 + 6 + 4 = 86, but 4 × 20 is only 80, so fewer than one-quarter do not attend any classes. Claim 3 is not correct. Only claims 1 and 2 are correct.

28 As 6 + 6 + 6 + 6 + 4 + 4 = 32, originally Avery could only see 32 cube faces. In the white solid: 5 + 5 + 3 + 3 + 5 + 5 = 26 and in the grey solid: 4 + 4 + 3 + 3 + 4 + 4 = 22. As 26 + 22 = 48, Avery can now see 48 cube faces. As 48 − 32 = 16, Avery can see 16 more faces.

29 There are 3 green balls so there are 6 blue balls (3 + 3 = 6). As 2 × 6 = 12, there are 12 red balls. As 3 + 6 + 12 = 21, then three-quarters of the balls represent 21 balls. As 21 ÷ 3 = 7, then a quarter of the balls is 7, and so 4 × 7 = 28 which means there are 28 balls in the box.

30

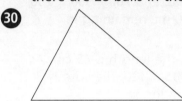

31 The pattern is 4, 12, 20 … The rule is 'Start with 4 and add 8'. The 4th term will be 28, and the 5th term will be 36. The perimeter will be 36 cm.

32 There are 8 odd numbers and 7 even numbers. This means it is more likely the number is odd. Statement 1 is correct. There are 4 numbers less than 4 and 5 numbers greater than 10. This means it is not equally likely. Statement 2 is not correct. There is one 11 and one 12 which means they are equally likely to be chosen. Statement 3 is not correct. This means the only correct statement is Statement 1.

33 As 105 × 4 is 420, Bruce gave $420 in total to his children. Now, 420 + 380 is 800, and 1000 − 800 is 200 so Bruce gave his sister $200.

34 All 3 statements are correct:

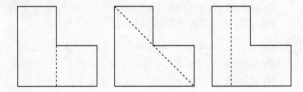

35 11 is impossible. 8 is 10 − 2; 9 is 14 − 5; 10 is 14 − 4; 12 is 17 − 5.

1 D **2** B **3** C **4** D **5** A **6** D **7** A **8** A **9** D
10 C **11** B **12** D **13** B **14** C **15** B **16** B **17** C
18 B **19** C **20** C **21** D **22** C **23** C **24** A **25** D
26 B **27** B **28** A **29** A **30** D

1 Abigail is directly opposite Bella, so there are two people between them on each side of the table. Now Cooper is next to Daniel so they are the two people on one side. Edward and Fiona must therefore be the two people on the other side. Edward must be next to Fiona.

Daniel might be next to Bella, but he might also be next to Abigail and not Bella. Cooper might be next to Abigail but he might also be next to Bella and not Abigail. Abigail might be next to Edward, but she might also be next to Fiona and not Edward. A, B and C are not options that **must** be true.

2 The projects are not due until 5 pm so the mistake made by Mr Flint is to assume that all the students submitting hard-copy projects had done so by that morning.

3 Rachael's home is unavailable. The next turn in alphabetical order is Brock's but he will be away on holiday. This means Jaxson will host the games night this week.

4 George has the highest total of the given scores. His total is 76 + 71 = 147.
Mia must have scored more than 147 in total to win the prize.
Now 147 − 64 = 83.
Mia had to score more than 83 to win the prize.
So the lowest mark that Mia could have scored is 84.

5 The statement that best expresses the main idea in the text is that fortune cookies were invented in Japan, not in China or America.

6 Square 5 has the same six pieces as square 3. If square 3 is flipped horizontally and then turned through a quarter turn in a clockwise direction, the result will be square 5:

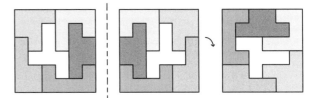

7 The top stripe is red, so the second stripe from the top will be either yellow or blue. If it is yellow, the next two stripes must be red and blue in some order. A red stripe will be next to a blue stripe. If it is blue, then a red stripe is next to a blue stripe. In either case a red stripe is next to a blue stripe.

The top stripe is red and the bottom is yellow. The middle three stripes might be yellow, red, blue or yellow, blue, red or blue, red, blue or blue, yellow, red or blue, yellow, blue. So B, C and D might be correct but they are not the options that **must** be correct.

8 Diane only suggests that Sam would *probably* enjoy the book. She does not assert that he definitely will, when she says: 'I told Sam that I thought he would probably enjoy reading it because it is very funny and I know he enjoys humorous books.' Tahlia asserts that Ilona would enjoy the book and read it through to the end. Tahlia acknowledges that Ilona is not much of a reader so she cannot know with certainty that Ilona will finish *Anne of Green Gables*. Therefore Tahlia's reasoning is incorrect.

9 This statement cannot be true. Peaches will graduate if she has learned two of the three core skills.

10 The one girl sitting between Jenna and Hailey cannot be Kahlia because she is not beside Hailey. The girl cannot be Isla because Laura is somewhere between Isla and Hailey. So the girl sitting between Jenna and Hailey must be Laura. Kahlia is beside Jenna and they must be left of Laura and Hailey. As Laura is somewhere between Hailey and Isla, Isla must be on Kahlia's left. So, in order from left to right, the girls are Isla, Kahlia, Jenna, Laura and Hailey. Jenna is sitting in the middle of the row.

11 Pashmina's argument is that English bull terriers are entertaining and funny to watch, especially when get over excited. She provides evidence of the behaviour to support her argument. The statement which best supports her claim is that English bull terriers are rowdy and clownish.

12 The argument is that the yo-yo must be the greatest toy ever invented. The statement that weakens that argument is **D** because anything that periodically goes out of fashion is not necessarily the greatest toy of all time.

13 Malven is east of Bankston and west of Araluen, so those three towns are in the centre row. The position of the other towns can then be marked:

```
•P    •R              N
                   NW ↑
•B   •M   •A     W—————E
                      ↓
•F   •H              S
```

Portland is north-west of Hapville.

14 Marc's conclusion is that Pearl will go shopping to buy a plain white t-shirt and leggings. The evidence he uses is that Pearl says she needs to go shopping after school because there's a dance concert coming up and she has to wear a plain white t-shirt and leggings. For Marc's conclusion to hold true, he must have assumed that Pearl does not already own a plain white t-shirt and leggings suitable for the concert.

15 First one post is placed between the two end posts to make 3 posts altogether. Then Joe puts a post in the gap between the first and second posts and he puts another post in the gap between the second and third post, making 5 posts altogether. There will now be 4 gaps between posts. Finally, a post is put in each of those 4 gaps to make 9 posts altogether. There will now be 8 gaps, each of 4 m, so the total distance is 8 × 4 m or 32 m.

16 When folded, if the blank face is on the bottom and the triangle on the front face, then the cross will be on the right side and the square on the top. The star will be on the back face and the circle on the left side. The face opposite the blank face will have the square.

17 The creator of the text wants you to accept that there are lifesaving actions you can take if caught in a blizzard. The rest of the text gives you reason to believe the main idea. It gives supporting information about some of these lifesaving actions.

18 The scientist's argument is that the evolution of tuskless elephants has a cost: lasting negative impacts on the ecosystem. The statement that elephants use their tusks in ways that help the long-term health of the ecosystem most strengthens this argument.

19 If 5 March is a Friday, then 1 March is a Monday. 8, 15, 22 and 29 March will also be Mondays. 31 March will be a Wednesday. Each week, if there are no Friday games, there are 3 training sessions. In the first week there will be 2 sessions, 3 in both the second and third weeks and 2 in the fourth week. Finally, there will be

sessions on Monday 29th and Wednesday 31st. So there will be 12 sessions altogether:

March						
S	M	T	W	T	F	S
	1	2	3	4	5	6
7	8	9	10	11	12	13
14	15	16	17	18	19	20
21	22	23	24	25	26	27
28	29	30	31			

20 According to the unit leader, if a scout has not made a major contribution to scouting then they do not stand a chance of winning a Scout of the Year award. Therefore none of the scouts who have not made a major contribution to scouting will win a Scout of the Year award.

21 The advertisement argues that the app is the best thing to expand your night-time astronomical explorations. The statement that looking at the bright screen of your phone will ruin your night vision weakens the argument, since ruined night vision will make it more difficult to explore the night sky rather than expand your explorations.

22 Because the $10 voucher is somewhere between the $50 and the $100 vouchers, and is in a lower numbered box than the $100, the $50 voucher must be in a lower-numbered box than both the $10 and $100. As that $50 voucher is in an odd-numbered box it must be in either Box 1 or Box 3. If it was in Box 3, the $10 would have to be in Box 4 and the $100 in Box 5. Then, however, there couldn't be two boxes between the $5 and $20 vouchers, so the $50 cannot be in Box 3. It must be in Box 1. The $5 and $20 vouchers must be in Boxes 2 and 5 in some order. The $10 would have to be in Box 3 and the $100 voucher in Box 4. The contestant should choose Box 4 to win the $100 voucher.

23 Finn took an hour to walk to his friend's house. If the return journey was 4 times faster, then it would have taken one-quarter of the time. So the return journey took a quarter of an hour. Now Finn arrived home at 4:50 pm, which is 2 h after he arrived at his friend's house. So the length of time he was at his friend's house is 2 h minus the quarter hour it took for him to travel home. Finn was at his friend's house for $1\frac{3}{4}$ h.

24 Eric's conclusion is that there is nothing wrong with staying up late to binge the series. He based this conclusion on the evidence that all his friends do the same. So, for his conclusion to hold, it must be assumed that if everyone else does something it's okay for you to do it too: all Eric's friends are staying up late to binge the series + if everyone else does something, it's okay for you to do it too = there is nothing wrong with Eric staying up late to binge the series.

25 The top row does not have a 1, 2 or 5. So the missing domino must have two of those numbers. The fourth column has both a 1 and a 2 so the missing number in the top row must be 5. The third column does not have a 1 or a 2, so either of those could be the missing number. However, the domino with a 1 and a 5 is used in the fifth column and each domino is only used once.

So the missing domino is  :

26 We know any student who has not completed and handed in their homework will not be allowed to go to the book fair. So Mila is correct in her reasoning that she won't be allowed to go since she left her homework at home. Hugo's reasoning is not correct. Hugo has made a mistake by saying he **definitely** will be allowed to go since there may be other reasons why a student is not allowed to go to the book fair.

27 Purple only appears in group 4. Green appears in group 1 and group 4. If Zena takes purple from group 4, she must take green from group 1. Blue appears in group 1 and group 2. Zena must take it from group 2, so the remaining colour must come from group 3. So Zena could choose red, white, orange or grey. She cannot choose black.

28 As the cupboard holding the plates is two away from the staples and three from the cookbooks, and the staples and cookbooks are not next to each other, the cupboards holding the staples and cookbooks are five cupboards apart. So the staples and cookbooks must be in the two end cupboards. The plates must be in one of the two middle cupboards. The cupboard holding the saucepans is between the cupboards holding the bowls and the cookbooks. So the bowls must also be in one of the middle cupboards. As the cupboard holding the cups is further left than that holding the bowls, the cups must be in the second cupboard from the left, meaning that the saucepans must be in the second cupboard from the right. The bowls must be in the third cupboard from the right:

left	staples	cups	plates	bowls	sauce-pans	cook-books	right

29 The middle symbol in the middle row can only be the square because there is already a triangle and star in that column and a circle and diamond in both diagonals. The diagonal from the top right to the bottom left needs the triangle and star. There is already a star in the second column so the second symbol in the fourth row must be the triangle and the first symbol in the bottom row must be the star. The other diagonal also needs a triangle and star, so it must have the star in the fourth row and the triangle in the bottom row. The fifth column must have its star in the third row and so it will have a circle in the fourth row. The circle in the third column must then be in the bottom row. The square in the bottom row will have to be in the second column and the diamond in the fourth column of the bottom row:

●	◆	▲	■	◆
▲	◆	◆	●	■
◆	●	■	▲	◆
■	▲	◆	◆	●
◆	■	●	◆	▲

30 The creator of the text wants you to accept that there is a difference between a need and a want and D is the statement in the list that best expresses this. The rest of the text gives you reason to believe the main idea. It gives supporting information about the differences between needs and wants.

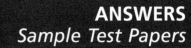
SCHOLARSHIP TEST
Part 1: Reading and Viewing   Pages 180–186

1 B **2** B **3** C **4** B **5** A **6** C **7** C **8** B **9** C
10 A **11** C **12** D **13** B **14** D **15** A **16** D **17** C
18 D **19** B **20** A **21** A **22** A **23** D **24** C **25** A

1 The second paragraph tells you this clearly, especially 'it was school that remained most in his mind. There, his difference from the other children would always be made apparent in all sorts of little ways'.

2 The end of paragraph 1 gives you the answer, especially 'The doctors could promise nothing'.

3 You have to work this out from the information that the accident happened when he was fourteen months old and that Andrew is in his last year of primary school.

4 In this type of question you have to look for the evidence for each statement. When you find statements that are true, cross them off so you won't be confused. There is no evidence that Andrew has **no** feeling in his right leg. In fact he says the opposite: 'But that silly, old, lifeless right leg—which wasn't really lifeless, but might as well have been'.

5 The second sentence of the last paragraph tells you this: 'But Andrew had spent far too long struggling to make his body do what he wanted it to do'. He may think about his parents' sacrifice (B) but we are not told this. He probably does try to think that it could be better tomorrow (D) but we are not told this. We know it is not C from everything said so far.

6 You need to understand that the poet is creating an image of the whole scene—he compares the tractor ploughing the field to a boat making its way across the ocean. Once you work out it is a boat of some kind (so not A or B), you have to look for

clues about what kind of boat: lines 6–8 make it clear it is a paddle-steamer, and not a speedboat.

7 It should be clear that the movement is difficult because the tractor is described as making its way across an 'ocean', and you know an ocean would probably not be flat. You also need to think about what you know about ploughing paddocks (fields) with tractors.

8 This should be easy if you read carefully— an 'excitement of seagulls'—clearly the word 'excitement' is being used to describe the group of birds and at the same time to describe their mood (excited).

9 If you got question 1 right, you should get this right. The poet continues to talk of the tractor as a boat, so the driver of the tractor is the captain.

10 It would help to know that 'casting off' is a term used when a ship is leaving shore, but you should be able to work out that the poet is referring to the tractor starting the motor to get going across the paddock (especially if you got questions 1 and 4 right).

11 The words 'father of science' (line 2) give you the answer. Line 8 also mentions that 'many scientists followed his example'. Thales did contribute to engineering, astronomy and mathematics, but you have to understand that his main contribution was to science as a whole.

12 You might have answered B because it is true that Thales' explanation was wrong. However, this was not the important thing. Lines 4–5 tell you clearly why his explanation was significant.

13 The answer is quite clearly given in the third paragraph. You might be tricked into C or D, however, because the text gives this information.

14 You have to do some sensible guesswork here and, if you can, use what you know of the way we number the BCE (Before Common Era) years. BCE years get smaller as time goes on, so 635 BCE is an earlier date than 543 BCE, so the answer is either B or D. The word circa means about or around. You could probably guess this: we don't usually know exact dates for people who lived thousands of years ago.

15 You have to work this out using all the clues in paragraph 2, and your own common sense.

16 Although this is not hard, you have to read all of paragraph 4 to get it right. You have to be especially careful with questions where all the answers are written in a similar sentence pattern—it is easy to make a silly mistake.

17 You must be sure to choose an answer that captures the whole text in this kind of question. B and D mention information that is covered in parts of the text only. Answer A is not right because it is about the present. C is the only answer that covers the meaning and purpose of the whole text.

18 Paragraph 4 gives you the answer quite clearly. You might have chosen C because in a way it could be true, but the writer does not explicitly state this.

19 Paragraph 6 gives you the answer clearly. All the other answers are mentioned in the text, so it could be easy to make a mistake if you do not take enough time.

20 Paragraph 5 gives the answer clearly. Be careful, however, in this kind of question. You should quickly check each answer even if you are sure you know it when you first read through them.

21 The answer is in paragraph 6. You should not have trouble finding it, but you need to be careful because there are many years and times mentioned in the text.

22 This kind of visually presented information can be tricky. You need to read carefully and concentrate. The first sentence of the text lists the types of fingerprints as loops, whorls and arches. This suggests the diagrams will be shown in the same order, so the third diagram is an arch (A).

23 You need to read closely and be sure you understand exactly what is being referred to by the two parts of fingerprints described in the text: deltas and cores. This first arrow points to a delta so the answer is none of these (D).

24 You need to read and think carefully. The text tells you there is only one type of fingerprint with both a delta and a core. The fact that there are two arrows on this diagram suggests the answer is either core or delta. If you worked out the last answer you should get this right. This arrow points to a core (C).

25 The text tells you that a whorl has at least two deltas, which suggests these arrows must point to deltas (A).

SCHOLARSHIP TEST
Part 2: Mathematics   Pages 187–188

1 D **2** D **3** D **4** A **5** B **6** E **7** C **8** B **9** C
10 D **11** E **12** A **13** E **14** B **15** D **16** E

1 Pitar can think of **any** number and he will always end with the answer of 6. For example, if he starts with 3: doubles to give 6, adds 3 to give 9, subtracts 1 to give 8, takes away the original number of 3 to give 5, adds 2 to give 7, takes away the original number of 3 to give 4, subtracts 2 to give 2, and adds 4 to give the final answer of 6.

2 Alexis is further away than Samuel or Frankie. Samuel is 2 vertical squares and 3 horizontal squares from Xan. This is the same as 3 vertical squares and 2 horizontal squares, which is the distance from Frankie to Xan:

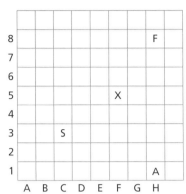

3 95 = 50 + 25 + 20; 115 = 50 + 25 + 20 + 20; 120 = 100 + 20; 145 = 100 + 25 + 20. But 135 is impossible.

4 There are 30 min from 2:40 pm to 3:10 pm. As 85 − 40 = 45, Rose has travelled 45 km in half an hour. This is an average speed of 90 km/h.

5 There are 60 min in an hour and so there are four 15-minutes in an hour. The temperature rises 2 °C every hour. As 30 − 23 = 7, the temperature has risen to 29 °C after 3 hours, and then 1 °C after another half an hour. This means the time will be 12:30 pm.

6 Starting from the bottom number 5, going up and to the right is 6. Now 5 + 6 = 11 which goes to the left of the second-last row. Continue the pattern and C = 11 + 13 = 24, B = 13 + 15 = 28 and A = 24 + 28 = 52.
Now A + B + C = 52 + 28 + 24 = 104.

7 As 6 × 8 is 48 it would take 1 person 48 h to paint the fence. Now as 48 ÷ 16 = 24 ÷ 8 = 3, it would take 16 people 3 h.

8 The square has been spilt into 2 rectangles. The top rectangle has been split into quarters. If the bottom rectangle has been split into quarters instead of thirds there would be 8 quarters. As 3 are shaded the fraction is $\frac{3}{8}$.

9 As 12 ÷ 3 = 4, Daphne has 4 chocolates. As 2 × 4 = 8, Noah has 8 chocolates. As 12 + 4 + 8 = 24, there were 24 chocolates in the box.

10

$1.30	10.00
$1.30	− 6.80
+ $4.20	$3.20
$6.80	

Harriet has 320 cents remaining and a pencil costs 80 cents. As 320 ÷ 80 = 32 ÷ 8 = 4, she can buy a maximum of 4 pencils.

11 As 45 − 8 = 37, Eva arrived at 10:37, which is 23 minutes to 11. As 25 + 12 = 37, and 37 − 23 = 14, Eva leaves at 11:14.

12 As 3 + 2 × 11 is 25, Mario scored 25 goals. As 11 + 25 = 36, Mario and Rafael scored a total of 36 goals. As 36 ÷ 2 − 2 is 16, Bruno scored 16 goals. As 11 + 25 + 16 = 52, the three players scored a total of 52 goals.

13 Piles of 3 with 2 left over: 5, 8, 11 … 44, 47. Piles of 4 with 3 left over: 7, 11, 15 … 43, 47. Piles of 5 with 2 left over: 7, 12, 17 … 42, 47. The only common number is 47. As 47 × 2 is 94, Lucy has $94.

14 As 15 − 12 = 3, the numbers are increasing by 3. The sequence of numbers are 0, 3, 6, 9, 12, 15 … The hundredth term is 100 × 3 − 3 which is 297. As 0 + 297 = 297, the sum is 297.

15 There are 6 ways of getting a total of 7: 1 and 6, 2 and 5, 3 and 4, 4 and 3, 5 and 2, 6 and 1. This is the most likely total.

16 There are 10 blue cars, 5 green cars and 9 yellow cars. As 10 + 5 + 9 = 24, then two-thirds of the cars equal 24. One-third is 24 ÷ 2 = 12, so 12 cars are red. As 12 × 3 = 36, Bronson has 36 cars.

ANSWERS
Sample Test Papers

Part 3: Writing   Pages 189–194

Your parents or teachers can use these checklists to give you feedback on your writing. The checklist they use will depend on the kind of writing you did. They might use points from more than one checklist to give you feedback.

Checklist for writing an 'Imagine if …' story

Did the student …

- start the story with a few sentences to capture the readers' attention and tell them what the story is about—who, what, when, where?

- include interesting, imaginative events and experiences?

- give the story an ending of some kind?

- use vivid, interesting language to describe the people, things and actions in the story?

- use correct and appropriate grammar, punctuation and spelling?

Checklist for writing a 'What would you do if …?' opinion text

Did the student …

- introduce the topic or question and give their overall opinion?

- give two or three good reasons for this opinion?

- use interesting, creative ideas to explain their reasons?

- develop these reasons with facts, examples or logical arguments?

- use signpost words to help the reader follow their ideas?

- write a short conclusion?

- use correct and appropriate grammar, punctuation and spelling?

Checklist for writing a narrative story

Did the student …

- start the story with a few sentences to capture the readers' attention and tell them who or what the story is about?

- include something interesting or unusual that makes the story worth telling?

- give the story an ending of some kind?

- use some vivid, interesting words to describe the people, things and actions in the story?

- use correct and appropriate grammar, punctuation and spelling?

Checklist for writing an 'agree or disagree' opinion text

Did the student …

- introduce the topic and give their overall opinion?

- give two or three good reasons for this opinion?

- develop their arguments with facts, examples or logical arguments?

- use signpost words to help the reader follow their ideas?

- write a short conclusion?

- use correct and appropriate grammar, punctuation and spelling?

240   *Excel* Revise in a Month Years 4–5 Opportunity Class and Scholarship Tests